Managing Risk and Uncertainty in International Trade

About the Book and Author

This book is addressed to those interested in an analysis of Canada's natural gas exports, North American natural gas market trends, and more generally, international trade in raw materials. The author outlines the development of Canada's natural gas industry and examines the country's management of natural gas exports, applying his findings to the more general international issues related to trade in primary commodities. Emphasis on risk management in uncertain, competitive environments provides useful parallels with other industries. Four major, interrelated conclusions are drawn concerning the nature of price appreciation and fluctuation for commodities, the tendency for governments to become involved in more and more aspects of commodity trade, the growing tendency for the basic ground rules for trade to be changed in mid-course, and the nature of how technological change affects the supply and demand for commodities on the international market.

<u>Alan R. Winberg</u> is assistant director of the Program Evaluation Division of the Department of Consumer and Corporate Affairs of the Canadian government.

Managing Risk and Uncertainty in International Trade

Canada's Natural Gas Exports

Alan R. Winberg

Routledge
Taylor & Francis Group
LONDON AND NEW YORK

First published 1987 by Westview Press, Inc.

Published 2019 by Routledge
52 Vanderbilt Avenue, New York, NY 10017
2 Park Square, Milton Park, Abingdon, Oxon OX14 4RN

Routledge is an imprint of the Taylor & Francis Group, an informa business

Copyright © 1987 Taylor & Francis

All rights reserved. No part of this book may be reprinted or reproduced or utilised in any form or by any electronic, mechanical, or other means, now known or hereafter invented, including photocopying and recording, or in any information storage or retrieval system, without permission in writing from the publishers.

Notice:
Product or corporate names may be trademarks or registered trademarks, and are used only for identification and explanation without intent to infringe.

Library of Congress Catalog Card Number: 86-51473

ISBN 13: 978-0-367-00864-2 (hbk)
ISBN 13: 978-0-367-15851-4 (pbk)
ISBN 13: 978-0-429-03850-1 (ebk)

For Donna Ruth

Contents

List of Tables and Figures		xi
Preface		xiii
Acknowledgments		xvii
Chapter 1	Introduction	1
Chapter 2	Natural Resource Exports	23
Chapter 3	Canada's Export Market for Natural Gas	43
Chapter 4	Canada's Natural Gas Industry	65
Chapter 5	Canada's Natural Gas Export Policy	107
Chapter 6	Uncertainty	113
Chapter 7	Substitution	129
Chapter 8	Foreign Ownership in Canada's Petroleum Sector	153
Chapter 9	The National Energy Board	169
Chapter 10	Export Prices	179
Chapter 11	Protecting Domestic Requirements for Natural Gas	203
Chapter 12	Alternative Regulatory Mechanisms	215
Chapter 13	Conclusions	231
Bibliography		245
Index		283

Tables and Figures

Table 3-1	Growth of Natural Gas Reserves and Consumption in the United States	47
Table 3-2	Average Wellhead Price and Marketed Production of Natural Gas in the United States: 1950-1983	57
Table 4-1	Marketable Natural Gas	85
Table 4-2	Length of Natural Gas Pipeline Network By Function of Lines	89
Table 4-3	Canadian Gas Supply Sensitivity by State: 1980	97
Table 4-4	Export Price of Natural Gas	101
Figure 6-1	Energy Consumption in Canada as Fuel Equivalent	116
Table 6-1	Consumption of Energy and Natural Gas in Canada	123
Table 6-2	Revenues from Natural Gas Sales by Class of Service	124
Table 7-1	Texas Natural Gas Statistics	151

Preface

The rate of development of a nation's capital stock of non-renewable resources and decisions on whether to export these commodities and on what terms are fundamental issues for nations that possess such resources. Some of the questions that arise are specific to the nation and/or the particular commodity; however, many are applicable in general to a variety of cases, including both renewable and non-renewable resources. The focus of this study is Canadian policy for the export of natural gas over the period of 1950 to 1985.

By examining the Canadian experience with natural gas, the study will attempt to clarify the issues involved and major considerations which come to bear in choosing between the policy options open to governments with natural resources, but which require an export component in order to achieve the optimal rate of development for these resources. The discussion provides an overview of the type of problems facing exporters of natural resources and the solutions being proposed to remedy some of these problems.

The regulation, by various levels of government, of the natural gas trade has been extensive in both Canada and the United States. In both countries, natural gas has been viewed as a commodity of strategic importance to the national welfare, and intervention in the industry by the federal level of government has involved the licensing of exports and imports and the regulation of various aspects of interprovincial and interstate trade. There is no question that trade regulation by the governments of Canada and the United States has altered the pattern of development which would have occurred had there been no restrictions on trade.

While this study focuses on the nature of and the effects of Canadian government intervention, Canada's export policies cannot be fully understood without a detailed examination of the situation in Canada's export market. In the first place, discussion focuses on why export policy for natural gas has had to be conceived in terms of the U.S. market. Following this, regulation of the industry in the United States is discussed, particularly as it relates to natural gas trade with Canada.

After an examination of the evolution of Canada's natural gas industry and exports, Canada's export policies are outlined and related to the goals being pursued. It will be shown that while the central goal of the government's policy has been to promote east-west ties, policy has been influenced by three key objectives. These are: the achievement of rapid delineation of the size of Canada's gas reserves; the optimal timing of the development of these reserves, and the extent to which exports are required to achieve this; and, the attainment of maximum value to Canadians in return for the appropriate volumes of natural gas exported to the United States.

Finally, Canadian export policy for natural gas is evaluated in terms of the policy objectives, and some of the major assertions of dependency theories of economic development. Export pricing, as well as Canada's policies and mechanisms to protect future requirements for natural gas, are examined. Discussion then turns to the matter of substitution of other forms of energy for natural gas and how the export price for natural gas is related to the price of substitutes and the overall demand for energy in North America and the world. Comparative observations are made with regard to policies pursued by the Netherlands government and Norway and also, at the sub-national level, by the state of Texas.

Special attention is given to the concept of uncertainty, and how it has been and could be treated in the policy-making process. Uncertainty has been one of the key factors in the evolution of Canada's natural gas export policies. Policy makers have weighed the risks and decided how both the petroleum industry and the Canadian public would share the costs required to avert some of the most unacceptable risks. Security of supply and Canadian nationalism were two of the major reasons that western reserves were connected with eastern markets at greater costs than would otherwise have been incurred. As for the problems involved in forecasting demand for and supply of natural gas and other energy sources, many factors, especially the world price of substitutes such as oil, are completely outside the control of a supplier such as Canada, and these add a further degree of uncertainty which must be addressed. The concept of uncertainty in the economics of natural gas exports is a major factor which has to be explicitly provided for in policy making in this sector, not only for decision makers in Canada, but also for authorities with similar responsibilities in countries or regions that must make similar judgements in the marketplace.

Alan R. Winberg

Acknowledgments

I would like to express my sincere thanks to Professor Susan Strange of the London School of Economics and Political Science for her patient guidance and thoughtful advice. I would also like to thank Professor Lawrence Alschuler of the University of Ottawa, Jonathan Stern of the Royal Institute of International Affairs in London and Peter Eglington of the Ottawa Energy Group Ltd. for their helpful comments and suggestions.

Thanks is also due to Melvin Conant of Conant Associates in Washington for his support in seeing this project through to publication.

A.R.W.

1

Introduction

Economic regulation always requires difficult compromises. Every regulatory decision reflects a balancing act between the solution that would be produced by the marketplace actors left to themselves, and the solution that would be produced through some weighted voting process by the various parties affected by the regulatory intervention. Despite a political authority's desire to introduce "stability and fairness" or to prevent so called "windfall" gains, the risks and uncertainties inherent to the discovery, production and trade of primary commodities like natural gas can never be removed by some regulatory decree. Additionally, export regulation of natural gas by Canada has had to be sensitive to changing conditions in the international energy markets and in the (regulated) U.S. energy markets.

Economic conditions change over time and with these changes, new winners and losers are created. Some changes may be expected well in advance; others come as surprises. It is seldom a surprise, however, for potential winners or losers to use every possible tool at their disposal to improve their economic position in the marketplace. In markets where the regulatory institutions are already in place, intense pressure is often put on regulatory measures in times of rapid economic change. In general, over time these types of regulatory intervention can moderate or redirect the flow and distribution of benefits and costs. They cannot, however, modify the fundamental economic shifts in supply and demand against which various political publics may wish to be insulated.

The North American natural gas industry is currently undergoing one of its most fundamental structural changes since the 1960s. Economic changes have overwhelmed the regulatory system in place and the different sectors which, together, make up the natural gas industry are relearning the basics of competition.

The inertia of the regulatory and accompanying legal environment is creating plenty of work for lawyers. The court cases of the 1970s reflected the seller's market, and involved the difficulties of pipeline companies that were unable to fulfill their delivery commitments to distributors and end users. The court cases that are taking place now, however, involve the suppliers of gas to the pipelines who wish to oblige the pipelines to respect purchase contract obligations. For the first time in two decades natural gas producers are discovering that they have to worry about selling their wares and that there are plenty of substitute fuels and gas sources that will back out high-priced natural gas. While the lawyers argue, while contracts are renegotiated, and while some players go bankrupt, the need to balance potential supply and actual requirements has taken over and a spot market, based on market-clearing prices, has developed.

U.S. imports from Canada and Mexico, have, of course, felt these competitive forces massively. Rather than compete, Mexico has decided to stop its export sales. Canada, on the other hand, has started to warm up to the idea of competitive and flexible export prices and is reacting with vigor to the new market reality. On October 31, 1985, a wide variety of measures were announced with the stated purpose of providing greater flexibility and sensitivity to market conditions for trade in natural gas both within Canada, and in export markets.[1]

The period under study includes times when natural gas markets were dominated by buyers (1950-1969), sellers (1970-1980), and again, by buyers (1981-1986). Once the traditional market cycles for commodities have been observed over time, various features are seen to occur repeatedly. In response to persistent observed, or potentially recurring difficulties, commodity exporting countries have expressed a variety of concerns related to the optimal development and sale of the commodity in question. Before looking at the general issues, applicable to exports of a variety of commodities, it is useful to consider an overview of the basic issues which have been debated in Canada over the question of natural gas exports.

The development of a natural gas industry, in a country like Canada, occurs within a global economic and governmental policy environment that changes over time. However, a major theme of Canada's economic

---

1. <u>Agreement Among the Governments of Canada, Alberta, British Columbia and Saskatchewan on Natural Gas Markets and Prices</u>, October 31, 1985.

development since the nation was founded (and indeed before) has been growth based on the export of natural resources.[2] Each particular resource export has presented unique issues to be dealt with by Canadians and their various levels of government. These issues will continue to be hotly debated in 1986 as the United States and Canada pursue negotiations for freer trade. The issue of the exportation of Canada's energy resources in particular has received public attention since the beginning of the twentieth century.

Federal legislation to control energy exports was introduced as early as 1907.[3] The concern at that time was the export of hydro electric power, however, petroleum resources were also covered under this legislation. Petroleum exports gained importance in the 1950s and 1960s. Particularly since the oil price increases achieved by OPEC during the 1970s, the subject has become one of utmost interest to Canadians, and indeed, to people everywhere. As we move into the fluctuating conditions of the 1980s, the questions are amplified further. The key issue for the 1980s is how Canadian exporters can best maintain export sales volumes and revenues.

As with many other nations, one of the foundations of Canada's economy is the natural resource sector. Taking a view to the longer term, the exploitation of these natural resources, in most cases, produces spin-offs to feed the industrial sector. For this to occur, careful coordination and efficient management are required[4] to ensure that labor and transportation bottlenecks do not occur in the production, transport and sale of the resource, to ensure that the best possible deals are struck for the sale of the resource, and to ensure that the wealth stream can be sustained for the long term.

Resource development must be managed. But there are no obvious solutions to the many management problems that must be faced. Timing of development is

---

2. See Innis (1954, 1956a, 1956b); Watkins (1963); Buckley (1958); McDougall (1982).

3. _The Electricity and Fluid Exportation Act_, S.C. 1907, c. 16.

4. Either by private industry or the government, and usually by a combination of the two. For an interesting discussion of why the structure of the Canadian federal system may tend to increase the role of the federal government in this area, see Courchene (1980).

always an issue; however, the answers are seldom straightforward. There is always a danger that resources are being exploited too quickly (that is at a non-sustainable or economically sub-optimal rate) as those who control the levers of the economy seek (through the use of carrots and sticks) to increase the national product and improve citizens' immediate well-being, boosting the business climate, corporate profits and government revenue in turn. Eventually, as economically recoverable resources are used up, economic activity shifts. These required shifts must be anticipated enough in advance to obtain a smooth transition with minimum waste of productive resources.

The management issues are somewhat different depending on whether the resources being considered are classed as "renewable" or "non-renewable. Considering in the first place the case of renewable resources such as timber, fish or cattle, there is a clear contradiction between, on the one hand, the immediate concern to produce more jobs and higher income and consumption, and, on the other hand, the longer term concern to sustain these sectors for the future and to maximize the total economic and social benefits derived from the nation's capacity to produce renewable natural resources. However, with careful planning, and provided there is a willingness to do so, over-exploited areas can be re-stocked and managed for continued profitable production. Systemic features such as the mix of public or private ownership of the resource can influence strongly the "willingness" issue. In a similar way, under-exploited sectors can be stimulated. Thus, in the case of renewables, the problems are to assess the extent to which a given area is under- or over-exploited and, where appropriate, to convince the concerned parties that the costs of stimulating production, or in the case of overuse, the costs of required conservation measures and re-stocking, are worthwhile to preserve the sector.

In the case of non-renewable resources, the problems are similar in that over- or under-exploitation may be the situation. In the case of under-exploitation (if the market signals are not getting through to increase supply and reduce demand), costs must be borne in order to stimulate activity. As for the case of over-exploitation, it may be equally difficult to convince the affected parties that the costs of reduced production from productive capacity already in place or, on the demand side, increased conservation, are worthwhile. With renewables the goal is to preserve (or increase) the size of the pie for all generations. With non-renewables, citizens may be asked to increase production costs to reduce wastage or to reduce consumption in order that what they conserve can be consumed by a distant generation. In such a case, no new wealth is created; rather, consumption is deferred to a generation that may well have alternatives to and/or substitutes for the commodity in question.[5]

A further argument that must be considered is that the ultimate size of a given reserve, in terms of how much can actually be produced, may appreciate

---

5. A far-reaching debate has gone on as to the extent to which a current, democratically-elected government, such as the Parliament of Canada, can and should efficiently and effectively be the trustee for unborn generations as well as for its present electors. The discussion can never be adequately resolved, as the heart of the matter transcends logic and rationality and enters the normative realm of philosophy and religion. The arguments are aptly summarized by Feldstein (1964). He cites writers such as Pigou, Dobb, Holzman and Sen as examples of analysts who are willing to impose on the public the responsibility and cost of protecting the welfare of future generations, and others such as Eckstein, Bain and Marglin, who argue that the interests of future generations should be recognized only to the extent that current electors sanction them through the democratic process. Feldstein's own view was to allow administrative determination of the weight to be given to the welfare of future generations by "democratic administrators". He argued that an administrative decision by an accountable government satisfied his notion of the "requirement of democracy" and added that democratic theory does not require that each decision represent a consensus, but that "government action as a whole" be acceptable to the electorate (Feldstein (1964) p. 253). This author agrees with Feldstein's view; however, he would add that because it is government action as a whole that must be acceptable to the majority of the electorate and because large numbers of individual electors, in general, can be expected to reflect, in their voting, preference for their immediate welfare (as opposed to future welfare, the welfare of citizens yet unborn, and the general state of things long after their lifetimes), the likelihood of a democratic government leaving decisions on a given issue to an administrative (as opposed to a political) decision-making process is decreased as both the political visibility of the decision and the perceived impact of the various alternatives on specific potentially affected publics increase.

substantially with advances in technology or new production techniques. The threshold of what grade of ore can be mined, or what percentage of reserves in place will be usefully recovered usually moves ahead (or declines) on a timetable that cannot be forecast with a high degree of accuracy. The development of substitutes and the relative prices of these substitutes are additional complicating factors.

The problem of assessing whether a non-renewable resource is being exploited too quickly, therefore, becomes more difficult to assess. As with many other countries which export non-renewable resources, there have been no simple answers in the case of Canada's petroleum resources. The estimated size of the resource base in this sector is most difficult (and expensive) to assess and can never be known exactly. Information is produced slowly from exploration efforts and much luck and intuition is involved. Decisions must be taken at any given time, based on a judgement of what economically recoverable reserves will ultimately be found over time both within and outside Canada.[6] Clearly, this introduces a high degree of uncertainty that has to be addressed at all decision levels.

In the case of natural gas, the period under study encompasses periods of development, expansion, and consolidation of Canada's natural gas industry and of Canada's natural gas trade with the United States. Over this period, and continuing to the present new period of intense competition, two general approaches have been advocated for the appropriate trade management of Canada's natural gas.[7] Setting aside the immediate concerns of how to sell Canadian natural gas in a time of apparent surplus, the macro-level question that comes up time and again is whether natural gas exports are appropriate under any circumstances. As would be expected, the arguments have fluctuating levels of political support, depending on the point in the market cycle at which the issues are being considered. While the size of support does fluctuate, the arguments do not change all that much over time.

---

6. See, for example, Van Meurs (1981) pp. 333-405. Some analysts have stated flatly that no one can predict with any assurance or precision future levels of energy use or supply, even in the medium term. See, for example, Rustow (1977) pp. 496-499.

7. See, for example, Waverman (1981).

One side of the debate argues that the more natural gas Canadians are able to sell abroad profitably, the better. In the current period of relatively high unemployment, these arguments meet with little opposition on this score as those who would like more exports can cite the economic stimulation and related benefits to be gained. They argue that Canada should strive for as many jobs, as much development, and as high export revenues as can be had based upon Canada's generous resource endowment.[8] While quiet during the current period of intense marketing, traditionally, others have argued the opposite. These individuals have maintained that natural gas is a strategic resource, too precious to sell to foreigners. In general, in the recent past this group has argued for very restrictive export control. At the extreme, they would like to see Canada's natural gas reserved solely for future use in Canada, in spite of the fact that this would mean that the immediate economic benefits of exports would be postponed.[9] This school of thought would argue that the export market generally "undervalues" energy resources. This is the approach now being taken by the government of Mexico, in contrast with the current Canadian attitude.

At times, and in particular, when energy markets have favored sellers over buyers, attempts have been made to link the question of energy exports to industrial and trade objectives and to attain further processing of exports, or access to restricted markets such as the United States, or Japan. In the late 1970s, for example, the provincial government of Alberta made a case for increased access to U.S. petrochemical markets in return for increased exports of natural gas. However, in the current, soft energy market environment, these considerations have become remote.

Where there are differences of opinion, if a market is allowed to work, the marketplace will likely reflect a compromise in pricing and other contractual terms that are agreed to by contracting parties. Sellers and buyers would be expected to make arguments, such as those that are made to a regulator, during contract negotiations. These issues could, therefore, be resolved by marketplace participants in private negotiations. In Canada, however, as in many other places,

---

8. See, for example, Manecon Associates Ltd. (1978).

9. See, for example, Willson (1977); McDougall (1977); Laxer (1977).

these arguments became attractive issues in the political process and governments quickly moved to correct perceived lacunae where the working of the market could not be trusted to protect various political constituencies. Put differently, this school argues that through political regulation, our lot as a collectivity would be improved; we would get a better deal than could be wrested from the marketplace itself (without government intervention).

Over the period under study, Canada's federal government has been, and continues to be, at the center of this debate in light of its constitutional control over interprovincial and external trade and commerce, and therefore, over energy exports.[10] It is this level of government that is responsible for weighing the various arguments and setting Canada's energy export policies. The federal level of government, with the advice of its administrative agencies and departments, and extensive consultation with interested parties, has considered when, under what terms, that is what volumes and prices, and to what extent energy exports serve Canada's broad national interest. Interactions with the U.S. purchasers have taken place in various sectors, and here too, the federal government has played a key role. The provinces, as owners of the natural resources located in the territories under their jurisdiction, have also played important roles, setting the terms and conditions by which resources may be removed from each province. In addition, the provinces, as owners of the resources located in their territories, earn royalty income from the production of these resources. Current regulatory policies affecting the key aspects of domestic and international trade in natural gas were put in place in an agreement signed jointly by the federal government and the three western provinces responsible for the bulk of Canada's natural gas production.[11]

In addition to regulation of exports on the Canadian side, the U.S. market, including both imports and exports, was regulated too by the U.S. Federal Power Commission and its later successors. When exporting into a regulated U.S. market, it is reasonable to expect that generally, there would be benefits to be derived from creating an equivalent statutory authority

---

10. <u>British North America Act</u>, Section 91 (2).

11. <u>Agreement Among the Governments of Canada, Alberta, British Columbia and Saskatchewan on Natural Gas Markets and Prices</u>, October 31, 1985.

on the Canadian side. Import approval requirements of a regulatory authority can thus be balanced with export approval requirements. In addition, exports of Canadian natural gas and other energy resources have, at times, become the subject of hot political debates, and regional concerns have had to be balanced in export decisions as well as the other factors discussed above. Also, pressures from both the international and domestic markets have, on occasion, played an important role.

Once a society steps back from a purely market-derived solution, decisions made with regard to a specific resource or economic sector are usually made within the framework of a state's (centralized or decentralized) planning to coordinate economic activities. As such, given the sheer volume of information to be coordinated, it is unlikely that, at the senior political levels, the minute details of a specific project or contract will be given close, detailed scrutiny. Even broader policy questions which are considered to be of a technical nature are usually referred to an administrative agency or commission for advice which is usually difficult to reject, leaving only relatively macro-level decisions and policies being brought to decision-makers at the highest levels. Public debate on any given issue, therefore, usually is focused on these macro-level issues, the nitty-gritty being left to the representatives of the special interest groups, impacted parties and specific politicians and/or bureaucrats responsible for advising the government on a given matter.

In this sense, once the macro-policy is established, the "technical" details (upon which the real impact of the macro-policy may ultimately depend) are worked out in an environment which may at times may be "political" but which may or may not directly involve elected representatives of the general public. If the judges or administrators are not elected, and hold a type of academic "tenure", and further, if they have little or no financial rewards or punishments for good, poor or mediocre management or decision-making, a huge element of systematic, regulatory conservatism, or inertia is introduced into the marketplace. When one board or tribunal or set of bureaucrats holds the reins of trade, the flexibilities, and ability for quick entrepreneurial actions that would otherwise exist in a diverse, less-regulated marketplace are lost. A regulator would generally be risk-averse, and therefore, very conservative in deviating from past precedents. While appropriate for a steady type of market, where marketplace conditions fluctuate rapidly, this type of regulated marketplace carries much more risk, from a societal viewpoint, than a marketplace characterized by a large number of diverse actors, all setting their own trade deals in accordance with their views of the future (rather than a set of rules set by a regulator). As the uncertainty associated with the future course of the market increases, so do the advantages of diverse decisions being made by diverse actors. This way, the marketplace, rather than a government regulator, is charged with rewarding the winners and the losers and creating incentives.

For example, one such "technical" issue is the specific price at which a given commodity is sold. In general, where a market is regulated, a macro-policy is usually set to sell at, above, or below a market or cost-determined benchmark price. Setting a specific price that conforms to the policy, at times open to wide interpretation, is then left to the administrative system.

In the case of natural gas exports, or the export of any resource for that matter, pricing and price expectations of buyer and seller are crucial. All future uncertainties must be translated to the present in the form of a price at the time a sale is made. When a supplier is selling into a large market relative to his own supply he can choose whether to sell sooner rather than later. In general, prices are expected to rise or fall over time. If prices are rising at an uncertain rate, the owner of a given resource, whether ownership is public or private, must face the problem of timing. He must choose whether to restrict production in anticipation of higher expected prices, or rather to accept the lower price sooner. When prices are falling, however, sellers must decide whether to accelerate deliveries or stop sales until the market improves. Depending on the owner's evaluation of an appropriate discount rate, which would include a very important risk factor, he would attempt to time development of a given reserve so that the present value of exploiting the resource at any given moment was equal to or greater than the value of doing so at any other moment.[12]

---

12. See, for example, Adelman (1972b) pp. 2-3; Bryan (1982) p. 99; Hotelling (1931); Solow (1974); Stiglitz (1976).

In the case of the exploitation of some energy resources, such as electricity,[13] a number of different non-price factors would come into play; however, price and revenue maximization have been among the chief explicit economic considerations regarding Canada's natural gas exports. Domestic security of supply, building east-west ties, regional development, and general economic conditions at different points in time have also been important factors. In general, Canadians have chosen to develop Canada's non-renewable natural resources, and reap the immediate and substantial advantages of development, rather than leave this endowment in the ground. Because of limited Canadian domestic markets, this choice to develop meant a choice to pursue export markets. This implies that export prices were considered attractive and the other terms of development, acceptable. However, even if exports have been considered attractive, restrictions have been maintained on the volumes committed to the export market. For commodities perceived to be strategic, and vital for the public welfare such as natural gas, various policies and regulatory procedures have been put in place to protect the future requirements of Canadian users. Sometimes, these measures have been used alone and sometimes jointly with private, market-oriented vehicles. Protecting future requirements either privately or through government regulation usually requires some degree of production deferral. In turn, deferral of production entails costs that must be borne by the various parties involved.

This whole question of deferring production, restricting volumes of export sales and keeping a quantity of natural gas in reserve to protect future Canadian requirements may seem somewhat academic in the current environment of intense competition to maintain and, where possible, increase export sales volumes. However, it remains a cornerstone of Canadian natural gas export policy, and was a constraint on export sales for much of the 1970s and the early 1980s. Refusing authorization for export sales and, therefore, deferring production from reserves which are known to be in place, imposes important costs on the owners of these reserves. While they may not show up in an accoun-

---

13. Electricity cannot generally be stored, and so is more of a "flow" resource or a stream of value over time than a storable "stock" of value. This is especially applicable in the case of the generation of electricity from hydro.

tant's notebook as actual cash expenditures, these costs are real and significant. In particular, as a result of these policies, some reserve owners face holding costs and foregone or postponed sales revenue. Although they may seem invisible, these costs can cause severe hardship to some reserve holders. Also, they are likely not to be equally shared across the entire industry as some fortunate producers may well hold sales contracts for their particular reserves. The costs borne as a result of this policy may, of course, be counterbalanced by subsequent price increases and resulting higher sales revenues in the future. When considering the relative attractiveness of currently available prices compared with price expectations, the value of current as opposed to future revenues and the expected impact of increasing current cash receipts are often crucial.

A fundamental issue is whether natural gas is indeed a strategic commodity, essential for the national welfare. It is strategic only when its absence would cause hardships. Time is a key factor. What is strategic at one time, may lose this quality once people invest in measures to reduce their strategic dependence. In the 1980s, a wide range of fuel substitutes are available. Substitutes to natural gas would include oil, coal, electricity and a variety of other liquid fuels. Once an investment has been made to allow gas users to shift to the substitutes when necessary, natural gas has nothing inherently strategic about it. Why should it deserve such special treatment? Non-strategic concerns provide the answer of why it did receive this special treatment and these are outlined in detail later on. But, as the debate in Canada and elsewhere has approached natural gas as a strategic commodity, it is worth pointing out the arguments based on this factor.

At the base of these arguments, one must understand that exploration and other investment in Canadian energy resources (and, a wide range of other raw materials) depends to a large extent upon the opportunity to sell them on either the domestic or the export market. Only when they are actually produced and used do these resources take on real value. Because of the limited domestic market, if and when the resources are found, the companies would be expected to seek the best prices and most effective sales opportunities available, both within Canada and abroad. Generally, once domestic market requirements were covered, provided transportation facilities were available, holders of reserves would be expected to pursue the export market. These firms are in the petroleum business and make money through finding petroleum resources, and developing what they find. In general, they would much prefer to earn an earlier return on their investment in exploration, rather than "bank" the reserves to earn an income stream sometime in the future. From the buyer's perspective, he is favored in two ways by a policy such as this that protects his future requirements. First there is the obvious advantage of being able to make the necessary capital expenditures to use the resource without having to worry about supply availability. In addition, he need not compete in a bidding situation with purchasers abroad. The existence of such a policy immediately sets up a situation where domestic prices can be lower than the prices that could be had for the commodity if potential foreign purchasers were allowed to bid on a given supply. Whether in fact domestic prices are lower than export prices then becomes a regulatory policy decision. With this background, the debate on exporting natural gas as a strategic commodity can be better appreciated.

In the 1970s, as the myth of natural gas as a "strategic" commodity was being raised by export opponents, the Canadian petroleum industry attempted and, to some extent, succeeded in turning the argument around. Export applicants pointed out that exports are a way of keeping up exploration efforts for this so-called strategic commodity. They argued that export sales provide the industry with the cash flow that is required to fund the exploration for new reserves. One notes that this statement assumes that exploration should be financed more through internally generated cash flow than through other financing vehicles.[14] Accepting this assumption, the statement makes sense from the financial point of view; however, the reasoning itself leads to new questions. Exports are used to fund exploration for new supplies to replace the exports. Authorizing exports provides the industry with cash to find more, but in the meantime, the Canadian resource base is depleted through these same exports. In turn, this depletion feeds the perceived "need to know", that is, the perceived requirement for more information about the location and extent of new reserves of the strategic commodity in question.

For those commodities considered to be "strategic", the main consideration in assessing the argument of using exports to provide cash flow to fund exploration is whether the expected benefits from exports, that is new discoveries, can reasonably be expected to exceed the cost in terms of the depletion of known

---

14. See, for example, Van Meurs (1981) pp. 237-250.

reserves. Through exports, a precious, strategic commodity is being used up. Acceptance of these arguments requires that an optimistic attitude be taken from the start. How much undiscovered resource is under the ground, waiting to be discovered? How sure are we that the companies will find more of the strategic commodity than they sell? Some would argue that the biggest, easiest to find reserves are more likely to be found first. Is it possible or likely that the principle of diminishing returns to exploration activity will come into play? This type of policy requires that expected future requirements be estimated and compared against discovered reserves and potential future discoveries and reserves additions. How important are future discoveries expected to be in relation to expected domestic requirements? Even accepting the unfounded basis that all Canada's natural gas is in fact a strategic commodity, this aspect of the debate rests on the uncertainties and on the confusion between Canada's estimated total resource base and proven reserves.

"Proven reserves," as used in Canada and many other countries, is a term rich in misconceptions. "Proven" as used here is prone to be misunderstood by many. While it sounds to be a rather straightforward use of the English language indicating a high level of reliability, the specific amounts of oil or natural gas calculated as "proven" is much more open to subjective judgement than one would normally expect. A distinction must also be made between reserves that are proven and those that are estimated to be recoverable and deliverable under current or forecast economic conditions. That portion of a reserve of oil or natural gas that is economically recoverable and deliverable is a function of market prices and advances in technology (and sometimes knowledge of geology). These variables are by no means stable and fluctuate substantially over time. It is possible that Canada's policies to protect future domestic requirements cause uneconomic investments to be made by exploration companies. A decision to "prove" resources, which is done by step-out drilling from discovered wells, as well as exploratory drilling, is an investment in better, more reliable information on a given pool. Undertaking this type of investment is similar in many ways to building up an "inventory" and can be done for political as well as economic and commercial reasons.[15]

---

15. See for example, a discussion of the motives of various companies, concession-holders and governments in the various OPEC states in Rustow (1977) pp. 500-503.

Additional arguments advanced by potential exporters, which build on the myth of natural gas as a strategic commodity, relate to the need for maintaining a base level of exploration activity. This argument is slightly different from the idea of using exports to finance the exploration effort discussed above. Rather, in this case, they look at the question of maintaining a "capacity to explore" in addition to the mere existence of a given level of proven reserves. Here they argue that there is no masterswitch that can be thrown to turn the exploration faucet on and off on short notice as and when required. While there is no question of this occurring in the near term, in the event that shortages of deliverable volumes of natural gas were to develop at a given point in time (as occurred in the mid-1970s), because of the long lags that may be involved between getting an exploration or a development effort started and actually getting natural gas flowing to a market, there may be difficulties in attempting to get instant exploration and to a lesser extent, development drilling.

While this reasoning is logical, the significant question here would be whether there were other substitutes available to replace the needed natural gas. Unlike oil, natural gas is not used to any great degree for transportation uses. Substitutes do exist. The industry's arguments to use exports to fund a base level of exploration for a strategic resource, therefore, are suspect. As they have started to do recently, potential exporters would be well-served not to adopt the "strategic-type" arguments, but rather to refute them. The strategic commodities of yesterday are not necessarily going to be strategic tomorrow.

Even apart from the "strategic" notion, these are weak arguments to support exports. If the gas is not there, no one will find it, no matter how hard they look. Thus, exploration does not create more natural gas resources; rather, it finds resources that are already there. More precisely, it increases knowledge regarding the likelihood of their existence at a specific location. The export issue, therefore, can be linked only to the rate of discovery, not to the actual amount of the resource in place. For example, if, by reducing the allowed level of exports, a government were to reduce industry cash flow, and consequently, reduce the level of exploration, the expected end result would be a slowing of the discovery process, not a reduction in the nation's total stock of natural gas. The risk here is that in the future prices may drop and the profitability of discovering and producing natural gas may become reduced from current levels. In such a case, a restrictive export policy which slowed the discovery process would result in a permanent loss to the Canadian economy as its natural gas asset declined in value and was perhaps never again worth looking for or producing.

Continuing the line of argument that exports are a good way of maintaining a base level of exploration, in addition to this point, export applicants have tried to use the uncertainties and the risks associated with exploration activities as a point in support of extra exports. These extra exports are portrayed as a type of insurance or policy cushion. Proponents have maintained that because of the uncertainty, it is not possible to know the precise level of exploration required to discover a continuing supply sufficient to meet domestic market requirements. In this manner, industry representatives have attempted to build a case for encouraging some measure of extra exploration to increase further the probability that future domestic needs will be met. Proponents point out that this extra exploration can be encouraged by allowing additional natural gas exports. In this case, exports are seen as preferable to other vehicles, which could be used but which could be a burden on government finances, such as fiscal incentives or the creation of a government-owned natural gas stockpile, or vehicles which would put additional costs on consumers, such as requiring domestic distribution companies to negotiate contracts for their expected requirements far into the future.

Political considerations, and objectives, including a desire to maintain or expand the level of economic activity in exploration areas; to promote the investment climate in Canada in general; to increase government tax revenues; and to promote national unity or national independence, have also played an important part in policy formulation.[16] These considerations and objectives may, in fact, be the deciding ones in a specific decision, over and above the more general, longer term objective of providing energy supplies to Canadians.

Of course, given the current climate of intense competition for export sales, and the recent (and continuing) political efforts of U.S. producers to back out Canadian supplies to the U.S. market through use of the U.S. regulatory process, this internal Canadian debate of the "strategic" importance of a given amount

---

16. See, for example, McDougall (1982).

of Canadian gas has been put on a back burner.[17] This could change again if the market does shift back in the longer term. However, the key question in the mid-1980s related to Canadian natural gas is not whether there exists an exportable surplus of gas in Canada, but rather, how much of the obvious surplus Canadian exporters will succeed in selling profitably. The "strategic commodity" argument no doubt will continue to be debated, and once these matters have been dealt with, export prices and revenues are the prime considerations. Assuming it is decided that some quantity of natural gas is perceived as being surplus to foreseeable domestic requirements, and therefore, available for export, price and other equally important issues arise which must be addressed. The issues are central to resource management of natural gas and many other traded commodities. These would include such matters as where and when the exports should occur, what specific reserves of natural gas (or other resources) should be exported, at what rate, at what price, by whom and to which importer.

There are a number of ways that these questions could be addressed by market participants and/or by government regulators. While natural gas exports from

---

17. In their agreement of October 31, 1985, the federal government and the producing provinces publicly anticipated a relaxation of the rules and procedures that restricted the volumes of natural gas available for export or removal from a producing province, and the resultant freer access to domestic and export markets (<u>Agreement Among the Governments of Canada, Alberta, British Columbia and Saskatchewan on Natural Gas Markets and Prices</u>, paragraph 16). On the other hand, the issue is not ice cold. For example, the province of Ontario, in a submission to the National Energy Board in November 1985, argued for preservation of the then existing 25-year exportable surplus determination procedure and reserves test (<u>Globe and Mail</u>, November 21, 1985, p. 34).

Canada have generally been at international prices,[18] some export opponents have argued that they have not necessarily been priced at their long-run marginal cost. "Long-run marginal cost" is a highly theoretical concept in the case of natural gas as there are a multitude of costs which could logically be either included or excluded from the calculations. In any case, giving those who support this view the benefit of the doubt, while there is a high degree of uncertainty, natural gas being exported under existing licenses may well turn out to be relatively low-cost compared to alternative frontier sources. This means that U.S. customers would get cheap gas now but that Canadian consumers of natural gas might have to turn to high-priced gas from the Atlantic or the Beauport sea for their requirements at some time in the distant future.[19] The high level of uncertainty of course is central to these types of buy, sell or hold questions. Many factors must be considered, all of which may be valued differently by different players in the marketplace. For these questions, there is the matter of whether government regulation would be expected to produce better results than could be had if private actors were left to use the tools available to private parties in the marketplace.

---

18. "International" market price in the case of Canada's natural gas exports, over the period before the OPEC oil price increases of 1973, is the price of equivalent natural gas supplies in accessible markets in the United States. This market was regulated by the U.S. Federal Power Commission over this period. The Commission based its price findings largely on the historic cost of natural gas production in the specific U.S. area concerned. In the 1973 to 1984 period, Canadian natural gas export prices were set in relation to the international crude oil price on a BTU equivalence basis. In the post-1984 period, export prices have reflected prices of alternative gas supplies and fuels in the U.S. market. Export prices are considered in detail in Chapter 10 of this study.

19. These arguments were put forward repeatedly in the late 1970s, and again, as recently as November 1985 at National Energy Board hearings (See Testimony of Ontario and of British Columbia Hydro and Power Authority reported in Globe and Mail, November 25, 1985, page B2; November 21, 1985, p. B4).

For the period before 1973, a wide range of export prices were negotiated by the contracting parties and contracts were reviewed by the federal regulator. From 1973 to 1984, both domestic and export natural gas prices were set by the federal government of Canada. Since 1984, prices have again been negotiated by contracting parties and reviewed by a federal regulator to ensure certain minimum conditions are met. A wide variety of factors influence the pricing of natural gas sales, and, in the current environment, the most important of these are the prices of competing, alternative energy sources. However, in spite of the wide range of potential factors, and the pressures of competition, it is reasonable to assume that one of the key factors is the cost of finding new supplies. Here again it is possible to argue that natural gas found as a result of an oil-directed exploration effort has a finding cost which is very low if not zero. Cost calculations, as evidenced by the acrobatics possible when competent accountants and lawyers role up their sleeves and argue about what should count and what should not, are open to a wide range of interpretation. However, for the purpose of this discussion, suffice it to say that since it is not possible to know the future cost of finding, producing and delivering Canada's frontier gas, there is an argument for restricting to frontier gas the eligibility for export. In effect, such a restriction would transfer to others the costs and uncertainties associated with these sources, while retaining the lower cost, established, conventional reserves for domestic use.[20] This type of approach, however, can only be successful when market conditions allow frontier reserves to be sold in competition with other sources and fuel substitutes. These considerations were at the base of the province of Alberta's initial export policy in authorizing exports from the Peace River district in the early 1950s. At that time, only natural gas from this seemingly "remote" area was considered surplus to provincial requirements and made available for removal from the province.

---

20. Politics aside, pricing a commodity domestically at a level below its value in the international marketplace, unless countered by a number of other measures to influence consumption patterns, would be expected to lead to "wasteful" consumption as consumers would not receive the proper signals which would cause them to increase the efficiency with which they consume that commodity.

Setting the export revenue question aside, for reasons of transportation and production economics, exports have often been essential in the development of Canada's reserves. The majority of these are found in Alberta and the other western provinces, and therefore, are distant from the major Canadian markets in Ontario and eastern Quebec. There is always a minimum market size threshold which must be met in order for a viable pipeline to be built to develop the reserves. Financing the large capital requirements for the construction of a natural gas pipeline has traditionally required that specific markets for the gas be identified and contracts be in place. In cases where the domestic natural gas market was too small to support the large up-front investment required in production and transportation infrastructure, exports were essential. Only with the economics of scale and the required larger markets made possible by exports could the investments be made and, therefore, could the development of the reserves proceed in the desired timeframe.

As will be shown, this has been the case in the development of Canada's major natural gas transmission lines, and could indeed represent itself in the future development of Canada's frontier reserves. To date, such reserves have been discovered in the high Arctic and the Mackenzie River Delta and offshore in the Atlantic Maritime region and in the Pacific, off the coast of British Columbia. In public statements related to these reserves, the export proponents' argument is that exports are necessary due to the economics of putting in place the delivery system and obtaining the required capital investments. Natural gas sales have to be made in competition with other fuels at the burner tip. Restricting sales solely to Canadian customers may not be possible as gas sales would not be competitive. Even in a case where sale of this gas was possible, costs to consumers in Canadian markets could well be much higher if exports and resulting economies of scale were not used to help lower the unit costs of producing and transporting the natural gas from the frontier areas. Faced with these very strong, well-founded arguments, export opponents have returned to the "strategic-type" concepts and pointed out that gas production from the frontier could be deferred for many years if natural gas from conventional areas were reserved for domestic use rather than committed for export. Again, we are back to the question of the extent to which natural gas is and will always remain a strategic commodity. Otherwise, what benefit is there to defer production from the frontier areas?

These issues and concerns and the arguments and counter arguments advanced are examined in detail in this study. They are discussed against the background of change which has pushed the industry through various market cycles. The market for natural gas, as for a variety of other commodities, is dynamic. Some emerging trends may well continue throughout the 1980s and beyond. In particular, the growing spot market for natural gas, disruption of long term arrangements and more flexible pricing agreements all point to a different market, requiring adaptation by market participants, including government regulators. The U.S. Natural Gas Policy Act of 1978 and its incentive pricing provisions, coupled with the worldwide business recession of 1980 and 1981 and falling world oil prices have brought about highly competitive marketing conditions between natural gas, and its fuel substitutes, including residual fuel oil in the industrial sector as well as distillate fuel oil in the commercial and residential sectors. Here, natural gas has lost its pricing edge, losing markets in all sectors in the United States. To make marketing even more competitive, higher prices under the 1978 legislation brought about more drilling in the United States and gas reserves increased dramatically. As would be expected, reduced demand and increased U.S. domestic supply, within the regulated United States marketplace, created new forces on regulators. Canadian exports, in particular dropped off dramatically in the period 1982 to 1984 as the new competitive situation made itself felt. As Canada permitted more flexible price regulation in late 1984, allowing export sales to be more competitive, volumes stopped declining and picked up again in 1985.

Regulators in the United States and Canada have had to adjust their regulatory approaches. The increasing importance of spot market activity and its vital role in providing needed market flexibility for what is now a non-strategic commodity is only slowly being understood.

In the chapters which follow, the market cycles for natural gas are considered. The problems of natural gas and marketplace regulation, however, are not really unique. These are shared by other commodities. Before proceeding with the discussion of natural gas in particular, the next chapter steps back and considers the more general issues of international trade in natural resources as a backdrop for the commodity specific analysis that follows.

2
Natural Resource Exports

The availability of adequate economic supplies of raw materials is a key factor in the economic growth and prosperity of nations, and the imperative of meeting this fundamental requirement has dominated relations among nations and regions throughout history.

In view of this reliance on natural resources, people have constantly feared the possibility of scarcities arising in the economic supply of these resources. Thomas Malthus' hypothesis, that the rate of population growth naturally tended to exceed the growth rate of supply of natural resources and that living standards would therefore fall if the rate of growth of population were not restrained, has appeared, with numerous variations, in economic and policy debates time and time again.

In recent years, pessimism regarding the earth's capacity to sustain current living standards has had a significant impact on public opinion towards economic growth and the management of natural resources. This pessimism reached its most recent peak in the mid-1970s, with the Club of Rome publication entitled "The Limits to Growth"[1] which, through an apparently scientific and sophisticated modelling approach, painted some very bleak scenarios regarding the future limited availability of natural resources and the consequent inevitable belt-tightening that would be required everywhere. In Limits to Growth, the authors concluded that if the global community were to avoid economic and social disaster in the coming decades, increased conservation of natural resources and more strict population and pollution controls would have to be combined

---

1. Meadows et al. (1972).

with controls on the rate of economic growth.[2]

Nowhere were these pessimistic hypotheses driven home more forcefully than in the energy sector. The actions of the Organization of Petroleum Exporting Countries (OPEC) in 1973-1974 resulted in dramatic, sudden increases in the international price of crude oil and underlined the vulnerability of oil importers. During the rest of the 1970s, the world witnessed the difficult beginning of an economic transition as people adjusted to accommodate this new energy situation. As we move into the 1980s a reverse of the trends is taking place. As sure as night follows day, perceptions of resource exhaustion in the near term tend to put in motion a number of mechanisms which, like the force of gravity, eventually pull the pendulum in the reverse direction.

As oil prices soared, so too did demand for regulated natural gas in North America. While Canadians faced eventual potential perceived shortages, real, regulatory-induced shortages hit the eastern United States and the Great Lakes areas in particular. Schools and factories closed down and the ordinary residential gas customer (read voter) became worried about actually freezing. There were, of course, political and economic reactions that soon created even greater market imbalances. Politically, new layers of complicated rules were added to the regulation of natural gas and federal jurisdiction was extended to all gas produced in the United States. Economically, gas users became worried and started to think about moving off gas to other fuels. Lower consumption would lead to lower utilization of pipeline capacity, and because pipelines are regulated utilities, to higher unit transportation costs for gas. Higher gas prices would impact on gas users' decisions on choice of fuel, and we are soon back to the beginning of a vicious circle on the demand side. Supply, of course, would be expected, by many, to react to higher prices and the regulated supply-price signals sent out in the late 1970s in both the United States and in Canada, had a much greater impact than was expected at the time. To

---

2. More specifically, Meadows et al. concluded that a society based on continued growth could not continue for another one hundred years unless steps were taken to limit growth in the very near term (p. 183), and in fact, during the decade of the 1970s (commentary on the Report by the Executive Committee of the Club of Rome – A. King, S. Okita, A. Peccei, E. Pestel, H. Thiemann, C. Wilson (p. 193).

address these phenomena in the context of natural gas trade, and in a broader context, which would apply to a wide range of traded commodities, we have to think back to the mid-1970s.

The success of OPEC gave rise to the possibility of raw material exporters forming similar united fronts to attempt to restructure the trading arrangements in place for a host of other commodities.[3] With the passage of time, however, it became clear that no other commodity shared the same kind of marketing opportunity as did oil, and that no other producer association could expect to duplicate OPEC's success.[4] Indeed,

---

3. In fact, many scholars directed their work to examining the hypothesis that as economic growth continued, advanced, industrial resource-importing countries could well become more dependent on particular exporters of specific commodities, and non-renewable commodities. See, for example, Connelly and Perlman (1975); Mathews (1975), pp. 85-86; Edwards (1975).

4. See, for example, Winberg (1976); (1979) pp. 178-182; Mikdashi (1976) pp. 196-205; International Bank for Reconstruction and Development (1973); Edwards (1975) pp. 18-19, 87-95; Singh (1976) pp. 89-91; Streeten (1976); Mikesell (1974). The author notes that there are also analysts who say that it is not OPEC as a cartel-type organization that is responsible for the oil price increase of the 1970s, but rather a market phenomenon of demand exceeding supply (see, for example, Johany (1982)). Although OPEC may not be a true cartel in the strictest sense of the word, the actions of Saudi Arabia, acting as a residual supplier, have had an effect very similar to a cartel which restricted supply to maintain a given price level. See, for example, McKie (1974); Stobaugh and Yergin (1979) pp. 31-37. The apparent disintegration of OPEC that became clearer in late 1985 has been assured by Saudi Arabia's change of policy announced in January 1986. If Saudi Arabia does, in fact, follow through on its stated intention to maintain its market share, then oil prices will continue to fall as there is nothing to make the OPEC system continue to function as a price-supporting element in the world oil market. Unless Saudi Arabia backs down, the next five years will witness great instability within OPEC and departures by at least half of the thirteen nations now in the organization. OPEC, as it stands at the time of this writing, is a group of states meeting purely for show. Different members have very different levels of oil

with the passage of time, people came to realize that the energy crisis was not as serious, in physical terms, as some were led to believe in the mid-1970s. Many now see that there are numerous reasons why the global system will most likely avoid the disasters predicted by Meadows et al.[5]

---

reserves and different needs for export revenues. The rhetoric of the meeting table is generally not followed through by concerted actions after the meetings. The interests are too varied; the pressures of the world marketplace are too strong. Those members that need immediate revenues will have to cheat and exceed their production quotas. Now that Saudi Arabia has decided to play hardball, the cheating will accelerate until the systemwide costs of cheating become astronomic. What will happen then is anyone's guess. Saudi Arabia is the key (**Business Week**, November 23, 1985, pp. 24-25).

5. See, for example, Cole, Freeman, Jahoda and Pavitt (1973); Connelly and Perlman (1975); Gordon (1973); Goldsmith et al. (1977); Madisson (1970) pp. 253-265; Kaysen (1972). In general, models such as those used in Meadows et al. (1972) can be faulted for having been erected on a very fragile and quite incomplete data base, and for the value biases which not only influence the models themselves but also any analysis which is attempted on the basis of these models. The specific reasons that could be cited are examined below in Chapter 6, entitled "Uncertainty", and include a number of factors which impact on supply and consumption including, most importantly, price. As stated by Kaysen (1972), "As a resource becomes scarce, the consequent rise in price leads to savings in use, to efforts to increase supply, and to technical innovation to offset the scarcity" (p. 665). Rising (or falling) prices of a depreciating natural resource commodity, particularly in relation to prices of other commodities which are complete or partial substitutes, would impact upon the development and use of substitutes, the utilization of known technology to extract the commodity from previously uneconomic or inhospitable environments, development of new or refined technology and efforts to increase rates of productivity in both the use and production of the commodity in question. With specific reference to the Meadows et al. (1972) model, pollution may be viewed as a type of "undesired commodity"; which, as it increases, the value of antipollution technology and measures also increases. In response to this increased value, one would expect improvements in

During the mid-1970s, however, the concerns of Meadows et al. were shared widely[6] and had a significant influence on world events. Immediately after the OPEC actions of 1973 and 1974, much diplomatic effort was spent to organize a dialogue between oil exporters and importers.[7] To this end, in April 1975 an international meeting was held in Paris, chaired by the French, but it soon broke down over the proper subject matter to be discussed.

Third World countries, led by the members of OPEC, wanted to discuss a wide range of raw materials and development problems; however, the industrialized world, led by the United States, wanted the discussions to be limited only to oil. The dynamics of each point of view were clear. If discussions were limited to oil, the meetings would put OPEC in a rather bad light -- the entire world of oil importers pitted against a handful of oil exporters. OPEC was economically strong, but wanted the rest of the Third World as political allies. If, therefore, OPEC had its expanded subject matter for the agenda, then the dialogue would be seen to occur more between the industrialized states and the less-developed countries (LDC's) including OPEC members.

---

technology to occur, and increased antipollution activities to be undertaken. Although analysts such as Georgescu-Roegen have presented some very thoughtful arguments pointing out the limitations of price and market adjustments (for example Georgescu-Roegen (1975) pp. 364-366), Georgescu-Roegen has agreed that the Meadows et al. conclusions lacked "a scientifically solid basis" (Ibid. p. 366).

6. See, for example, Commoner (1972); Daly (1973), (1974); Leiss (1976); Muir (1975); Schumacher (1973). A Second Report of the Club of Rome was published in 1974, which attempted to refine the original model and answer some of the criticisms that were made against the 1972 report. The conclusions were consistent with those of the 1972 report and recommended a global, integrated solution, with a view to the long term costs of pursuing short term gains and proposing the ethic of conservation as a choice which cannot be delayed (Mesarovic and Pestel 1974). See also Leiss (1976) which outlines the advantages to society if a limit to growth is accepted.

7. See, for example, Hurni (1975).

Although the April 1975 Paris talks broke down, in May 1975, the United States and other industrialized states accepted that raw materials and a variety of development problems be discussed, along with oil and energy. However, the dialogue was to be pursued in four different commissions: oil and energy would be discussed in one, raw materials in another. The other two commissions covered finance and development aid.

Over the following two years, discussions were pursued related to stabilizing the price of oil at a "fair" level, indexing the price to the rate of inflation in the industrialized world, ensuring adequate supplies to consumers, and, in general, trying to guarantee an overall "orderly" market. Needless to say, these discussions did not meet the expressed objectives, and in fact, in 1979, oil prices shot up again with resultant shocks to the world economy as significant as in 1973-1974.

While the finance and aid commissions served mainly as additional international forums for a continuing exchange of ideas which were largely duplicated in other international organizations, the commission on raw materials saw its subject matter discussed in sub-committees which looked at commodities on an individual basis. These were rolled into similar groups within the United Nations Conference on Trade and Development (UNCTAD) after the UNCTAD IV meetings were held in Nairobi, Kenya in May 1976.

Until the mid-1970s, mainstream theories of economic development focused almost exclusively on internal changes that less-developed nations had to bring about in order to obtain economic growth and prosperity. Some economists, however, made various arguments that changes in the structure of the global economic system were the essential elements for LDC's to achieve economic success. Following the changes brought about by the new energy situation, this new economic reasoning has been advocated by the Group of 77 who have advanced arguments for changes in the international development aid dispensing process, in the rules and laws governing international trade and commerce and in the control of foreign investment.[8]

Following the 1976 UNCTAD IV meetings, the dialogue on commodity trade between industrialized and less-developed countries continued to evolve, and has taken a central place in international affairs.[9] Over

---

8. See, for example, Kahail (1979) p. 530; Streeten (1976); Helleiner (1976).

9. Singh (1976).

time, raw material exporters have enumerated an extensive list of problems that they wish to remedy. Some are very dependent upon fluctuating revenues derived from the export of a few products and there are often few alternatives open to raw material exporters. Many commodities are subject to wide price fluctuations. Generally growth in export volumes is very slow. As regards some commodities, the governments of exporting states may be at a disadvantage with regard to transnational firms in negotiations for the sharing of economic rents which may be generated over time. Also, in some cases, there may be difficult barriers for exporters to increase their share of final market prices by further transformation of the products they export.

While the problems apply to the whole range of traded commodities, "exhaustible" natural resources have been a prime concern. In all countries, both industrialized and less developed, the rate of development and use of domestic "exhaustible" resources presents difficult decisions.[10] The development of these resources for export presents a further layer of questions that must be addressed.

In the case of export-oriented development, governments have attempted to take measures to maximize the net benefits accruing to their citizens, derived from exports. At the same time, governments have attempted to protect the interests of domestic citizens (including future generations) impacted by the development of resources for export, and to protect the country's future requirements for the resource in question. In addition, where appropriate, and to the greatest extent possible, governments have attempted to use resource exports to strengthen their negotiating position, to obtain trade and other concessions, and to promote further processing and resource-based industrial development.

Canada's natural gas exports and the policies put in place by the Canadian government in pursuit of its goals are a case in point. Before attempting to approach the specific issues of that case, however, it is useful first to step back to look at the questions of general concern to exporters of natural resources and to examine the types of policy options open to governments with natural resources (be they domestical-

---

10. See, for example, Appelby (1976); Arrow (1973); Barnett and Morse (1963); Bradly (1973); Gray (1914); Hotelling (1931); Helliwell (1975); Solow (1974); Tullock (1979).

ly or foreign-owned or controlled) but which need an external market for their optimal development.

Dialogue on Commodity Trade

The objectives of the changes sought by LDC primary commodity exporters and which developed importers have been willing to discuss at recent international meetings may be summarized as follows:[11]

1) to stabilize prices at levels which remain remunerative to producers and equitable to consumers and consistent with the balance between production and consumption as this evolves within expanding world commodity trade;
2) to encourage economic development through the stability of export receipts of LDC's, in particular from commodities, and through increasing foreign currency earnings by diversifying production, improving productivity and expanding the processing of primary commodities;
3) to encourage conditions favorable to increasing trade and production in ways conducive to development which facilitate the provision of investment finance, promote exploration, build up the necessary managerial and technological capabilities and lead to increased production and local processing;
4) to give LDC's an opportunity to participate in the marketing, distribution and transport of their commodity exports;
5) to encourage research and development on the problems of natural products competing with synthetics; and
6) to seek to improve market access and reliability of supply for primary products and the processed products thereof.

Also, states have agreed that special attention must be given to the problems of the poorest LDC's and to LDC's which are net importers of raw materials.

Before considering the matter further, it is necessary to point out some fundamental characteristics of trade in raw materials and low per capita income countries. It would be improper to assume that

---

11. United Nations, UNCTAD Information Unit (1976) pp. 2-4.

improvements accruing to net exporters of raw materials would automatically make the present international division of wealth and power more equitable, an explicit goal of the LDC's. Certainly, real resources may flow from net importers to net exporters. But this would occur within the existing market structures and the workings of a market are usually independent from considerations of justice or equity. The advanced, industrial nations are the greatest net importers, but many developing countries would also be affected, as they were by the dramatic real increases in oil prices during the 1970s. Developing countries which are net importers of commodities in which markets can be transformed would find themselves in a even less favorable position.[12] Also, some industrial countries such as Australia, Canada, South Africa, Sweden and USSR are net exporters. Some of these exporters, or members of successful producer groups, may indeed share some portion of their wealth with developing states; in this regard, there would be a greater probability that the world's wealth and power would be divided more equitably between all nation-states.[13] This probability would be further increased if mechanisms were established to assure the resource poor complete compensation for the losses they face stemming from higher import prices.[14] Chances of such mechanisms being established in the near future are very remote.[15]

---

12. See, for example, Streeten (1976) especially p. 82.

13. Campbell and Mytelka (1975) discuss the "recycling of petro-dollars" and the advantages given by OPEC states to a select group of LDC's.

14. Examples of such schemes are discussed in Mikdashi (1976) pp. 188-194.

15. The author here is discussing a matter of probability rather than preference. As Pinicus (1967) has pointed out, if the effects of the UNCTAD policies regarding international trade turn out to be substantial, they are unlikely to be adopted; whereas measures that are likely to be adopted are also likely to be unimportant as sources of increased capital or trade (p. 294). As stated by a Saudi Minister for Finance and National Economy (Kahail, 1979): "Neither the North-South dialogue nor the discussion between industrial and developing countries in UNCTAD and at other international forums has succeeded in bringing about a change of attitudes and policies in the industrial world" (p. 530).

If current trends continue, eventually a significant portion of trade in all commodities, including investment, production and consumption decisions, may come under some form of intergovernmental regulation. Economic forces remain important, but they are being overshadowed by political forces. In the current system, these political forces are centered around individual nation-states, each competing to pursue its own particular interests. Often this leads to a relatively short-sighted perspective by each state, more interested in its immediate needs and goals than in the problems of the global community.[16]

Furthermore, with regard to the development of domestic conditions which would allow people to achieve their full human potential,[17] the changes being considered may not have much relevance. There are always domestic groups which profit very well from primary commodity exports in spite of the above problems. These groups may have a large input into the formulation of domestic decisions regarding how gains or losses are distributed domestically, and it is these domestic decisions which determine the degree of "justice" arising from new international trade structures.

While the unique characteristics of every commodity require different approaches to be examined for each case, a well-defined range of measures have received attention by nations at recent international

---

16. See, for example, Lieber's (1979) discussion of the improbability of getting effective international co-operation on energy in which he quoted a German energy official who felt the "myopic selfishness" of peoples and governments was standing in the way of effective cooperation between energy importers and a solution to the energy problem.

17. The concept of "development" is defined normatively in Galtung (1975). The questions of "dualism", or the continuing co-existence of a "modern" sector and a "traditional" sector within the domestic economic framework of an LDC are examined in Myint (1971) pp. 315-347. See also Vaitsos (1975), who agrees that gains that could be obtained from a new international economic order could benefit only a small part of the population in LDC's unless internal changes take place but points out that external dependence affects internal inequality and hence redressing external relations is necessary even if not sufficient for social and economic development (p. 41).

meetings. In general, they are based on consumer-producer cooperation and take account of commodity arrangements already in existence or under consideration. Such agreements usually include features such as pricing agreements where prices fluctuate between a specified range and are reviewed periodically;[18] buffer stocks or export controls; facilitation of long term contracts; systems of export earnings stabilization; improvement of market access by multilateral trade negotiations including special measures for LDC's; and other measures which are designed to meet the objectives stated above.

Since 1945, international commodity agreements (ICA's) have been negotiated on seven commodities: wheat, sugar, tin, cocoa, coffee, olive oil and natural rubber. Because of the economic, technical and political difficulties of successfully implementing such measures, none of these ICA's has been very successful except for the tin agreement which lasted until November 1985.[19] Its relative success, can be accounted for in part by the fact that vertically integrated transnational firms, responsible for tin extraction as well as distribution, influenced production decisions and consumption levels. Until the agreement fell apart, these firms successfully demonstrated a clear parity of interest to decision makers on both sides of

---

18. The benefits of price stabilization to developing exporters are open to question. For example, using a linear model, E. M. Brook and E. R. Grilli found that developing countries as exporters would benefit in terms of income and welfare only in two agricultural commodities: coffee and cocoa. They showed that there were no likely benefits to developing countries from price stabilization of minerals and metals (and explained that this could, in fact, benefit developed importers). See Brook and Grilli (1977). Similar results were found by A. Ritter (Professor of Economics, Carleton University), presentation to the Economics and Policy Analysis Sector of the Canadian Department of Energy, Mines and Resources, Arnprior, Ontario, February, 1980. Pinicus (1976) states that there is no evidence that growth of the GNP is accelerated by smoothing out fluctuations in the trend of export earnings and concludes that "stabilization of earnings is not worth much to LDCs" (p. 367).

19. See, for example, Rogers (1976).

the negotiating table.[20] The downfall of the tin agreement hinged on the inability of the fund managers to use realistic forecasts of demand in setting the floor price for tin and in the entry into the market of non-member suppliers. The artificially high prices maintained by the International Tin Council during the 1980s also increased use of substitutes such as aluminium and plastic, further reducing demand for tin.

In general, the technical, political and economic problems of ICA's are interrelated. While every commodity has its own characteristics, technically, because of the large number of independent variables, it is very difficult, if not impossible, to accurately predict long term trends in consumption and production. How is one to predict totally unexpected changes in weather conditions, civil uprisings, strikes, new discoveries, new technology and other like factors which may occur either with regard to the commodity being considered or for one of its substitutes? This technical difficulty makes it difficult for states that are signatory to a given ICA to agree on what the price range should be. ICA's require a continuous flow of information on the supply and demand of the commodity and of possible substitutes. This problem is amplified by states which may not wish to divulge full facts about their particular situation. Often changes over time require that price ranges be renegotiated during the course of an ICA and this provides members with an occasion to reopen other issues leading to renewal of disagreements. Short term fluctuations from the long term trend require some sort of stabilizing method. Buffer stocks may be suitable for some commodities, but financing is always a problem. Would they be financed by direct contributions to the fund by exporters, importers or a combination of both? Other possible sources of financing include levies on international trade, commercial borrowing, "soft" loans from international lending institutions or individual countries, private investment with some kind of governmental guarantees, contributions by existing international institutions or contributions by new international institutions.

---

20. See Mikdashi (1976) pp. 118-136 for a good overview of the workings of the international tin agreements; also, C. P. Brown (1980) pp. 11-20; Fawcett and Parry (1981) pp. 63-67, 70-77; Edwards (1975) pp. 80-84.

In this regard LDC's have requested the establishment of a common fund linking the available resources of a number of a buffer stocks.[21] As currently conceived, this fund is meant to be like a bank which in itself would have no powers, but would be a source of funds for the various buffer stock authorities to draw upon. Thus control of the use of funds could operate through the mechanism of producer-consumer consensus in the context of individual agreements. In one sense, it may be seen as a kind of insurance scheme, whereby less total financing would be required than if each buffer stock had to establish a separate fund. A further advantage of a relatively large common fund is that it would discourage speculators. For example, a fund manager would only need to buy or sell a quantity of this commodity and the threat of further intervention would be enough to discourage speculation. It has been suggested that this common fund could also serve as a source of counter-cyclic financing, especially for those commodities which are less suitable for stockpiling.

The size of a buffer stock is of course crucial. It must be able to accommodate all fluctuations from the long term trend. This element is usually a source of disagreement between exporters and importers in ICA's. This would likely become an area of heated discussion among stock managers if stocks were financed from a common fund. Costs increase very quickly with the size of the stock. Costs will also vary with the nature of the commodity. For example, while minerals such as tin can be stocked very cheaply because of low volume and no deterioration in quality, many agricultural products have completely opposite characteristics and, therefore, are quite unsuitable for stockpiling since costs would be astronomic. Where stocks are physically held -- in exporting countries or in importing countries or some combination -- is another difficult point to be negotiated.

A further problem to be dealt with is that presently much stockpiling is done privately by producers and consumers of primary goods. If large stockpiles were to be accumulated by international authorities and if a large common fund guaranteed that managers would be able to maintain a narrow price range, it is to be expected that present holders of stocks would reduce the size of their normal holdings and let the international authority bear the costs associated with holding stocks. This means that, to be effective, the international stockpiles would probably have to be much larger

---

21. Singh (1976); Rogers (1976).

than the sizes described at recent UNCTAD meetings. Other difficult problems include choosing and monitoring fund managers, agreeing upon the timing of market interventions and guarding against individuals or groups which may attempt to profit financially from the stock's operations.

For most commodities, short term fluctuations from long term trends cannot be completely accommodated by buffer stocks, and a form of export controls will be necessary, and this in combination with the buffer stock system. Here the problems become exceedingly difficult, as seen in previous ICA's. Problems involved include not only the allocation of quotas, but also having exporters and importers respect these quotas. In addition, it is necessary to monitor the exports of non-members as past experience has shown that there is usually a tendency for these states to attempt to increase their market shares at the expense of the complying members.

The international coffee agreements which came into force in 1976 and 1980 provided examples of the kinds of problems to be expected.[22] These agreements are based on a system of export quotas to deal with conditions of serious over-supply. Quotas come into effect when coffee prices fall to an agreed trigger price. Previous agreements were only mildly successful in overcoming the cyclic problem of coffee, which involves excess planting in periods of high prices leading to constant overcapacity.[23] Most trees bear fruit for over twenty years. Although almost all coffee is exported from developing countries, neither of these agreements is meant to be an instrument to transfer resources on an "aid" basis, but rather a price stabilization scheme. For coffee producers, it has proved most difficult to respect export quotas. Unlike some other commodities such as oil, it is most difficult to physically cut back coffee production. For oil producers, it is a matter of turning a tap and leaving the oil in the ground; not many persons are thrown out of work (although financial difficulties may be created for the state from cutting back production). Coffee production is much more difficult to curtail in the short term.

---

22. International Coffee Association (1976), (1980).

23. For further evaluation of the main features of the international coffee market, and problems faced by coffee exporters see Winberg (1981); Kravis (1968); Edwards (1975).

New investment can be diverted out of coffee production by heavier taxation, lower (imposed) domestic prices, or access to credit for diversification. The variable costs involved in coffee production, however, are very low, and it would take drastic measures to cut back production quickly. Trees could be destroyed, but even such programs have been known to fail as peasant farmers destroy only the low-productivity trees, or farm the remaining trees more efficiently. If trees were to be destroyed on a large scale, many people would become unemployed and in most countries it would be difficult to find alternative employment. The other alternative for producers wishing to restrict supply is to pick and store the beans. This is very expensive, and the existence of huge producers' stocks is a constant temptation especially to those producers in extreme need of foreign exchange.

This is why in previous coffee agreements there was a constant tendency to sell outside the ICA quotas at cut prices. In times of oversupply, competition for markets in non-member countries has always become most intense; prices have fallen, encouraging non-members to import large amounts of coffee and to immediately sell this "tourist" coffee to quota markets at a profit.

As occurred in the coffee agreement, the only way to increase the efficiency of export quotas is to enlist the help of importing countries to enforce the quotas. Importers will usually assist in achieving the goal of stabilizing prices. However, understandably, they usually are not very keen on cooperating to increase general price trends, or to "stabilize" prices at artificially high levels. One of the strongest arguments against quotas is that they discriminate against new low-cost producers and do not provide pressures for cost reduction which would exist were there no agreement in force.[24]

The industrial countries as a group have agreed that price targets should be remunerative to efficient producers and fair to consumers. In this regard, developing exporters have requested that export prices of primary goods should be indexed automatically to the price of manufactured goods which they import from industrial producers. They argue that this is the only measure which would halt the perceived problem of deteriorating commodity terms of trade.

Important industrial countries such as Japan and Germany have taken very rigid positions against indexing, and there is very little chance of this measure

---

24. See Kravis (1968), especially pp. 305-317.

being negotiated into ICA's in the near future. The argument against automatic indexing on most commodities is that it can distort markets, leading to misallocation of resources. If prices become too high, supplies increase, leading to a breakdown in the original agreement to index. In addition, high prices may reduce consumption, causing producers' income terms of trade (which takes account of export prices and export volumes) to deteriorate. One way to stop the tendency to oversupply where a commodity price is indexed is for all exporters to levy an index-derived tax in a uniform manner. Still, such a tax would not reduce incentives of non-member exporters and of new producers to enter the market and to sell at lower prices. Furthermore, opponents argue that their domestic societies would not support indexing since it would accelerate domestic inflation; also, politicians in these importing countries would be criticised for paying more than was necessary for these products. On the other hand, if these over-payments were regarded as a form of development "aid" a reduction in a country's regular aid spending may be demanded. Certainly the continuation of "aid" in the form of "artificially high" commodity prices would be subject to all the criteria applied by governments to their present "aid" programs.

It is noted that for some commodities indexation may be viable, given required market conditions. During the heydays of the late 1970s, oil producers indicated that they would attempt to index the price of oil whether or not consumers agreed to this indexing. Of course, when oil markets became soft, all discussion of indexing stopped. Another example is Jamaica, which has taken unilateral action and has levied an export tax on bauxite, indexed to the price of aluminum.[25] Possibilities of success in such cases are increased if all exporters first form common fronts, as did the oil producers.

Compensatory financing mechanisms currently in use or under study are meant to smooth out erratic fluctuation in primary commodity export earnings or to assist in temporary balance of payments problems. In general, funds are made available in periods of shortfall, and in most cases must be repaid when export earnings return to higher levels. These schemes tend to meet with the approval of most industrial countries because

---

25. In 1974 Jamaica imposed a production levy (in addition to higher royalties) equivalent to 7.5 percent of the price of aluminum imports in the world market (Edwards (1975) p. 42).

they do not tamper very much with traditional market mechanisms and are in no way designed to alter the terms of trade. The purpose of these schemes is to stabilize rather than distribute income. However, as evidenced by trends appearing in Stabex and the Lomé Convention, there may eventually be some agreement to increase automatic concessions to the poorest developing nations.

It should be noted that compensatory financing and indexing have been criticised as methods of "buying off" exporters from forming producer associations or from taking inflexible positions in ICA negotiations.

Certainly, compensatory financing at this point has little to do with the establishment of a new, more just, economic order. Schemes currently in operation tend to reinforce traditional trade patterns, and by their nature, ensure a steady supply of raw materials to industrial states. Also, they could well have a distorting effect on market mechanisms, as they reduce the incentive to cut back production created by a fall in price. Clearly, such an effect would favor importers. As for Stabex and the Lomé Convention,[26] they only cover a short list of products exported to the EEC. These schemes tend to institutionalize patterns established during the colonial period and reduce incentives to diversify into domestic agricultural production or to process commodities in the producing nations. A further drawback is that earnings ranges and targets are expressed in nominal as opposed to real terms, and this means that over time, inflation will work in favor of importers (unless some form of indexing is introduced).

The above discussion demonstrates that the modifications presently under consideration cannot reasonably be expected to do much to improve the situation facing raw material exporters.[27] In general, existing structures and patterns are reinforced by these modifications and incentives for change or diversification are greatly reduced.[28] Those modifications which distort market mechanisms in favor of producers are met with

---

26. A good description of the Lomé Convention is provided in Friedberg (1975) who, in addition, points out its many positive aspects. See also Singh (1976) p. 95; Society for International Development (1975); Rogers (1976).

27. See, for example, Johnson (1977).

28. See also, Campbell and Mytelka (1975).

firm opposition by industrial countries on the grounds that they lead to misallocation of the world's limited resources. However, there is much less opposition to measures which improve security of supplies such as the creation of ICA's, buffer stocks, or compensatory financing schemes although they too may lead to misallocation of resources by encouraging high cost producers to remain in production and in some cases to increase production.

Conventional wisdom indicates that, in the longer term, as the population of the globe grows and society's requirements for key raw materials increase, commodity issues will take on increasing significance in relations between states.[29] In fact, industrial society has always required access to various key raw materials, and as technology has advanced, various raw materials have taken on strategic importance while others have lost their "key" status. Holders of these strategic commodities have consequently seen their relative wealth and power ebb and flow over time.

Energy commodities have long been regarded as key commercial and strategic goods and this view is underlined by the energy market upheavals that occurred in the 1970s, fueled by the oil sector. Canada's exports of natural gas are subject to concerns similar to those expressed above with regard to natural resources in general. These concerns include determining the appropriate rate of production and timing of exploration and development; determining whether the commodity should be exported, and if so, to whom, under what terms and conditions, over which timeframes, in what quantities and at what prices; and assessing whether it is possible to use natural gas exports to strengthen Canada's negotiating position, to obtain trade and other concessions and to promote other economic, industrial or social goals.

Certainly, natural gas has some unique features which distinguish it from the other commodities discussed above. First, over the period under study, it could be transported efficiently in quantity only by pipelines, although recent technological developments have opened the possibility of economic transport of natural gas in a liquid form by LNG vessels.

This transportation constraint means that transport and distribution facilities for natural gas require large up-front costs to be borne and financed or paid for over a given period of amortization. This has

---

29. See, for example, Rogers (1976) pp. 104-105; Helleiner (1976).

clear implications for security of supply, and size of reservoir needed to support a given transportation network and set of customers. Consequently, contracts have an important time component and deliverability component. Sales over a given period of a specific quantity may be valued differently from sales at a different point in time, for a different duration and for a quantity that can be delivered using available deliverable capacity in a pipeline, or one which requires additional transport facilities.

A second unique characteristic is that natural gas is generally discovered and/or produced with crude oil and discoveries of and production of natural gas are closely related to these activities related to crude oil. A large part of natural gas supply is produced as a type of by-product of the production of crude oil. If the oil is produced, so is the natural gas.

Natural gas shares many of the features of other non-agricultural, depletable resources. For example, there is only a fixed stock of natural gas in the world and in specific geographic locations. It can be left in place forever without deterioration. Once it is discovered, and once production facilities are in place, little additional labor or capital expenditure is required to produce the natural gas.

As with other minerals and fuel deposits, reserve estimates are highly uncertain. The limits of a given deposit can only be ascertained by additional drilling and production testing. The actual quantities that can be recovered from a given reservoir can never really be precisely known until after the reservoir has been produced. How Canada has attempted to deal with the problems as well as the opportunities presented by natural gas exports is examined in detail in this study.

3
Canada's Export Market for Natural Gas

Canada's sole external market for natural gas has always been the United States. Sales of liquified natural gas (LNG) outside the North American continent were not economically feasible, nor were they technologically feasible until the mid-1970s.[1] Thus, geography, technology and transportation economics have limited Canada's market to the United States.[2]

---

1. Commercial operation of LNG vessels began on a very small scale in the 1960s and by 1975, seventeen such vessels were in service (Mankabady (1975) pp. 655-656). By 1981, 1.6 tcf of LNG was traded worldwide, with over half going to Japan. Most of the rest went to Western European countries. Very small imports of 40 bcf were received by the United States and were imported by Distrigas Corporation (Tussing and Barlow (1984) pp. 63-65).

2. At time of writing, proposals have been made to liquify natural gas in the High Arctic for sale to the U.S. market and Japan. Petro-Canada's Arctic Pilot Project was the subject of regulatory hearings in 1982, and would involve delivering natural gas from Melville Island to a receiving station in southern Canada built by TransCanada Pipelines. (National Energy Board Hearings, 1982). A second project, proposed by Petro-Canada, TransCanada Pipelines and two West German companies, Ruhrgas AG and Gelsenberg AG, would see gas from the King Christian Island area of the High Arctic, liquified and exported to customers in Europe. Canadian liquified gas would give European utilities additional security of supply in the face of declining quantities available from the Netherlands, and would permit a degree of diversification of supply sources aside from the North Sea, the Soviet Union and northern Africa (Globe and Mail, April 20, 1982, p. B1).

As there was in effect only one external market for Canadian natural gas, Canadian export policy had to be conceived in terms of the U.S. market. In essence, Canadian exports, if they were to occur, had to be competitive with potential importers' alternative fuel supplies. As the natural gas industry in the United States was closely regulated over the period under study, the concept of Canadian exports being "competitive" needs close examination and definition.

In this chapter, the policies adopted by U.S. regulatory authorities over American producers and transmission companies are examined and how these regulators viewed imports and exports is considered. Regulation of the industry in the United States is discussed particularly as it relates to Canada's natural gas exports.

Evolution of the U.S. Natural Gas Industry

Natural gas has long been used as a fuel in North America but, before the major advances in pipeline technology which occurred in the 1930s, it was not commercially viable to transport natural gas over long distances.[3] At that time, natural gas had to be used where it was produced. Oil, on the other hand, was much more cheaply and easily transported. This transportation constraint affected the potential market sizes and, consequently, the relative values of natural gas and oil.

Because markets for natural gas were geographically limited compared with oil, and because this constraint limited natural gas prices, production of oil was more profitable. Thus, from the beginning of the twentieth century to the late 1930s, oil was the primary goal of petroleum exploration in the United States. When extensive oil discoveries were made in the states of Texas, Louisiana, Kansas, Oklahoma, and New Mexico, the associated natural gas found was of only minor value, more of a nuisance than a prize. Very large volumes of natural gas were flared at the wellhead. Some natural gas was sold locally for pennies per Mcf, often for the purpose of making carbon black, which is used in rubber and ink manufacture.

Basic to the understanding of petroleum exploration is the fact that oil and natural gas occur alone or together, at random, in similar geologic structures. Only to a limited extent can an exploration

---

3. Van Meurs (1981) pp. 620-621, 624-625, 632-633; Davis R. (1964); Brown, K.C. (1972), (1975).

effort be directed to oil as opposed to natural gas. Geologists have made important strides in this area in recent years; however no one has yet found the magic formula and indeed no such formula may exist. Consequently, successful exploration efforts may lead to the discovery of oil or natural gas or both. In addition, bringing an oil well into production will usually put the "oil" producer into the natural gas business to some degree. Almost all crude oil contains some natural gas. Thus, in order to pump crude oil, some natural gas too will be produced as a by-product. Roughly 25 percent to 30 percent of established U.S. natural gas reserves are associated with oil and must be separated from the oil by various processing methods before sale to pipelines.

Depending on marketability, location relative to transport facilities and a producer's netback, it may be profitable to gather and market the natural gas which is produced as a by-product of crude oil production. An additional physical factor affecting the profitability of natural gas exploration and production is that most natural gas contains a variety of hydrocarbons which can be separated from the stream of natural gas and liquified. If the natural gas can be processed economically, that is, if a natural gas plant is available and can take additional volumes of natural gas, separating these valuable hydrocarbons from the natural gas stream is generally a profitable proposition. These natural gas liquids are relatively easy to transport, and are usually readily marketable.

In the 1930s, advances in pipeline transmission technology lowered the construction and operating costs of thin-walled, high pressure pipelines. Consequently, in a relatively short period of time, natural gas was made available in a much larger geographical market area. Adequate supplies were not the problem. There was plenty of natural gas. This meant that demand for this fuel could increase dramatically before purchasers would have to bid competitively amongst each other for new natural gas supplies. From the suppliers' point of view, natural gas quickly changed from a near-worthless nuisance, to a source of some cash flow, in addition to the revenues generated from the sale of crude oil.

After the Second World War, in the absence of any constraints on natural gas supplies, retail prices of alternative fuel sources rose considerably faster than the retail price of natural gas. As one would expect, demand for natural gas increased dramatically. During the period between 1945 and 1960, a great many long, interstate pipelines were constructed in the United States (and Canada). By the end of the 1950s a transmission network bringing natural gas to almost all states in the continental United States was in place. Natural gas had a price advantage over competing fuels in most United States markets. In addition to being less costly, gas was a high quality, clean-burning fuel, leaving no solid residues. For these reasons, natural gas rapidly came to supply a large share of American energy requirements in the residential, commercial and industrial sectors for non-transportation related uses. To illustrate this rapid growth, it is estimated that over the period from 1950 to 1960, energy supplied from natural gas in the United States increased from 20 percent to 33 percent of total U.S. energy requirements.[4] Table 3-1 shows the growth in reserves and consumption of natural gas in the United States over the period 1920 to 1984.

---

4. American Gas Association (1977) Table 16, p. 15.

TABLE 3-1

GROWTH OF NATURAL GAS RESERVES AND CONSUMPTION IN THE UNITED STATES[5]
(Trillion cubic feet)

	(1) Estimated Proved-Reserves at Year-End	(2) Annual Marketed Production[6]	(3) Annual Reserve Growth[6]	(4) Column 1 / Column 2
1920	15.00	0.76	.76	19.7
1925	23.00	0.95	2.55	24.2
1930	46.00	1.64	6.24	28.0
1935	62.00	1.70	4.90	36.5
1940	85.00	2.40	7.00	35.4
1945	144.29	3.38	15.24	42.7
1950	184.58	6.28	5.18	29.4
1951	192.76	7.46	8.17	25.8
1952	198.63	8.01	5.87	24.8
1953	210.30	8.40	11.67	25.0
1954	210.56	8.74	0.26	24.1
1955	222.48	9.41	11.92	23.6
1956	236.48	10.08	14.00	23.5
1957	245.23	10.68	8.75	23.0
1958	252.76	11.03	7.53	22.9
1959	261.17	12.05	8.41	21.7
1960	262.33	12.77	1.16	20.5
1961	266.27	13.25	3.95	20.1
1962	272.28	13.88	6.01	19.6
1963	276.15	14.75	3.87	18.7
1964	281.25	15.46	5.10	18.2
1965	286.47	16.04	5.22	17.9
1966	289.33	17.21	2.86	16.8
1967	292.91	18.17	3.57	16.1
1968	287.35	19.32	(5.56)	14.9
1969	275.11	20.70	(12.24)	13.3
1970	290.75	21.92	15.64	13.3
1971	278.81	22.49	(11.94)	12.4
1972	266.08	22.53	(12.72)	11.8
1973	249.95	22.65	(16.13)	11.0
1974	237.13	21.60	(12.82)	11.1
1975	228.20	20.11	(8.93)	11.4

TABLE 3-1 (Cont'd)

GROWTH OF NATURAL GAS RESERVES AND CONSUMPTION IN THE UNITED STATES[5]
(Trillion cubic feet)

	(1) Estimated Proved-Reserves at Year-End	(2) Annual Marketed Production[6]	(3) Annual Reserve Growth[6]	(4) Column 1 / Column 2
1976	216.03	19.95	(12.17)	10.8
1977	208.88	20.21	(7.15)	10.3
1978	200.30	19.97	(8.58)	10.3
1979	200.99	20.47	0.69	9.8
1980	199.02	20.38	(1.98)	9.8
1981	201.73	20.10	2.71	10.0
1982	201.51	18.73	(0.22)	10.8
1983	200.25	16.80	(1.26)	11.9
1984	197.46(e)	17.60(e)	(2.79)(e)	11.22(e)

---

5. 1920 to 1945: Canada, Royal Commission on Energy (1958) p. 9. This information was submitted to the Commission by the British American Oil Company Limited. 1950 to 1975: American Gas Association (1977) Table 3, 11, pp. 4, 11. 1976 to 1980: American Gas Association, Gas Facts, Annual. Updated 1979, 1980, 1981, 1984, figures provided in telephone interviews with L. Cover (April 11, 1983), T. Murphy (October 23, 1984) and S. Brown (January 22, 1986), Statistics Department, American Gas Association. 1984 annual marketed production estimate from U.S. Energy Information Administration as reported in Petroleum Economist, September, 1984, p. 358.

6. Note that annual reserve growth and annual consumption data for the period 1920 to 1945 represent 5-year averages.

U.S. Supply/Demand Balance

Until the producing fields were connected to most of the major U.S. natural gas markets, the potential economic supply of natural gas was far in excess of requirements. Even once the markets were connected, it often took a period of years for the market to become fully developed. Thus, over this development period, there was little upward pressure on U.S. natural gas prices. Producers were often obtaining an attractive return on their crude oil production, and additional revenues obtained from increased sales of natural gas were the "icing on the cake" that enhanced further the return on investment in petroleum exploration and development.

This apparent excess of available supply over requirements remained throughout the period up until the late 1960s. In 1967, net total proven U.S. gas reserves stopped growing; that is to say, new discoveries of natural gas in the United States fell below the level of U.S. gas production.[7] During this period, interstate prices, including the cost of this gas at the wellhead as well as the cost of transporting the gas from the wellhead to the consumer, were set by federal regulation. At the prices which had been set, some customers of U.S. interstate pipelines were not able to contract to purchase all the gas they could otherwise profitably transport and sell. A regulation-induced shortage of natural gas had come into being. As prices were set by a federal regulator, there was no practical way for potential interstate customers to bid for gas supplies against other potential customers.

This problem of shortages would not go away on its own. As with many regulatory systems which attempt to hold prices below the market-clearing level for extended periods of time, things just continued to become worse. An excess of potential demand over deliverable supply (at the regulated prices) persisted in the case of many U.S. interstate pipelines in the late 1960s and became larger in the 1970s. This excess of demand for natural gas over supply required some interstate pipelines to curtail deliveries of gas to some of their customers. Different categories of customers were created in order to achieve politically equitable distribution of available natural gas. In short, a

---

7. Production first exceeded total discoveries, reserve revisions and extensions in 1967. See American Gas Association, <u>Historical Statistics</u>, Table 3, p. 4.

type of rationing scheme was put in place in the United States. From the Canadian exporters' point of view the U.S. natural gas market area was wide open to accept any and all the gas the government would permit to be exported.

While there are differing opinions as to the key factors which could account for the market imbalance in the United States over that period, the regulation of natural gas prices was without doubt of major importance.[8] Regulatory changes made after 1978, the economic recession of 1980-81 and recently, a large increase in deliverable supplies of oil and other gas substitutes have had the impact of reversing the market, and an excess deliverable supply over actual demand has developed. The U.S. market structure and Canadian exports are of course impacted by this market reversal.

Regulation of Commerce in Natural Gas Within the United States

As a result of the history of the natural gas industry and its evolution, there are four distinct sectors within the industry. Each sector has own economic purpose and structural characteristics. The four sectors are: the exploration, development and production sector, which finds and produces the natural gas; the natural gas pipeline transmission sector, which carries the gas from producers to utilities in market areas; the local distribution sector, which carries the gas to ultimate natural gas users such as residences, business and industry; and direct industrial customers. It is noteworthy that in the case of other major energy sources such as electricity and oil, there is no such separation of functions carried out by separate and distinct commercial entities. Rather, in these cases, generally speaking, in at least a large part of the industry there is near-complete vertical integration with exploration, production, transmission, storage, refining and distribution usually carried on or controlled through ownership by single commercial organizations.

In the U.S. natural gas industry, both natural gas producers and natural gas distributors are engaged in a restricted, geographically limited operation. In general producers and distributors have been regulated

---

8. See, for example, Breyer and MacAvoy (1974); Brown, K.C. (1972), (1975); Di Bona (1973); Erickson and Spann (1971); Kahn (1960); MacAvoy and Pindyck (1973), (1975); Wheatly (1971).

by state regulatory bodies. As regards producers, state conservation commissions have attempted to reduce waste in the industry. To meet this objective, the state commissions have promulgated and enforced regulations designed to improve production methods and to restrict the volumes of gas flared at the wellhead, or vented into the atmosphere. Other measures have been taken to ensure that the maximum quantity of hydrocarbons are eventually recovered from producing formations. These include such things as specifying well-spacing requirements, setting a producer's ratable take[9] and taking similar conservation measures. On the distribution side, during the shortage situation that existed until the 1980s, state utility commissions generally attempted to ensure that there was no discrimination between the same classes of customers and that the tolls charged were just and reasonable in relation to the interest of the citizens of that state. In some states, regulation of distribution companies is left to the municipal level of government.[10]

As for the pipeline transmission sector of the industry, until 1938 it was essentially unregulated, because the commerce clause of the U.S. Constitution precluded interstate pipelines from being regulated by the individual states.[11] However, subsequent sales of (interstate) gas within a given state by a distribution company to consumers within that state were judged to be under state regulatory jurisdiction.[12] After 1938, of course, all this changed and federal regulation of interstate pipelines was put in place.

The Natural Gas Act of 1938

The U.S. political system is very responsive to the expressed concerns of large political constituencies. When some people cried out against unfair profits, in 1938 there was a large number of politi-

---

9. Setting a producer's "ratable take" refers to specifying production rates slow enough to maximize recovery over the life of the well.

10. For example, the state of Texas. See McClesky (1966) pp. 335-337; Brown, K.C., (1972), (1975).

11. See for example, Missouri v. Kansas Gas Co., 265 U.S. 298 (1924); East Ohio Gas Co. v. Tax Commission, 283 U.S. 465 (1931).

12. Public Utilities Commission v. Attleboro Co., 273 U.S. 83 (1927).

cians prepared to listen to and act upon their wishes. There were significant and growing numbers of natural gas consumers. Congress responded to their expressed potential problems with popular legislation. Briefly put, the Supreme Court had ruled that the states did not have the jurisdiction required to protect the interests of natural gas consumers.[13] Because there was a general public concern that a pipeline monopolist could unjustly increase its rates to a captive customer distribution company, or discriminate in the rates charged distribution companies in different cities,[14] in 1938 Congress passed The Natural Gas Act.[15] The act was a major new factor for the natural gas industry in its period of very rapid growth. It set the ground rules. The act provided for the federal regulation of the construction and operation of interstate pipelines. The federal regulator, therefore, would have a major say over which interstate pipelines were put in place, where they were put in place and how they were constructed and operated. In addition, the act authorized federal regulation of the interstate sale of gas that was to be resold, and for the import and export of natural gas. Responsibility for the enforcement of the act was given to the Federal Power Commission (FPC).

Under its jurisdiction over pipelines, the FPC regulated pipelines' earnings using the traditional "cost of service" criteria. This was a standard regulatory method which was applied by various regulatory authorities in the United States to a wide variety of

---

13. The House Report stated that the federal legislation was designed to occupy the area in which "the Supreme Court has held that the States may not act." H. Rept. 709, 75 Cong. 1 sess. (1937); Davis (1964).

14. See, for example, the opinion of Justice Jackson, FPC v. Hope Natural Gas Co., 320 U.S. 591, 638 (1944). Here, referring to complaints made by people living in the area served by the depleted Applachian fields, he says that "the public came to feel that the companies were exploiting the growing scarcity of local gas." Early development of natural gas in the United States was centered in the Appalachian region, with most production coming from West Virginia, western Pennsylvania and southern Ohio. Production from this area passed its peak by the early 1920s (FPC v. Hope Natural Gas Co., 591, 629-34).

15. Natural Gas Act of 1938, 52 Stat. 821, as amended, 15 U.S.C. pars. 717ff; Davis (1964); Brown, K.C. (1972), (1975).

public utilities. The general principle behind this approach is that public utilities should be allowed to recover their costs and make a fair profit. Using the regulatory jargon, the idea is that, as a natural monopoly under public regulation, a utility such as a natural gas pipeline should be controlled as to the tolls and tariffs it may change. It should only be permitted to collect from its customers gross revenue sufficient to pay all prudently incurred operating expenses and to earn a rate of return on used and useful capital assets high enough to attract and hold the capital required for the utility's continued operation.[16] In addition, these rates of return should take into account the capital structure of the utility and the market rates required to finance the utility using an appropriate mix of both debt and equity.

In this regard, when the act was first promulgated, payments by pipeline companies to natural gas producers were generally allowed as recoverable operating expenses. Consequently, in general, the FPC allowed the pipeline companies under its jurisdiction to recover this expense from its customers. One notes that under this type of regulatory system under the market conditions at that time, the transmission companies would make the same amount of money regardless of what they paid for their natural gas supplies (as long as these payments were considered prudent expenditures). If the prices that interstate pipelines were required to pay to acquire natural gas increased, the pipelines would generally be allowed to increase the prices charged when the gas was delivered by a similar amount. Clearly, producers would not be expected to suffer in this type of regulatory regime. Thus, although Congress enacted the <u>Natural Gas Act of 1938</u> to protect the users of natural gas, the producers as well as the transmission companies did not fare badly, at least over the early years after its enactment.

Of course, this regulatory system of passing on costs only works when the cost of the gas at the burner tip remains competitive with other fuels that could be purchased to do the same job. This was the case over the period to 1981. However, once natural gas at the burner tip lost its competitive pricing edge, the need for pipeline companies to aggressively market gas in order to maintain throughput volumes became obvious. This applies not only to U.S. domestic gas production, but also to imports from Canada and elsewhere.

---

16. Although easily stated, this principle is very difficult to apply. See, for example, Davidson (1972).

Phillips Case of 1954

As the focus of the FPC regulation was on the pipeline transmission companies themselves, between 1938 and 1954 the FPC did not attempt to regulate the prices paid to producers who were not owned by or otherwise affiliated with the pipeline purchasing the gas. All this changed, however, after 1954 when the U.S. Supreme Court ruled on what came to be called the Phillips Case. In response to a request by Wisconsin, a "consumer state", the U.S. Supreme Court ruled that the Natural Gas Act required the FPC to regulate the sales prices and other terms of sale for all natural gas moving into interstate pipelines.[17] This left some loopholes in the regulatory system but they were quickly blocked by the Supreme Court in later decisions. The Supreme Court ruled that FPC jurisdiction extended to absolutely all sales to interstate pipelines, regardless of whether the specific sale was made at the wellhead or whether it occurred after gathering and processing. This was the beginning of a regulatory nightmare as the FPC moved to fulfill its responsibilities as judged by the U.S. Supreme Court.

In response to the Court's rulings, over the period 1954 to 1960 the FPC attempted to regulate the price paid by interstate pipelines to individual natural gas producers on a case-by-case basis, a task which eventually proved to be totally unworkable. Producer regulation presented the FPC with a variety of difficult regulatory problems. Although its jurisdiction was clear, utility-type regulation of independent natural gas producers, the largest of which were vertically-integrated oil companies, had never before been attempted in the United States. It was like a new ball game, but there was no rulebook. Also, regulating field prices was an extremely subjective exercise. There simply did not exist any generally accepted standards against which to judge "just and reasonable"[18] natural gas field prices.[19] The relatively

---

17. *Phillips Petroleum Co. v. Wisconsin*, 347 U.S. 627 (1954); Davis (1964); Brown, K.C. (1972), (1975).

18. Under section 717c and 717d of the Natural Gas Act, natural gas prices were to be "just and reasonable", that is, permitting recovery of the costs of producing gas plus a reasonable rate of return. 15 U.S.C. pars 717c, 717d. U.S. Congress. The National Energy Act (1979) p. 37; Davidson (1972).

19. Breyer and Macavoy (1974) pp. 66-69.

clear rules of the U.S. marketplace were replaced by the then fuzzy rules of a federal regulator. Unfortunately, things got more and more fuzzy and confused as time passed. Only the eventual total breakdown in the regulatory system paved the way for the policy makers to reverse the regulatory pendulum in this sector.

One major problem in regulating natural gas field prices was how the federal regulatory agency was to assess the reasonableness and justness of field prices for natural gas when the gas was most often a by-product of exploration for the discovery and production of crude oil. One readily sees the wide range of argumentation that could be made on any specific case. In addition, if a traditional rate of return to "used and useful" or "prudently acquired" assets was to be used, how was the regulator to allocate common production costs between jointly produced natural gas and oil? Again, very subjective judgements are required.

A second major problem for the regulator was the physical, administrative complexity of dealing with very large numbers of natural gas producers. There were an estimated 5000 to 8000 competing independent U.S. producers having wide variations in size, ownership and manner of operation, and operating in different geographic areas and under different degrees of (geological) risk.

Another issue which the FPC had to address was the appropriate rate of return to be allowed natural gas producers compared with pipeline operators, and what rate of return was to be allowed for the exploratory activities of producers and pipeline companies.[20] The riskiness of various activities was very hard to judge in a manner that all concerned would agree on what was fair and reasonable in relation to the risks involved. Clearly, a development well, drilled close to a producing well was far less risky than a wildcat well, drilled hundreds of miles from the nearest producing field and far from any existing pipelines. However, between these two extremes, there are lots of shades of grey.

Due to these very difficult regulatory issues, the administrative and regulatory complexities of regulating prices paid to individual producers turned out to be a totally unmanageable headache. As expected, some FPC decisions were criticised for appearing to be arbitrary and inefficient. Eventually, these criticisms and problems of regulation of individual producers led to a change in method by the FPC in 1960.[21]

---

20. Kahn (1960); Brown, K.C. (1975).

21. Breyer and Macavoy (1974) pp. 68-72.

It was decided that rather than to attempt to regulate specific prices paid to individual producers on the basis of separate investigations of their separate costs, ceiling prices would be set for all natural gas produced in designated geographical areas.[22]

Under the new policy, the FPC's stated objective was still very ambitious. It aimed to set prices for each natural gas producing area in the United States that would be just high enough to maintain "adequate" natural gas production, but no higher. In evaluating what these prices would be, the FPC stated that it would continue to consider costs of production on the basis of historic costs. Also, it would assess a range of other important factors. These would include forecasts of supply as well as market analysis and demand forecasts, trends in drilling productivity, reserves and additions to reserves, potential deliverability, and risks and prospective rewards of natural gas producers. The FPC recognized that wellhead prices would affect the level of exploration, but in addition, gave itself the difficult problem of forecasting the extent to which private exploration efforts would result in actual discoveries and additions to reserves. In addition, although it complicated the process somewhat, the FPC wisely adopted the policy of allowing a variety of ceiling prices within a given area depending on the regulatory category in which a given sales contract was deemed to belong. In general, newer contracts were allowed higher sales prices than older contracts.

The FPC's first area rate case decision, involving the gas fields of the Permian Basin in southwestern Texas and southeastern New Mexico, was handed down in August 1965.[23] At that time, this area produced about eleven percent of all interstate natural gas. To give an idea of the time lags involved in hearing these cases, the FPC's second decision, involving the southern Louisiana producing area, was handed down in September 1968.[24] This area produced about one third of the U.S. marketed natural gas at that time.

---

22. Phillips Petroleum Co., 24 FPC 537 (1960). The FPC's termination of the original Phillips proceeding was sustained by the Supreme Court in **Wisconsin v. FPC**, 373 U.S. 294 (1963).

23. Area Rate Proceeding, AR-61-1, 34 FPC 159; Davidson (1972).

24. Area Rate Processing, AR-61-2, 40 FPC 530.

Over the period under consideration, the U.S. average wellhead price of natural gas increased from 6.5 cents per Mcf in 1950 to 17.1 cents per Mcf in 1970, 149.6 cents per Mcf in 1980, and about $2.63 per Mcf in 1984 as shown in Table 3-2.

TABLE 3-2

AVERAGE WELLHEAD PRICE AND MARKETED

PRODUCTION OF NATURAL GAS IN THE UNITED STATES, 1950-1983[25]

Year	Average Wellhead Price (Cents per Mcf) (¢)	Marketed Production[26] (Million cubic feet)
1950	6.5	6,282,060
1951	7.3	7,457,359
1952	7.8	8,013,457
1953	9.2	8,396,916
1954	10.1	8,742,546
1955	10.4	9,405,351
1956	10.8	10,081,923
1957	11.3	10,680,258
1958	11.9	11,030,248
1959	12.9	12,046,115
1960	14.0	12,771,038
1961	15.1	13,254,025
1962	15.5	13,876,622
1963	15.8	14,746,663
1964	15.4	16,462,143
1965	15.6	16,039,753

---

25. U.S. Bureau of Mines. <u>Natural Gas Annual</u>, as compiled in American Gas Association, Historical Statistics 1966 to 1975, p. 125, and <u>Gas Facts Annual</u>.

26. Marketed production as reported by the Bureau of Mines is equivalent to natural gas production usefully consumed. It includes natural gas sold by producers and other non-utilities to industrial consumers and includes natural gas mixed with manufactured gas for consumption. Figures for 1980 and thereafter, provided

TABLE 3-2 (Cont'd)

AVERAGE WELLHEAD PRICE AND MARKETED

PRODUCTION OF NATURAL GAS IN THE UNITED STATES, 1950-1983[25]

Year	Average Wellhead Price (Cents per Mcf) (¢)	Marketed Production[26] (Million cubic feet)
1966	15.7	17,206,628
1967	16.0	18,171,325
1968	16.4	19,322,400
1969	16.7	20,698,240
1970	17.1	21,920,642
1971	18.2	22,493,012
1972	18.6	22,531,698
1973	21.6	22,647,547
1974	30.4	21,600,522
1975	44.5	20,108,661
1976	58.0	19,952,438
1977	79.0	20,025,463
1978	90.5	19,974,033
1979	117.8	20,471,260
1980	149.6	20,378,787
1981	198.2	20,177,701
1982	245.7	18,728,171
1983	259.3	17,000,000
1984	263.0	17,600,000(e)

As seen in the above table, natural gas prices moved slowly upwards in nominal terms throughout the 1950s, leveled off in nominal terms throughout the 1960s (real decreases), and increased significantly during the 1970s and early 1980s. The increases allowed during the seventies reflected the declining reserves to annual production ratio and an implicit

---

by Statistics Department, American Gas Association, are calculated in a manner that varies slightly from the method used by the Bureau of Mines up to and including 1979 (Interviews with L. Cover (April 11, 1983) and T. Murphy (October 23, 1984), American Gas Association).

recognition that field prices impacted directly on exploration activity. In addition, increases were justified by the increased average costs of finding and producing natural gas in general, and the value of natural gas in relation to other competing fuel sources. The average price figures for the 1980s really camouflage the very wide range that exists between the various categories of old regulated gas and the high incentive prices permitted by the <u>Natural Gas Policy Act of 1978</u>.

In assessing the FPC regulation of wellhead prices, it is useful to briefly discuss the impact of state taxes on U.S. natural gas prices. As mentioned above, state regulatory commissions are generally mandated with the "prevention of waste" and conservation. As such, a state body does not have have legal authority to attempt direct control of the prices paid to natural gas producers in its state.[27] However, producing states do have the power to charge a severance tax on each unit of gas which is produced, provided that there is no attempt to tax gas moving into interstate commerce differently than gas used intrastate. In its

---

27. For example, the regulatory commission in Oklahama attempted to set a minimum price for sales of interstate gas in 1972, but was unsuccessful. In October 1972, the Oklahoma Corporation Commission noted that state law authorized it to prevent "wasteful" consumption of natural gas. Based on this legal mandate, the Commission ruled that gas which was sold to any pipelines at sales prices less than 20 cents per Mcf (and higher prices for wells which exceeded certain depths) was, by definition, being sold for wasteful purposes. Consequently the Oklahoma Corporation Commission issued orders prohibiting such sales, regardless of whether sales were being made to inter-or intra-state pipelines. The FPC, however, refused to grant price increases conforming to the Oklahoma Corporation Commission's ruling. Rather, the FPC filed a complaint with the United States District Court for the Western District of Oklahoma asking the Court to declare that the orders of the Oklahoma Corporation Commission constituted an unlawful infringement of the jurisdiction of the FPC over interstate natural gas. The court upheld the FPC, confirming that state regulatory commissions did not have authority to set minimum prices, at least for sales of interstate gas. This regulatory regime, eventually led to natural gas sales prices differing depending on whether the gas was to be consumed within a state rather than outside the state.

setting of ceiling prices, the FPC did allow actual state taxes paid to be included as a component of a producer's average production cost. In turn, this average production cost was a major factor in the FPC's determination of area ceilings. One may conclude, therefore, that, in general, until the soft markets of the 1980s, if a producing state were to increase its severance taxes, the FPC would allow ceiling prices within the state to be increased by a like amount, and this increase would then be passed on to natural gas consumers.

Returning now to the evolution of FPC price regulation, in July 1974, all ceiling prices were scrapped by the FPC. Partially in response to the dramatic increase in oil prices, the FPC set rates for new natural gas on a nationwide basis for the first time. This seemingly more straightforward regulatory approach soon got wrapped in several layers of complicated red tape and soon there was nothing but a tangled mess and huge shortages of interstate gas. Over time, as pressures built up, the Commission set new, higher nationwide rates for several categories of "new" and "old" natural gas. However, even these new, higher rates did not reverse the trend of declining natural gas supplies for the interstate market. As new deliverable gas supplies did not materialize in spite of the improved incentives, this caused extensive curtailments of firm industrial service and occasional threats to essential residential and small commercial service. While shortages grew in the interstate market, prices for natural gas in the (unregulated) intrastate markets increased to reflect the value of natural gas compared with alternative fuel sources. This allowed utilities serving these markets to maintain, and in some cases to expand, natural gas service. Because of this difference between the interstate and intrastate markets, in 1977 and 1978, surpluses of natural gas accumulated in the intrastate market.

In order to deal with this growing problem, and as part of a comprehensive package intended to reduce the oil import needs of the United States and to achieve more efficient and equitable use of energy in the United States, U.S. President Carter introduced the Natural Gas Policy Act of 1978.[28]

---

28. U.S. Congress, Committee on Energy and National Resources, The National Energy Act. Publication No. 96-1, January, 1979. Natural Gas Policy Act of 1978, Public Law 95-621, November 9, 1978.

At the time the act was passed, an impact of the disparity between the interstate and intrastate markets for natural gas was a requirement for increased oil imports in those states served by the interstate system. Furthermore, the accumulation of surpluses in intrastate markets would certainly have been expected to lead to a reduction of so-called natural gas-oriented exploration and development in the producing states as market forces reacted to the surpluses.

Carter's Natural Gas Policy Act of 1978 was designed to address these problems by establishing prices for natural gas that were thought to be "certain" and applicable to both interstate and intrastate systems. The price ceiling system was designed to provide the highest incentives for more risky exploratory drilling, while restraining price increases on previously discovered gas to prevent so-called "windfall" gain and "unnecessary" inflationary impacts.

In addition, the act provided for the protection of residential and small commercial consumers from dramatic price increases through incremental pricing of higher cost gas supplies to industrial consumers; emergency authorities to ensure continued supplies for high priority uses; and protection of essential agricultural users and industrial feedstock and process users from curtailment of gas supplies.

Carter's Federal Energy Regulatory Commission, which replaced the Federal Power Commission, had primary federal responsibility for implementing the Natural Gas Policy Act of 1978. President Carter's initiatives were soon overtaken by a new round of international oil price increases in 1979, and then by the additional steps taken or attempted by the Reagan administration for further deregulation of natural gas prices.

To be fair, the 1978 legislation tried to achieve an even, predictable deregulation of natural gas prices. It was intended that gas prices would come unregulated in phases and all gas would be deregulated by 1985. Twenty eight categories of gas were created based on the year the gas was committed to sale, production-related factors and company-related factors. One type of frontier gas, called "deep" gas, was immediately decontrolled. Deep gas came from wells over 15,000 feet deep.

The market problems being felt today started to materialize when oil prices shot up in 1978-80. At that time, conventional wisdom was that oil prices were headed up indefinitely and were going totally out of sight. For example, Canada's 1980 National Energy Program, which reflected the thinking by experts at that time, was that at a minimum, real oil prices would continue to increase at a rate of 2 percent above the general rate of inflation for at least the next ten years. During the years 1979 to 1982 U.S. pipelines purchased gas everywhere at prices which were considered reasonable, although well above the prices at which gas could then be sold to final customers. Some deep gas sold for the astronomic prices of $8.00 to $10.00 per Mcf. Virtually all contracts included take-or-pay provisions as standard clauses. At prices like that from U.S. producers in, say, the Gulf of Mexico, Canadian exports at $4.94 looked cheap. Many new deals were signed and Canadian exporters thought they would move large additional quantities at these attractive prices. Canadian exports began to look like even better deals, compared to proposed U.S. imports of LNG from Algeria at landed prices that were about twice the Canadian border price.

Unfortunately, most natural gas contracts, including export contracts, had standard clauses other than "take-or-pay". One of these was a "market-out" clause, by which pipelines could get out of their contractual commitments under certain circumstances. These circumstances began to occur in late 1982 and became more and more amplified in 1983 and 1984, continuing into 1985. Oil prices fell, quickly and dramatically. Natural gas prices, however, could not respond with any real flexibility. They continued to increase as newer, higher priced supplies were produced, sold and taken or at least paid for under the recently signed contracts.

As relative prices of alternative fuels moved closer together, consumption shifted. Large segments of the market stopped buying natural gas and, in its place, purchased more oil, coal and electricity. Conservation efforts increased as well. Consequently, pipeline throughout fell, creating increased unit transmission charges. This accentuated further the shifts in demand. In the end it was simple. Pipelines could not charge enough for the natural gas to cover the costs and profits to which they were "entitled" under the U.S. regulatory system. If they tried to charge that much, no one would buy the natural gas.

The final price at which natural gas would be competitive and be purchased was beyond the control of the regulators. As the system collapsed, the lawyers had plenty of work. Every trader in the system appealed to the various regulators. Traders attempted to oblige the other players to give up the money to which they were "entitled" by one rule or another in order to allow themselves to get their "fair" share. The solution is very messy, and may well be resolved only by massive financial restructuring and bankruptcies.

One key element was of course U.S. imports from Canada and Mexico. For a while Canada maintained its export price and watched export volumes drop dramatically. As the U.S. market situation came to be understood, prices were dropped and greater flexibility was allowed to be negotiated into contracts. As for the U.S. imports from Mexico, which account for roughly one percent of U.S. demand (as compared with roughly four percent of total demand accounted for by imports from Canada), Mexico decided to cut off all U.S. gas exports and use the gas domestically rather than sell into the soft U.S. market.

But as the dust settles, a new industry is in place, one that has relearned competitive pricing, flexibility in contracts and spot market transactions. Additionally, while one of the chief concerns in previous deals was whether regulatory approval could be obtained, new deals will look to sound economics and market needs rather than regulatory approval as a basis for business decisions. Regulatory approval and legal documents are no longer guarantees of success and profits. Good management and quick adaptation to flexible and changing markets are absolutely vital for future success. This applies not only to Canadian export contracts, but to all aspects of the U.S. natural gas industry.

Over the period under study, U.S. federal regulation of natural gas prices did have a significant impact on Canadian natural gas exports, in terms of both volumes and prices. This impact cannot be considered without first discussing the evolution of the Canadian industry, which is examined in the following two chapters.

4

Canada's Natural Gas Industry

The time from 1950 to 1986 can be divided into three distinct periods. A development period occurred from about 1947 to 1959, during which natural gas reserves were proved up and transmission systems were put in place. A period of expansion lasted from 1960 to 1970. During this period the emphasis was on marketing discoveries and stimulating continued rapid growth in the petroleum sector. The third period started as a period of consolidation which lasted from 1971 to 1980. During these years the growth rate of petroleum supplies slowed, prices rose, and conservation and security of supply came to the fore as vital issues. During this time, the provincial and federal governments in Canada became more active in energy resource management. The latter part of this period, 1981 to 1986, was a period of relatively soft markets, during which deliverable supply exceeded actual requirements within both Canada and the United States. This chapter examines the major developments in the petroleum sector during each of these periods.

The Development Period

Before discussing the events of the 1950s, it is useful to provide some background of the early development of Canada's natural gas industry and the rise and decline of exports from Ontario at the turn of the twentieth century.

The first commercial gas well in Canada was drilled in 1855 in Welland County in southwestern Ontario. Significant subsequent gas discoveries were made in 1888 in nearby Essex County.[1] These discoveries were rapidly exploited, supplying gas by pipeline

---

1. Miller (1970) p. 74; Gray (1970) p. 60. Much of the historical data for the development period is drawn from Davis (1964).

to markets in southern Ontario and export markets in Michigan and upper New York State. These reserves were produced quickly and, as southern Ontario markets were small, exports contributed to the relatively rapid depletion of these fields.

Natural gas customers in southern Ontario became concerned that the province's known gas reservoirs were becoming rapidly depleted and succeeded in making this point to the members of the Ontario legislature. Consequently, the Ontario government took steps to restrict natural gas exports. It imposed a volume limitation on exports in 1898, and in 1900 cancelled a licence which was issued in 1899 to construct a pipeline from Essex County to Detroit. As well as restricting export volumes, the Ontario government stipulated that the rates charged within Canada were to be 10 percent lower than those charged outside Canada. By 1907, the Ontario government was imposing an excise tax of two cents per Mcf on all natural gas production, with 90 percent of the tax remitted on gas consumed within the province. In response to a growing domestic market and declining reserves, exports of natural gas from Ontario stopped in 1909. Since that time, gas has continued to be produced in Ontario but later finds have never been adequate to meet the province's ever-growing needs. Consequently, there has never been a surplus of Ontario-produced gas for export.[2]

Concern over constitutional jurisdiction between the federal and provincial governments over trade in natural resources led to the enactment of legislation by the federal parliament in 1907. The undisputed constitutional authority for this federal legislation was section 91 (2) of the British North America Act, which authorized the federal government to regulate Canada's external trade and commerce. After the passage of the Electricity and Fluid Exportation Act in 1907, applicants wishing to export natural gas had to obtain a licence from the federal government.[3] The federal legislation specified that exports would be limited to those quantities which were surplus to Canadian requirements as determined by the federal government, and that export applicants would have to distribute supplies to Canadian customers before being allowed to export.[4] All of these provisions were

---

2.   Miller (1970) pp. 75-76; 223-234.

3.   Electricity and Fluid Exportation Act, S.C. 1907, c. 16.

4.   Ibid., s. 5.

consistent with the regulatory regime then in place in the province of Ontario. They still form the basis for Canada's present day natural gas export policies.

In the early twentieth century, the main exploration for natural gas and oil in Canada shifted to the province of Alberta, where natural gas had been discovered as early as 1883 during the construction of the Canadian Pacific Railway. By the 1940s, substantial discoveries of natural gas had been made in western Canada in the course of the growing exploration for oil.

As had occurred in the United States, throughout the first half of this century exploration efforts in Canada were directed at locating oil rather than natural gas. The Canadian experience with natural gas was similar to the American experience in many respects. Until the 1950s natural gas was only of marginal importance, difficult to transport, and sold only in local markets at relatively low prices. In the province of Alberta, large amounts of natural gas which could not be sold in local markets were vented into the atmosphere or flared at the well, and wasted. Due to this flaring, some producing formations were irreparably damaged, reducing the amount of oil that could eventually be recovered. The provincial government moved to address this problem. In 1938, the province of Alberta established its Petroleum and Natural Gas Conservation Board to regulate the petroleum industry and deal with the problem of inefficient operations, poor conservation practices and wastage of natural gas.

Apart from the instructive cycle of the rise and decline of exports of natural gas from southwestern Ontario to Michigan and upper New York State in the late nineteenth and early twentieth centuries, there were no significant exports of natural gas from Canada until the early 1950s.[5]

In the early years following the 1947 discovery of the Leduc oil fields in Alberta, large reserves of natural gas were discovered. The value of this gas was rather limited. Distant markets, transportation difficulties, geographical barriers and market uncertainty continued to be barriers to profitable natural gas production. At this time, oil was the petroleum commodity that could be most profitably produced. However, technological changes in the transmission sector after

---

5. For accounts of the early development of Canada's petroleum industry, see Miller (1970) pp. 74-80; Canada (1979) pp. 8-9; Gould (1976) pp. 40-58; The Petroleum Resources Communication Foundation (1979) pp. 12-22.

World War II soon changed the transportation costs and, consequently, the value of natural gas. As outlined earlier, during this period, thin-walled transmission lines were developed which made long distance transmission of natural gas economically feasible, and an extensive inter-state transmission system was put in place across the United States. Overall growth in demand for natural gas in North America was dramatic. The existence of large proven gas supplies in Alberta and rapid growth in U.S. demand soon combined to produce attractive opportunities for entrepreneurs in the sector. A number of proposals were developed to export Canadian gas by pipeline to potential markets in the states of Washington and Oregon, still not connected to the U.S. pipeline network. Other potential exporters proposed to move Alberta natural gas east to Winnipeg and then south to markets in the U.S. midwest.[6]

As had been the case in exports from southwestern Ontario at the turn of the century, there was concern that new exports to the United States from Alberta could threaten domestic supply. The <u>Electricity and Fluid Exportation Act</u> was the federal legislation then in place under which the government had a responsibility to fulfill. Consequently, the federal government appointed the Director of the Geological Survey of Canada to assess potential Alberta supplies with a view to addressing whether there existed gas supplies in excess of domestic requirements and therefore, available for export. Federal control of natural gas exports and of the transport of gas within Canada took on additional importance with the passing of <u>The Pipelines Act</u> in 1949.[7] Under this legislation, a federal licence was required to construct or operate any interprovincial or international pipelines in Canada.[8] Also of significance, the federal Board of Transport Commissioners retained supervisory control over the operation of these pipelines.[9]

Within the province of Alberta, there was public concern that gas exports would increase gas prices to Albertans as export customers bid for this commodity. There were also fears that exports would deplete sup-

---

6. Gray (1970) p. 164; Fisher (1971); Davis (1964).

7. The Pipelines Act, S.C. 1949, vol. 1, c. 20. McDougall (1982) pp. 59-60.

8. Ibid., s. 5.

9. Ibid., s. 11, 51.

plies required to meet Alberta's needs[10] and would result in the loss to the province of industries dependent on gas, which could locate elsewhere than Alberta if gas was made available elsewhere through exports. A commission of inquiry was appointed, the Dining Commission, which estimated Alberta's gas supply and requirements to 1999. The Dining Commission recommended that some exports could be allowed but that Albertans should have prior claim on the province's resources.[11]

Consequently, in 1949, the Alberta legislature passed the Gas Resources Preservation Act[12] by which potential exporters, that is firms wishing to remove gas from the province of Alberta, were required to obtain an export permit from that province's Oil and Gas Conservation Board[13]. In addition, in parallel with the federal legislation, the act stated that only gas supplies considered surplus to Alberta's future, foreseeable requirements could be authorized for export by the Board.[14]

Commencement of Exports

Commencing in 1949, several natural gas transmission companies[15] were incorporated by Special Acts of the federal Parliament, for the purpose of carrying natural gas between Canadian provinces and from Canada to the United States. In 1950, in accordance with the provincial regulatory requirements, a number of applications were filed with Alberta's Oil and Gas Conservation Board for permits to remove natural gas from Alberta. These proposed exports were planned to serve

---

10. McDougall (1982), p. 60.

11. Gray (1970) pp. 164-165; Davis (1964).

12. Gas Resources Preservation Act, S.A. 1949, c. 17, subsequently re-enacted as the Gas Resources Preservation Act, 1956, R.S.A. 1970, c. 157, which is the basis of current Alberta control. See also Energy Resources Conservation Act S.A. 1971, c. 30.

13. Ibid., s. 4.

14. Ibid., s. 3, 7.

15. These included Interprovincial Pipeline Company, Westcoast Transmission Company, Western Pipelines, Alberta Natural Gas Company and Prairie Transmission Lines Limited (McDougall (1982) pp. 61-62).

markets in eastern Canada, and export markets in the U.S. Pacific coastal states and Montana.[16]

In early 1951, the Alberta Oil and Gas Conservation Board refused all the applications. As grounds for its decision, the Board pointed out that it had not yet completed its survey of provincial gas reserves and was unable to determine to what extent reserves were sufficient to protect Alberta's requirements. Consequently, it dismissed the applications and invited the applicants to reapply after September 1951.

The parties reapplied in late 1951. In 1952 the Board allowed only Westcoast's application. The others were refused on the grounds that established reserves were not sufficient to protect reasonably foreseeable provincial requirements. The successful applicant, Westcoast, was applying to remove gas from the Peace River district in northwestern Alberta. These reserves were considered "remote", and thus surplus to the requirements of Alberta. Having obtained the provincial permit, Westcoast applied to the Canadian federal government for an export licence. In 1951, the application from Montana Power's subsidiary, Canadian-Montana, was given special consideration, and limited exports were allowed. This export project and other projects which eventually led to the establishment of Canada's current natural gas transmission system are discussed briefly below.

Canadian-Montana Pipeline Company

Canada's first significant export of natural gas to the United States occurred in 1952. At that time, metal industries in Montana, under the pressure of the Korean War, had significant requirements for volumes of natural gas in excess of what was locally available.[17] The U.S. Department of Defense became concerned that the military could run short of vital supplies of zinc, manganese and copper if Montana Power was obliged to curtail deliveries to its largest customer, the Anaconda Copper Mining Company. Consequently, the Canadian Department of Defence was asked to intercede with the province of Alberta to ensure that the removal of the required supplemental natural gas supplies would be

---

16. Applicants included Westcoast Transmission Limited, Canadian Delhi Oil, Western PipeLines, and Canadian-Montana Pipeline, a subsidiary of Montana Power Company; Davis (1964).

17. Miller (1970) pp. 95-99; Davis (1964).

authorized. As a result, legislation was passed by the province of Alberta,[18] authorizing the removal of up to 10 bcf per year at a daily rate of up to 40,000 Mcf from specified gas fields, for the exclusive benefit of the Anaconda Copper Mining Company.

For its part, in 1951, the Canadian federal government instructed its Minister of Trade and Commerce to grant an export licence under the Electricity and Fluid Exportation Act.[19] In turn, the Canadian federal Board of Transport Commissioners authorized the necessary pipeline construction in Canada under the Pipe Lines Act.[20] The American Federal Power Commission authorized the imports in 1952, limited to the volumes specified in the provincial authorization.[21]

From this initial, limited export, authorized export volumes grew to 20 bcf per year and 100,000 Mcf per day in 1955. The American and Alberta authorities authorized the additional import and export for a twenty-year term.[22] The federal export permit granted in 1955, initially a five year permit, was renewed in 1960 by an export permit expiring May 1, 1974.

Canadian authorities may have had some reservations about having a major U.S. customer dependent upon a strategic supply of natural gas from Alberta. As early as 1960, Canadian authorities warned Montana Power to maintain and improve its United States sources of gas supply. They pointed out that it might not always be in the Canadian public interest to approve applications to export additional supplies of natural gas from Canada. However, further increased volumes for export from Canada were authorized in 1960, 1965, and 1967.[23] These exports were the subject of some concern when possible shortages became an issue in the mid-1970s. Of course, in the period of the weak

---

18. Gas Export Act, S.A. 1951, c. 36.

19. Electricity and Fluid Exportation Act, S.C. 1907, c. 16.

20. Pipe Lines Act, S.C. 1949, c. 20. Eighteen miles of 16-inch pipeline were constructed by Canadian-Montana Pipeline, a subsidiary of Montana Power Company; Davis (1964).

21. 11 F.P.C. 1 (1952).

22. 14 F.P.C. 227 (1955).

23. Canada, National Energy Board (1960a); (1967b).

markets of the 1980s, Montana Power is seen as a valued, long term customer, and any additional Canadian export orders, be they short term or long term have become very welcome.

The Westcoast Project

Westcoast Gas Transmission Company Limited was incorporated in 1949 by a Special Act of the Canadian Parliament. Westcoast was formed to transport natural gas from the Peace River area of northwestern British Columbia through the interior of British Columbia to Vancouver and to the Pacific northwest of the United States. The British Columbia markets alone could not support, at that time, the costs of a large-diameter gas transmission line. Volumes of natural gas which could be sold in markets in the Pacific northwest of the United States were essential to achieve economies of scale sufficient to make natural gas competitive with other energy sources, including oil, hydroelectric power and coal, available in both the Canadian and American energy markets.

Westcoast contracted for gas reserves, in the Peace River districts of northeastern British Columbia and northwestern Alberta, sufficient to support its proposed 600-mile pipeline to Vancouver and to the American border. It planned to deliver this natural gas to its American subsidiary, Westcoast Transmission Inc., which could build and operate a 400-mile pipeline in the U.S. Pacific northwest. At this time, there was no natural gas transmission system in place in the Pacific northwest.

Westcoast received the required natural gas removal permit from Alberta in June 1952, and the federal export license was issued in 1953. However, in June 1954, the American Federal Power Commission refused to grant Westcoast's American subsidiary the required import permit.[24]

In the proceedings before the Federal Power Commission, Westcoast's application was heard with a competing application by Pacific Northwest Pipeline. Pacific Northwest proposed to supply the U.S. Pacific northwest market with natural gas transmitted from fields in New Mexico. The Federal Power Commission in approving Pacific Northwest's application, stated that it did not wish to permit an important American region to become totally dependent upon a foreign supply of natural gas, over which it had no jurisdiction. The Commission did mention that it would be prepared to

---

24. 13 F.P.C. 221 (1954); Davis (1964).

consider imports as a supplementary or interruptible supply of gas to the Pacific northwest.

Without an import permit, the Westcoast project could not proceed. Sale of natural gas to the American market was essential to the successful financing of Westcoast Transmission's pipeline. However, as allowed under the American <u>Natural Gas Act</u>,[25] Westcoast appealed the FPC's refusal to the American courts. The uncertainties created by Westcoast's court action paralysed the financing of the Pacific Northwest project, which required loans of about $160 million. Predictably, negotiations for an out-of-court settlement went on between Westcoast and Pacific Northwest. The result of these negotiations was that Westcoast agreed to drop its court action, and, for its part, Pacific Northwest agreed to purchase gas from Westcoast as a supplementary source of supply. The settlement between Westcoast and Pacific Northwest was approved, and the required permits issued by the government of Alberta, and Canada and by the American FPC, which then viewed Westcoast's proposal as a supplementary supply source.[26] Westcoast's pipeline was successfully financed and completed, and natural gas transmission started in October 1957.[27]

Because Westcoast required access to export markets in order to make its project viable, it was in a rather weak bargaining position vis à vis Pacific Northwest, and this was reflected by what were later perceived as unfavorable prices in its 1954 sales contract with Pacific Northwest. The key issue behind much of the public and political concern was the fact that the export price was significantly lower than the price paid by Canadian customers in Vancouver.

The terms of the export contract were that Pacific Northwest could purchase up to 300,000 Mcf per day, and assuming a ninety per cent load factor, sales would be at a price of 22.25 cents per Mcf until January 1, 1959 and 22 cents per Mcf during the remaining years of the twenty-year contract. Furthermore, Pacific Northwest obtained an option to purchase an additional 100,000 Mcf per day at the 22 cent price beginning in November

---

25. <u>Natural Gas Act</u>, 1938. U.S.C., 1976 edition, ch. 15B, para. 717r, sub. b.

26. 14 F.P.C. 157 (1955); Miller (1970) pp. 103-104; Canada, Royal Commission on Energy (1958) fn. 15 pp. 13-24.

27. Westcoast Transmission Company Limited (1958).

1959. Finally, Pacific Northwest was granted an option to purchase fifty per cent of the outstanding common shares of Westcoast.[28] For comparison, later sales made to customers in southern British Columbia were priced at 32 cents per Mcf.

Although the Canadian authorities authorized the exports at the contracted for prices in order to get the project launched, Westcoast's exports were a source of much difficulty between regulatory agencies of both Canada and the United States and among the pipeline companies and provincial and state entities concerned. Although the development of the Peace River natural gas reserves was considered to be beneficial to the country, the export pricing arrangements were criticized within Canada for years after.

In 1957, the Royal Commission on Canada's Economic Prospects published its report in which it criticized the structure of the export arrangements; noted the power of the American FPC, and the resulting unfavorable effect on Canadian natural gas export prices; and recommended the creation of a national energy regulatory authority in Canada.[29] The controversy over the Westcoast exports was one of the Canadian government's major concerns behind the appointment in 1958 of the Royal Commission on Energy.

This Commission gave extensive consideration to the Westcoast contracts, heard testimony and hired expert consultants to examine various aspects of the financing of the Westcoast project. The Commission stated in its report that in 1954 Westcoast was not in a position to bargain with Pacific Northwest on an equal footing and was forced to take practically whatever terms the American firm was prepared to offer.[30]

Consultants hired by the Commission found that the operating profits of Westcoast were coming solely from the Canadian deliveries, and no profits were earned in carrying out the export contracts. Westcoast hired other consultants, who gave evidence supporting alternative conclusions. This whole area of cost and revenue allocation is rather subjective and many assumptions must be made in order to draw conclusions. The Commission recommended further inquiry into this matter

---

28. Canada, Royal Commission on Energy (1958) pp. 16-21.

29. Canada, Royal Commission on Canada's Economic Prospects (1957) Chapter 7.

30. Canada, Royal Commission on Energy (1958) p. 23.

which, it believed, could be rectified if new export licences were requested by Westcoast.[31]

TransCanada Pipelines

Soon after the Westcoast Transmission Company came into operation, the TransCanada Pipelines transmission system was developed to transport natural gas supplies eastward from Alberta. The ultimate corporate make-up of this transmission system was a result of pressure from the federal and Alberta governments.

Since 1951, two companies had been competing for about two years for permission, from the Alberta Oil and Gas Conservation Board, to remove natural gas from that province. One company, Canadian Delhi Oil, was seeking supplies for transmission to eastern Canada;[32] the other company, Western Pipe Lines, wanted to sell natural gas in Canada to communities as far east as Winnipeg and, from there, to export natural gas into the United States.

After much interaction between the federal government through the Minister of Trade and Commerce, C.D. Howe, and the government of Alberta, through Premier Earnest Manning, a compromise solution was identified. Having considered the applications from both companies for permission to remove gas from the province, the Alberta government announced that it would approve a proposal made by a joint venture formed by the two companies concerned. In January 1954, the two companies merged under the name of Trans-Canada Pipe Lines Limited. In May 1954, provincial approval was given to Trans-Canada Pipe Lines to remove natural gas from Alberta. Trans-Canada's proposal had the primary purpose of supplying markets in Canada east of Alberta. As a secondary purpose, Trans-Canada wished to export such natural gas as might be considered surplus to Canadian requirements to markets in the United States.[33] This example casts light on the interplay between provincial and federal interests in trade in natural gas.

---

31. Ibid., pp. 23-24.

32. Canadian Delhi obtained a charter for a wholly-owned subsidiary, Trans-Canada Pipe Lines, under the federal <u>PipeLines Act</u> (S.C. 1949, c. 20, R.S.C. 1952). This pipeline was to reach as far east as Montreal, Quebec; Davis (1964).

33. Kilbourn (1970) pp. 34ff; Davis (1964).

Federal Export Policy

Having constitutional jurisdiction over external trade and commerce, the federal government was able to use its control of natural gas exports to obtain concessions from the province of Alberta. Canadian export policy on oil and gas was explicitly set out in a speech given in March 1953 by C.D. Howe, the then Canadian Minister of Trade and Commerce.[34] The essence of his intended message was that no natural gas exports from Canada would be allowed unless natural gas markets in eastern Canada were connected to the Alberta reserves by a pipeline situated within Canada.

In this speech, Howe drew a clear distinction between exports of oil and natural gas. He stated that Canada's national policy regarding oil was to move it from the wellhead to refineries within economic distance by the cheapest means possible, and to arrange for markets for that portion of Canadian production that could not be economically used in Canadian refineries in the market that offered the highest return to the producer.[35] In this respect, oil was regarded as an industrial fuel which (until 1973) moved freely between international boundaries, as did other basic commodities such as iron ore or wheat. There being a variety of competing sources of supply worldwide, oil was regulated with an eye to maximizing returns from the resource rather than to achieve some strategic or security-oriented advantage. This remained the basis of Canadian oil export policy until 1973.

In Howe's policy statement, the sale and distribution of natural gas was viewed from an entirely different perspective. Howe argued that as with electricity, natural gas exports required important investment in facilities in the United States, and that this obligated Canada to maintain a continuous supply of natural gas once exports were allowed to commence. Howe concluded, therefore, that Canadian policy would be to refuse the export of natural gas by pipeline until such time as the government was convinced that there could be no economic use, present or future, for that natural gas within Canada.

Howe never intended that this statement be taken literally. He was taking a position to deal with Alberta and the petroleum industry. One would have to

---

34. Canada, House of Commons, Debates, March 13, 1953, pp. 2927-2931.

35. Ibid., p. 2928.

wonder how a government could ever be convinced that there would never be an economic use within Canada for an energy source like natural gas. In the rest of his speech, the Minister clarified the government's position by implying that new gas exports to the United States would only be possible once a pipeline was built totally within Canada to connect western Canada's gas reserves to markets in Ontario and Quebec.[36]

The construction of this pipeline was the federal government's true goal, and natural gas exports were the tools to be used to help attain the goal. As with the construction of the Trans-Canada Railroad, the political desire to promote east-west ties within Canada was one of the major motivations behind the federal government's effort to modify the economic attractiveness of north-south lines of trade in natural gas. Work done by Waverman[37] and Debanné[38] has estimated the greater economic costs of the resultant existing natural gas pipeline system compared with one that would have been put in place if sources of supply had been allowed to be connected to their most economic markets.

A rather unequal perceived relationship between Canada and the United States is revealed in Howe's 1953 speech. In stating government policy, Howe explained that eastern Canada could not depend on American sources of supply for natural gas. He cited attempts which had been made to obtain a supply of natural gas for southern Ontario from the United States. He quoted the following passage from an export permit issued by the American regulatory agency to a pipeline from Texas (which extended its line to Windsor, Ontario).

> The delivery of natural gas to the Union Gas Company of Canada shall be curtailed or interrupted whenever it is required for the protection of deliveries of gas to any or all of the pipelines' customers in the United States -- it being the intention that at all times, persons and municipalities in the

---

36. Ibid., p. 2929.

37. Waverman (1973).

38. Debanné (1975).

United States are to receive preferential service over that given to the Union Gas Company of Canada.[39]

Howe explained that as a result of this clause, deliveries of gas to Union Gas had been made only in summer months, and very little gas had been delivered. He pointed out that if deliveries of gas to Canada from the United States had to be subject to this clause in every case, it would not be possible for Canada to obtain a reliable source of supply in the United States.

Howe's argument was rather inconsistent. He first stated that the export of natural gas was different from that of oil, because once gas exports were approved, Canada would have to offer the American purchasers a reliable, continuous supply. However, in the next breath, he stated that Canada could not rely on American sources of supply because these sources could be curtailed at any time if required to meet requirements in the United States.

Howe concluded his speech by stating that gas swaps on a geographic basis whereby Canadian gas would be sold in the U.S. Pacific northwestern states in return for an equivalent supply delivered into southwestern Ontario from Texas would not be possible due to the attitude of the American regulatory agency. He concluded by stating that the only reliable supply of natural gas for Ontario and Quebec would have to be from western Canada by means of a pipeline situated totally within Canada.[40]

Howe and the government to which he belonged were committed to the principle of an all-Canadian pipeline, located entirely on Canadian territory to supply Alberta gas to eastern Canada. However, these criteria complicated the financing of the project, and it appeared that the proposal could not be financed

---

39. Canada, House of Commons, Debates, March 12, 1953, p. 2930. It is noteworthy that, to the author's knowledge, no similar statement has ever been made by the Canadian regulatory agency. In fact, during the period under study and particularly in the mid-1970s, when there was a possibility that curtailments would be required, it was generally stated that if curtailments were ever required in Canada, domestic purchasers would share the burden on an equal basis with export customers.

40. Loc. cit.

through normal commercial channels without additional Canadian or export sales contracts. The problem was rather circular since neither Canadian nor export sales contracts were likely to be concluded unless it was demonstrated that the pipeline would in fact be built. To resolve this problem, the federal government, in conjunction with the government of Ontario, set up a Crown corporation, the Northern Ontario Pipeline Crown Corporation. The mandate of this company was to build and own some 675 miles of the 30-inch TransCanada natural gas transmission system through northern Ontario. A key feature of this mandate was that the operations were to proceed on terms which made it practicable for TransCanada to carry the charges on this line through its development period, and made it attractive, although not obligatory, for TransCanada to buy the Crown line once the system was operating at normal capacity.

To assist in the financing of the Crown line, an export component and a temporary "swap" arrangement were built into the project. By these arrangements, TransCanada was to build the first section of its pipeline from Alberta to Manitoba and transport part of the natural gas to the Manitoba border at a point near Emerson. At the border it would be delivered to Midwestern Gas Transmission, a subsidiary of Tennessee Gas Transmission. For its part, Tennessee Gas would transport gas from American sources to the U.S. border at Niagara to supply the Ontario market. This swap arrangement made good economic sense. During the construction of the Crown line in northern Ontario, the Ontario natural gas market could be developed with temporary imports. Also, this arrangement allowed TransCanada's western pipeline facilities to be utilized at an economic capacity while the Crown pipeline was being put in place. The plan was that once the transmission line was completed, the imports would stop, and a small export of Canadian natural gas would be allowed at Niagara. The export at Emerson, Manitoba would continue, but at a reduced level.

After due consideration by the federal parliament,[41] the proposal was approved.[42] With this kind of backing from the federal government, purchase contracts covering the anticipated requirements of the major cities in central Canada were quickly put into place. This in turn allowed the Crown corporation to secure its remaining capital requirements.

Royal Commissions Established

When the Diefenbaker government took power after the 1957 general elections, the TransCanada issue, and the issue of natural gas exports in general were the subject of much controversy. Two Royal Commissions were established to report on these and other related matters. The first Commission, the Royal Commission on Canada's Economic Prospects, which had been established before the elections by the St. Laurent government, sponsored a study of Canada's energy resources[43] which

---

41. Time was critical to the project and its financing since TransCanada's contracts covering both supply and sales had escape clauses which made the arrangements void if they were not put into effect before certain deadlines. Consequently, to facilitate the success of the project, the Liberal government tried to force the legislation creating the Crown corporation through Parliament in 1956. This led to what historians have called the "Great Pipeline Debate". The sound economic basis for the overall plan was obvious, and not the real focus of the debate. Rather, there was some confusion as to some specific details of the plan. Some argued that private parties could benefit from government assistance in the financing. The debate centered less on the details of the pipeline proposal than on the manner in which the government of Louis St. Laurent was dealing with the issues in Parliament. Certainly, this was one of the issues on which the government of St. Laurent was defeated in 1957 by John Diefenbaker; Davis (1964); Kilbourn (1970).

42. The Northern Ontario Pipe Line Crown Corporation was created June 7, 1956. The Corporation was established to (a) construct the northern Ontario section, and (b) make short-term loans to TransCanada on behalf of the Crown for the construction of TransCanada's western section of the line. These loans were to cover up to 90 percent of the cost of the western section (but were not to exceed $80 million); Davis (1964).

43. Davis (1957).

examined energy supplies and markets, including exports. In its report, published in November 1957, the Commission recommended that a comprehensive national energy policy be formulated, and that a national energy regulatory authority be established. The proposed mandate for this authority was to advise the federal government on energy matters in general, and to approve all contracts for the export of natural gas, oil and electric power.[44]

The political reality that a controversy over an energy-related matter had led to the downfall of the previous government was not lost on the newly elected government. It seemed to be a good idea to pursue the recommendation to establish a regulatory agency, removed somewhat from the arena of politics, to deal with exports and the energy transmission companies. As a preliminary to establishing such an agency and in an attempt to defuse the political excitement then surrounding the various issues, in October 1957 the Diefenbaker government established the Royal Commission on Energy. The terms of reference for the Commission were generally to study the energy situation in Canada and to inquire into and make recommendations concerning: energy exports; the regulation of pipelines; the creation of a National Energy Board to administer various aspects of federal energy policy; and certain aspects of the arrangements between Trans-Canada Pipe Lines and the Northern Ontario Pipeline Crown Corporation.[45]

In its First Report, published in October 1958, the Royal Commission on Energy examined the export contracts and the financing of Westcoast Transmission,[46] and the financing of TransCanada Pipe Lines and its arrangements with the Northern Ontario Crown Corporation.[47] In their report, the Commissioners pointed out

---

44. Canada, Royal Commission on Canada's Economic Prospects (1957) Chapter 7; Davis (1964).

45. Canada, Order in Council, P.C. 1957-1386. This Commission was chaired by Mr. Henry Borden, and is often referred to as the Borden Commission. The Commission consisted of six Commissioners including the Chairman. The other five Commissioners were J. Louis Levesque, G.E. Brinell, G.G. Cushing, R.D. Howland and L.J. Ladner.

46. Canada, Royal Commission on Energy (1958) pp. 13-24.

47. Ibid., pp. 54-88.

the major problems of regulating Canada's natural gas exports to ensure that Canada's best interests were protected. Three basic problem areas were identified:

1) The size of the resource base was uncertain. Although policy would be based on incomplete information, it would have to be based on an informed judgement, founded upon the very best available information regarding how much natural gas would ultimately be discovered in Canada, and in the western Canadian sedimentary basin in particular. The Commission suggested that export decisions must be based on a continuous appraisal of the supply and demand situation in Canada.[48]
2) The rate at which the Canadian market for natural gas could be expected to expand was largely judgemental.[49]
3) Natural gas export prices should aim at ensuring that the minimum prices which are obtained reflect the true value of the exported commodity in terms of the prices of alternative energy resources in markets served, and that the development and transport costs incurred to service an export market are borne appropriately by the pipeline customers who benefit.[50]

---

48. Ibid., p. 8.

49. Ibid., pp. 7-8. The Commission did not undertake to prepare precise forecasts of future Canadian supply and demand for natural gas. Rather, the Commission took the highest estimate of demand submitted to it by intervenors and compared this estimate with a "conservative" estimate of future supply. From this comparison, the Commission stated that there was a large supply over the next 30 years (1957 to 1987) compared to expected Canadian market demand.

50. Ibid., pp. 8-12. More specifically, the Commission noted that: "While, in the first instance, the terms and conditions of an export contract are matters of negotiation between the Canadian exporter and the purchaser of natural gas, these terms and conditions should be examined when application is made for an export licence. The Government should be satisfied, not only with respect to the technical aspects of the contract, but also with respect to its price provisions.

The Commission recommended that a National Energy Board should be established to deal with various energy-related matters, including the regulation of natural gas exports.

It is noteworthy that, while acknowledging the uncertainties involved, the Commission took an "optimistic" approach, and made the assumption that Canada's ultimate potential, that is the size of Canada's undiscovered, but economically producible reserves, was relatively very large. For example, the Commission stated that it was "reasonable to anticipate, under favorable economic conditions, an ultimate discovery of some 300 Tcf of natural gas in the Western Canadian Sedimentary Basin".[51] This compares with a January 1983 estimate of 174 Tcf by Canada's National Energy Board, up from its 1981 estimate of 162 Tcf, and its 1978 estimate of 146 Tcf.[52]

Thus, the Commissioners, having assumed that scarcity was not an important constraint to exports, were able to encourage an export-oriented policy. The Commission reasoned that by expanding markets for Canadian gas, earnings in the industry would be expected to increase and exploration and development would be encouraged; also potential economies of scale on transmission costs could be achieved.[53]

"It is necessary to ensure that the minimum export price is fair and reasonable. Where sales to Canadian distributors as well as export sales are involved, the price relationship, between Canadian sales and sales for export, should be such that Canadian sales will not contribute more than a fair and reasonable proportion of the total return to the shareholders on their investment in the gas transmission company.

"The export contract should contain fair and reasonable provisions for price adjustments during the term of the contract, so that the exporter, and in turn the gas producers, will participate in any benefits accruing from general price increases occurring in the export markets."

51. Ibid., p. 3.

52. Canada, National Energy Board (1983) p. 17; (1979) pp. 3-13. Included in these totals is some 40 Tcf which has already been produced.

53. Canada, Royal Commission on Energy (1958) pp. 8-9.

Taking into account the domestic pressures in western Canada, the Commissioners' optimism was perhaps to be expected. The economy of western Canada was "taking off" due to investments in the petroleum industry. By 1955, more than $900 million had been invested in the various sectors of the petroleum industry.[54] Drilling results were very encouraging. The industry was finding large volumes of natural gas. Once found, the gas only produced export revenues for the economy, profits to industry and taxes and royalties to the federal and provincial governments once it was flowing to market in a pipeline. Understandably, the Commissioners heard a lot of evidence from a large number of intervenors to encourage the formulation of an optimistic opinion on Canada's wealth in natural gas reserves.

The government acted with speed on the recommendation of the Commission, and in May 1959 introduced legislation to create a National Energy Board. The National Energy Board Act was passed in July 1959[55] and by November 1959 the Board had been established. Of key importance, the Commission's export orientation was translated into the National Energy Board Act. Exports of oil, natural gas and electric power were to be allowed if the volumes were "surplus to Canadian requirements" and provided the price was "fair and reasonable".

With the establishment of the National Energy Board, the "expansion phase" in the development of Canada's natural gas resources began. Table 4-1 demonstrates the growth in Canadian gas exports over the period under study.

---

54. Davis (1957) p. 325.

55. National Energy Board Act, S.C. 1959, c. 46.

Table 4-1

MARKETABLE NATURAL GAS[56]
(Billion cubic feet)

Year	Canadian Production	Exports	Export Revenues ($ million)
1950	60	.002	not available
1951	67	.004	not available
1952	73	7.94	not available
1953	84	8.01	not available
1954	100	6.99	not available
1955	124	11.37	not available
1956	136	10.84	not available
1957	168	15.73	2.32
1958	281	86.97	17.98
1959	363	84.76	16.95
1960	450	91.05	18.05
1961	561	168.18	41.69
1962	776	319.57	72.42
1963	847	340.95	75.63
1964	944	404.14	97.61
1965	1,029	403.91	104.28
1966	1,107	426.22	108.75
1967	1,217	505.16	123.66
1968	1,384	598.14	153.75
1969	1,606	669.82	176.19
1970	1,838	768.11	205.99
1971	2,028	905.05	250.72
1972	2,299	1,007.05	306.84
1973	2,444	1,030.91	350.75
1974	2,420	960.71	493.64
1975	2,446	949.47	1,092.17
1976	2,459	954.05	1,616.49
1977	2,591	993.80	2,028.05
1978	2,475	882.59	2,190.33
1979	2,660	990.49	2,889.05

Table 4-1 (Cont'd)

MARKETABLE NATURAL GAS[56]
(Billion cubic feet)

Year	Canadian Production	Exports	Export Revenues ($ million)
1980	2,465	810.94	3,983.85
1981	2,395	765.88	4,370.05
1982	2,446	779.47	4,807.60
1983	2,299	707.04	3,940.80
1984	2,576(e)	743.69(e)	3,920.30(e)

Developments in the 1960s: Expansion of Exports

Throughout the period from 1960 to 1970, policies were adopted to facilitate the development and expansion of the Canadian petroleum industry. This was done by expanding domestic and export markets for both oil and natural gas. Natural gas exports played an important role.

National Oil Policy

In 1961, Canada put in place a "National Oil Policy" (NOP), the purpose of which was to gain a large enough market, domestic and foreign, to develop and maintain a healthy petroleum industry in western Canada. The NOP split the domestic Canadian oil market into two sectors. Crude oil markets west of the Ottawa River valley were reserved for indigenous crude while lower-priced imported oil was allowed to be used only in areas east of the Ottawa River valley. The NOP also sought to expand American markets for Canadian crude oil and natural gas.

Since the federal government guaranteed western Canadian producers a portion of the Canadian market, and made a commitment to seek greater export markets, this greatly improved the Canadian petroleum industry's

---

56. Statistics Canada publications 57-205, 65-004; Commodity code: 26-431 in Export in Commodities Classification. Revenues from export of natural gas for the period before 1957 are not available from Statistics Canada. Export revenues 1982 to 1984 are from National Energy Board, _1984 Annual Report_, p. 22. Figures shown for 1984 are preliminary estimates.

potential to develop Canada's oil and natural gas resources. The NOP allowed eastern Canada, including Quebec, to retain access to then considerably lower-priced imported crude oil.

In going along with the higher crude oil prices paid by consumers in Ontario, the Ontario government certainly bore in mind the prospects of increased refining activity in Ontario, considerably protected from competition with refineries east of the Ottawa River valley. Over time, of course, the potential regional gains from continued adherence to this NOP changed considerably as resources in Canada's western provinces became developed to their potential and as the international oil markets underwent significant changes in the 1970s.

Under the NOP, during the 1960s, the Canadian government sought to expand exports and, through negotiations with the United States, succeeded in obtaining exemptions for Canadian crude oil from the strict U.S. import controls. In the 1950s, in order to protect the U.S. oil producers, and to maintain regulated crude oil prices in the United States (at levels usually above the cost of imported crude) production from many of the more productive wells in the United States was prorated. By the mid-1950s, imports of crude oil into the United States had reached levels which were considered a potential threat to U.S. national security. In response, U.S. President Eisenhower imposed informal import quotas on crude oil imports. These quotas were made formal in 1959 and remained in force throughout the 1960s.[57] In return for gradually increased access to midwestern and Pacific coastal American oil markets, Canada allowed unrestricted entry of American coal (used largely for generation of electricity in Ontario) and agreed to accept the compliance costs of maintaining exports at levels proposed by the United States government. As a result of this agreement, the National Energy Board was charged with the responsibility of overseeing Canadian export sales in the American market and keeping exports in line with limits set by the American government. The United States lifted quotas on all oil imports in 1972.

---

57. These quotas kept up the price of oil to U.S. consumers and created an impetus to substitute other energy sources such as natural gas and coal for oil in U.S. markets. See, for example, Odell (1975) p. 35. Interestingly, both Canada and Mexico were granted exemptions to the U.S. quota system, but in contrast, Venezuela was not granted any exemptions to these quotas (Odell (1975) p. 41).

Increased Exports of Natural Gas

Applications to export large volumes of natural gas awaited the National Energy Board upon its creation in 1959. Natural gas export licences were issued by the Board throughout the 1960s, and exports grew steadily from about 87 Bcf/yr in 1959 to about 800 Bcf/yr in 1970 and peaked at just over 1000 Bcf/yr in 1972. At hearings for export licences held in 1971, licences were refused on the grounds that there was no natural gas surplus to domestic requirements.[58] No significant new export licences were granted again until 1980, when circumstances had changed considerably.[59]

Significant Developments During the Expansion Period 1960-71

Several significant developments during the period of export expansion are noted below. Most important during this period is the expansion of the pipeline transmission systems within Canada and the putting in place of additional transmission systems to service export markets. Table 4-2 demonstrates the steady rapid growth in Canada's natural gas pipeline transmission system over the period 1960-71. Lines of transmission system pipeline almost doubled from over ten thousand miles in place in 1960 to over twenty thousand miles in 1971.

Alberta-California Project

A major natural gas transmission system was put in place in 1961 to link some Alberta natural gas fields with the markets of northern California. This is often referred to as the Alberta-California project or the Alberta and Southern export project. The Canadian firms involved are Alberta and Southern Gas Company as the purchaser of gas and Alberta Natural Gas Company as the transmission company. The United States purchasing utility is the Pacific Gas and Electric Company. Although the primary objective of this natural gas project was and remains the export of Canadian natural gas, the system has provided service to a few small Canadian communities along its route, and in the late 1960s and 1970s, provided substantial quantities of gas from its contracted reserves to meet the growing requirements of Alberta utilities.

---

58. Canada, National Energy Board (1971b).

59. Canada, National Energy Board (1979).

Table 4-2

**LENGTH OF NATURAL GAS PIPELINE NETWORK
BY FUNCTION OF LINES**[60]
(Miles)

YEAR	Gathering	Transmission	Distribution	Total
1960	3,680	10,716	18,419	32,815
1961	4,464	11,217	19,545	35,225
1962	4,568	11,845	20,940	37,352
1963	4,692	12,388	22.459	39,540
1964	4,918	13,311	23,644	41,862
1965	5,206	14,206	24,661	44,073
1966	5,319	14,935	25,728	45,982
1967	5,376	15,613	27,305	48,295
1968	5,905	16,535	29,892	52,322
1969	6,517	17,872	31,980	56,370
1970	6,791	19,282	33,840	59,913
1971	7,175	20,601	35,116	62,892
1972	7,256	22,880	37,103	67,239
1973	8,064	24,505	38,088	70,657
1974	8,613	25,107	39,292	73,012
1975	9,635	25,962	41,410	77,007
1976	11,979	27,147	43,750	82,876
1977	12,578	28,581	46,735	87,893
1978	12,578	28,577	51,376	92,531
1979	13,112	28,768	50,431	92,310
1980	14,425	28,934	53,135	96,493
1981	15,404	29,829	55,219	100,452
1982	16,769	31,200	57,133	105,103
1983	18,938	32,206	62,018	113,163

---

60. Canadian Gas Association (1982) p. 41; (1985) pp. 34-37; Statistics Canada, Publication 57-205 Annual.

TransCanada's Great Lakes Project

When TransCanada's northern line had been completed, because of the rapid growth of gas markets in southern Ontario, soon additional transmission capacity was needed. The company proposed that a second line be built south of the Great Lakes to delivery points at Sault Ste. Marie and Sarnia, Ontario, with some export sales being made to U.S. customers along the way. The National Energy Board recommended approval of this line but pointed out to Cabinet in its reasons for decision that the Great Lakes Line, being 36-inch diameter compared with the 30-inch diameter northern line, could become TransCanada's main line. In turn, the Board cautioned that this could expose natural gas supplies for Ontario and Quebec to the uncertainties of passage through another jurisdiction. On the basis of this warning, the Cabinet initially denied approval for the Great Lakes project. TransCanada reacted by contracting with the Canadian government to maintain its northern line as its main line. In addition, TransCanada promised to ensure that specified and increasing minimum percentages of its requirements for eastern Canada would flow through the northern line, and to commence looping or twinning that line. With these undertakings, Cabinet approved the proposed export licences and the construction of the transmission facilities in Canada associated with the Great Lakes project.

Another important feature of the planning stage of the Great Lakes Line was a short-term import of American gas at Niagara Falls which served to bridge the supply gap while the Great Lakes Line was being built. This was for an initial amount of 25 billion cubic feet per year, diminishing by 5 billion cubic feet per year over a five-year period. This was a parallel to an arrangement for importation of natural gas from 1954 to 1958, to build up the Toronto and Montreal natural gas markets pending construction of the original Trans-Canada system.

One interesting feature of the operation of the Great Lakes Line is an exchange of volumes which takes place. Some 500 million cubic feet per day are provided by Great Lakes to U.S. customers in Wisconsin and Michigan and an equivalent amount is injected into the Great Lakes Line at the Farwell storage area in Michigan, some 330 miles further east along the line. The resultant substantial savings in transmission expense benefit both the American and Canadian customers. The existence of this transmission system would permit the expansion of such geographic exchanges if this were judged to be in both countries' interest as perceived

91

Diagram of Canada/U.S. Natural Gas Pipeline System[61]

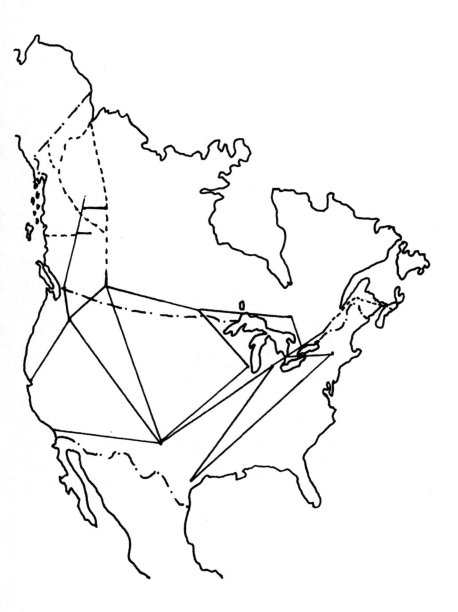

61. National Energy Board <u>1984 Annual Report</u>, p. 32; Economic Council of Canada (1985) p. 58.

by the respective regulatory agencies. In many instances, economic considerations would favor the development of geographic exchanges such as this. The biggest obstacle in the late 1970s when the idea was floated very seriously was the doubt about whether the supplies subject to the exchange were secure.

Developments in the 1970s: A period of consolidation

The third period considered in this study, 1971 to 1980, was a period of consolidation. While reserves continued to grow, the pace of growth was slower than in the 1950s and 1960s. Consensus and collaboration between the federal and provincial governments and the petroleum industry, which generally characterized the earlier two periods, was replaced by conflict and confrontation.[62] Although reserves and sales volumes did not appreciate dramatically, sales revenues, taxes and other payments to governments including royalties and land bonuses, and producer netbacks all soared as a result of domestic and export price increases for oil and natural gas which followed OPEC increases in the world oil price after 1973.

Whereas, in the first two periods, the petroleum industry took the initiative in developing Canada's petroleum sector and making trading arrangements, with governments monitoring and approving arrangements, contracts and projects sought by the private firms, in this third period, the different levels of government took a much more active role. Most significantly, governments at all levels established a strong presence in the sector through ownership of corporations[63] actively involved in petroleum exploration, production, transportation and marketing.

Even before the oil price shocks brought on by OPEC in the wake of the 1973 Middle East War, potential limitations on natural gas supply were recognized and significant price increases began to occur. At its 1971 export hearings, the National Energy Board refused all the natural gas export applications on the basis that there were not enough reserves to protect Canadian requirements.[64]

---

62. See, for example, Toner and Bregha (1981).

63. Some of these include: Petro-Canada, Alberta Energy Corporation, British Columbia Petroleum Corporation, Ontario Energy Corporation and SOQUIP (Quebec).

64. Canada, National Energy Board (1971b).

Shortages of natural gas in the U.S. interstate market became a subject of much political debate. Widespread curtailments in the mid-1970s took on crisis proportions in the winter of 1976-1977, and accelerated the movement towards the decontrol of natural gas prices in the United States. Although no Canadian gas user or export customer ever had deliveries curtailed, for a short period in 1974 and 1975 it appeared that there would be insufficient deliverable gas to meet expected growth in the Canadian market.[65] In this regard, increased netbacks[66] to natural gas producers in the period 1974 to 1979 led to accelerated exploration and development drilling which was very successful. This success led to rapid growth in reserves, and renewed pressure for additional exports during the latter part of the period.[67] In 1977, authorization was given to build a pipeline across Canada, the Foothills line, to connect Alaska natural gas reserves to U.S. Midwest and Pacific Markets, and at the same time, to connect Canadian reserves in the Mackenzie Delta to southern markets in Canada. Within two years, however, the supply/demand situation had shifted considerably to the point that a "surplus" had accumulated and in 1979, additional gas exports were authorized. The following year, construction of the southern leg of the Foothills pipeline was authorized to carry Alberta gas to the United States which would later be replaced (for sale in Canada) with Alaskan gas. This "pre-build" was intended to provide immediate cash flow to the builders of the line (and Alberta gas producers and governments) and facilitate the financing and construction of the rest of the pipeline.[68]

The period 1970 to 1980 was thus a period of consolidation. At the beginning of the period, natural

---

65. Canada, National Energy Board (1975a) p. 84.

66. Netbacks to producers increased eightfold over this period.

67. The idea of allowing price competition through deregulation of prices or of reducing domestic prices for natural gas or reducing producer netbacks for natural gas as a solution to this problem was not given serious consideration during this period.

68. At the time of this writing, the sponsors of this line have still been unable to secure financing for the northern part of the line, and it is far from certain that the line will be built in the near future.

gas supplies were viewed as limited and export market development was stopped. At the end of this period, natural gas reserve additions created export opportunities which started a new sales and marketing initiative after 1980.

Several developments during this period are noteworthy in the context of this study, and are now outlined. These developments include changes in Canadian export policy for oil and natural gas, export prices and the creation of Petro-Canada.

Canadian Oil Exports

As has been pointed out, shortages of crude oil in the United States in the early 1970s pushed up U.S. domestic prices even before the OPEC price hikes which were instituted after November 1973. Under the NOP, Canadian crude oil prices west of the Ottawa Valley were tied to prices set for oil landed in Chicago. Thus, as oil prices increased in the United States, so did Canadian prices west of the Ottawa Valley. As U.S. prices started to creep upward, pressure mounted from Canadian consumers to cut loose this pricing policy. The argument was that U.S. shortages should not force Canadians to pay higher prices for Canadian crude. The arguments against a change in policy, of course, came from crude oil producers, who would be foregoing revenues if they made sales to domestic customers rather than to export customers, willing to bid higher prices.

In September 1973 (prior to the OPEC embargo, which went into effect in November), the Canadian government froze domestic oil prices at $4.00 per barrel. Although this removed much of the political pressure applied by oil consumers, it was inequitable to oil producers in that those who exported all or part of their production had an advantage over producers serving the domestic market.

To achieve equity between producers and to remove the incentive to export rather than serve the domestic market, the federal government instituted a tax on crude oil and oil product exports. This export tax in effect created a two-price marketing system for crude oil produced in Canada.

In October 1973, the tax was 40 cents per barrel. After the OPEC embargo and pricing actions during the fall of 1973 and winter of 1974, the export tax increased to $6.40 a barrel in February 1974. The tax was calculated on the difference between the landed price of oil imported into Montreal and the lower, regulated wellhead price of oil in Alberta. The government adopted the policy that the difference between Alberta wellhead prices and international prices would be steadily reduced in an orderly fashion through regular increases in the domestic wellhead price. As the price gap diminished, so too would the export tax.

One argument used to justify the export tax was that Canadians were receiving the same price for exports as they were paying for imports. Also, a subsidy program was put in place to reimburse importers the difference between the cost of imports and the cost of equivalent crudes if supplied domestically. As gross exports were generally of the same magnitude as gross imports, the revenues obtained from export taxes could be equated roughly with subsidies paid to compensate importers. However, as oil exports to the United States were cut back after 1974, net imports grew. The difference between world prices and controlled domestic wellhead prices increased (especially after the 1979 OPEC increases), and the import compensation subsidy payments became much larger than revenues received from the tax on oil and oil product exports. It is worth noting here that Canadian cutbacks of oil exports were phased in gradually to accommodate the needs of some U.S. refiners in border areas. This example is illustrative of Canada's sensitivity to minimizing the negative impacts its actions may have on vulnerable areas in the United States.

Natural Gas Exports

Natural gas exports differ from oil exports in three important aspects:

1) Natural gas in both Canada and the U.S. was priced below its value as an energy commodity throughout its history as a source of fuel. Export prices for natural gas were therefore lower than those for oil on a value-for-heat basis.
2) While oil exports are contracted for on a short-term basis for relatively small quantities (generally thirty-day contracts), Canadian natural gas exports have been sold under long-term (generally about 20 years) contracts. This contract term appears to be changing rapidly in current, evolving markets and with the development of a spot market. However, looking at the pre-1982 situation, in view of the capital expenditures which are made and amortized over a given period, on the basis of a given, reliable contracted for supply, a certain type of moral obligation

may have been perceived for Canadian exporters to honor contracts in place and for the Canadian federal government to allow exporters to meet the commitments of contracts for which export licences had been issued.

3) In times of tight supply, such as the mid-1970s, cutting back a natural gas export contract would certainly require market adjustments in the U.S. market which would be much more difficult than in the case of oil. While oil can be transported by a number of modes, over the period under study there were no efficient alternatives to pipelines for natural gas. Putting a pipeline in place requires a very large capital expenditure, and therefore is undertaken only on the basis of assurances of long-term supply availability. In the future, long term supply availability may have to be matched with **well-backed** guarantees that specific delivery volumes will be purchased.

For these reasons, natural gas exports were treated differently than oil exports. For a relatively short period in 1975-76, it appeared that gas shortages could occur in Canada, but higher netbacks granted producers led to rapid reserves additions and no shortages ever materialized. Thus, the question of how curtailments would be shared between the domestic and export markets never had to be addressed in the hard terms of deciding on actual cutbacks. In the current environment of oversupply, these concerns have become rather remote.

The aspect of the importance of Canada's exports to total U.S. supply is worth examining in some detail. In terms of the total U.S. market, Canadian exports make up a relatively small share, roughly four percent of total U.S. requirements. In specific, regional U.S. markets, however, imports from Canada are very important and account for a very large portion of natural gas supply. This is illustrated in Table 4-3.

Table 4-3

CANADIAN GAS SUPPLY SENSITIVITY BY STATE[69]
1980

State/Area	Estimated Gas Utility Sales (Trillion Btu)	Approximate Percent Canadian Gas
California	1,656.2	20
Colorado	237.3	8
Idaho	47.0	57
Illinois	1,114.0	4
Michigan	830.2	12
Minnesota	260.7	6
Montana	60.4	40
Nevada	70.2	32
New York State St. Lawrence County	6.4	100
North Dakota	23.6	20
Oregon	88.5	52
Vermont	4.2	100
Washington	147.2	49
Wisconsin	341.5	19
Wyoming	53.2	18

Export Prices

As oil export prices increased, so too did export prices for natural gas. A detailed discussion of export prices is presented in Chapter 10. Major events during the 1970s are now pointed out.

In July 1974, the National Energy Board issued a report[70] on the pricing of natural gas exports. The Board found that there had been a significant increase in prices for competing natural gas supplies and for alternative energy sources in U.S. markets. The Board

---

69. Where Canadian imports are less than four percent of supply in a state, these states are not shown. Source: "Status of Canadian/U.S. Natural Gas Arrangements," *Gas Energy Review*, February 1982, Vol. 10, No. 2, pp. 12-19.

70. Canada, National Energy Board Report (1974).

concluded that the prices in existing export licences, which ranged from 23 to 60 cents per Mcf, were too low, or, in the language used by the Board, prices were no longer just and reasonable in relation to the public interest. A regulation had been passed as early as 1970 which stated that export prices could be set by the federal government to replace prices set out in natural gas export contracts.[71]

---

71. Regulation 11A was added to the National Energy Board's Part IV Regulations by Order in Council, P.C. 1970-1706. The Minister of Energy, Mines and Resources, Mr. J.J. Green, issued a Press Release on September 29, 1970, describing the functions of Regulation 11A as follows:

> "The Government considers that the price arrangements should be such as to call for a review should there be a significant increase in prices in the United States market for competing gas supplies or for alternative energy sources, and in this regard, the Governor in Council has made new regulations under Section 85 of the <u>National Energy Board Act</u>. The National Energy Board will keep under close review the adequacy of the pricing arrangements under contracts for the export of gas, and the report of the Board arising from such review will be considered by the Government in determining appropriate action."

Regulation 11A reads as follows:

1) Every Licence for the exportation of gas is, in addition to any other terms and conditions imposed by or under the Act, subject to the condition that the prices to be charged for the gas, the export of which is authorized under the licence, shall be subject to review by the Board, and where, in the opinion of the Board there has been a significant increase in prices for competing gas supplies or for alternative energy sources, the Board shall report its findings and recommendations to the Governor in Council.

2) "Where the price to be charged for gas, the export of which is authorized under a licence, is reviewed and reported on by the Board pursuant to subsection (1),

In its 1974 report, the Board recommended that the minimum border price in each licence be increased to $1.00 per Mcf or the "commodity-value", whichever is less. The report also recommended that natural gas export prices be redetermined annually to ensure that the full "commodity-value" prices, were achieved over a number of years. "Commodity-value" referred to the maximum price at which natural gas would still be competitive with energy sources available to an American importer. Depending on the location, oil heating fuels, electricity, and in some instances, coal were used as reference points for pricing purposes. As it gained experience in applying this concept, the Board came to advocate using a weighting system based on available alternative fuels in setting the Canadian export price, whenever this was possible.

As a result of the Board's July 1974 report on natural gas export prices, the export price of substantially all gas exported from Canada was raised to $1.00 per Mcf effective November 1, 1974. In the spring of 1975, the Board re-examined the "commodity-value" aspects of natural gas export prices in a report to Cabinet. The government, in accepting the Board's report, increased the export price to $1.40 per Mcf effective August 1, 1975 and to $1.60 per Mcf effective November 1, 1975. The delays in implementing the Board's recommendation, and the two-stage increase in prices, may reflect the sensitivity of the Canadian government in avoiding abrupt and sudden increases in the export price of gas. While this policy may be viewed as good customer relations, some have argued

---

the Governor in Council may, by order, establish a new price below which gas exported under the authority of the licence may not be sold or delivered after such date as may be specified in the order.

3) "Where an order is made pursuant to subsection (2), it is a condition of the licence in relation to which the order is made that gas exported under the authority of that licence shall not be sold or delivered at a price below the new price after the date specified in the order."

In addition to Regulation 11A and the authority of the Board under the <u>National Energy Board Act</u>, the <u>Petroleum Administration Act</u>, S.C. 1974-75-76, c. 47, was passed to provide further legislative authority for the National Energy Board to regulate the price of natural gas in interprovincial and export trade.

that it reflects the dependency status of Canada. The argument that follows is that that if the gas is not sold at prices reflecting its full commodity value, then it should not be exported, but rather, left in the ground for sale at a later time to the U.S. market or for use in the future by Canadian customers.

In 1976, the Board recommended that the prices of natural gas exports be increased to varying levels ranging from $1.60 per Mcf to $2.10 per Mcf. These prices reflected the Board's assessment of factors which were based on the commodity-value of natural gas in various export market areas. The government, in considering the Board's recommendations, also considered the views of the United States government. When consulted, the U.S. authorities stated a preference for a uniform border price for Canadian natural gas. As a result of these and perhaps other considerations, and in spite of the expected advantages of varied export prices in specific markets that were estimated by the Board, the government decided that it would retain a uniform boarder price which would increase to $1.80 per Mcf effective September 10, 1976 and to $1.94 per Mcf effective January 1, 1977.

In its 1977 review of prices in Canadian natural gas export markets the Board considered the commodity value of alternative energy sources, the costs to Canadians of foreign crude oil, the natural gas shortages that were then occurring and their impact on United States domestic prices and other economic and environmental factors. Based upon these considerations the Board recommended that the uniform border price of natural gas exports be denominated in United States dollars[72] and increased to $2.25 (U.S.) per Mcf. In the government's review of the Board's recommendation, it decided that the concept of substitution value or replacement cost, based on the BTU equivalent value of the international price of crude oil, was more appropriate than the commodity value calculation then in use. Consequently, the new export price was set at $2.16 (U.S.) per Mcf, effective September 21, 1977. One notes that in both 1976 and 1977, the approved prices were less than the full commodity and then substitution values estimated by the National Energy Board.

---

72. Over the period 1970 to 1977 the Canadian dollar traded at a rate close to par with the U.S. dollar. However, in 1977 the Canadian dollar depreciated significantly with respect to the U.S. dollar and has continued to depreciate up to the time of this writing.

The substitution value concept remained in use into the 1980s and export prices were increased in a steady and dramatic manner, corresponding to the steady and dramatic increases in world oil prices, reaching a high of $4.94 (U.S.) in 1981.[73] The following table summarizes the history of increases in the export price of Canadian natural gas since 1972.

Table 4-4

EXPORT PRICE OF NATURAL GAS[74]

		Canadian dollars per MMBTU	U.S. dollars per MMBTU
Average	1972		0.30
Average	1973		0.34
Average	1974		0.54
January	1975	1.00	–
August	1975	1.40	–
November	1975	1.60	–
September	1976	1.80	–
January	1977	1.94	–
September	1977	2.32	2.16
May	1978	2.66	2.30
August	1979	3.28	2.80
November	1979	4.08	3.45
February	1980	5.17	4.47
April	1981	5.88	4.94
April	1983	5.50	4.40
October	1984	negotiated prices provided certain minimum conditions are met	

---

73. Upon reaching this peak no further increases took place, and in April 1983, Canada's export price was reduced to $4.40 in view of declining world oil prices and low levels of natural gas export sales.

74. NEB files (1975 to 1983); <u>Gas Energy Review</u>, February 1982, Vol. 10. No. 2, pp. 12-19 (1972 to 1974). Prices shown for period 1972 to 1974 are average prices for the calendar year.

Starting with the 1973 price increases, and until November 1984, Canada maintained a two-price system for both oil and natural gas. During this period, oil sold within Canada was priced below the international level. As natural gas sold within Canada was priced in relation to the domestic oil price, and discounted to cost less than oil on a BTU equivalence basis in eastern Canadian markets, natural gas export prices were held higher than domestic prices. In the fall of 1984, oil prices were raised to the international level and decontrolled. Natural gas export prices at the Canadian border have been partially unregulated, and at the time of writing, are negotiated between contracting parties. Provided they meet certain minimum conditions, including being greater than Canadian natural gas prices in areas near the point of export, the contracts would likely be approved.

Oil exports were taxed with the export tax flowing into the federal treasury to help pay for crude oil imports. Natural gas exports, however, have been treated very differently. No export tax has been levied. Rather, the difference between the export price and domestic price has flowed back to all gas producers. That is, the difference has been channelled back to producers, producing gas for any market, in proportion to the size of their production in relation to total production. All gas producers, therefore, in addition, to the price they have received for their gas at the wellhead, have received a share of the additional revenues earned on the export market. This means that _all_ producers of natural gas have had a special interest in additional natural gas being exported by any given producer. These flowback payments were very significant in the late 1970s and early 1980s. At the time of writing, this flowback system is still in operation with flowback payments down to about 3 cents per Mcf. As export prices continue to drop, these flowback payments will likely disappear completely in the near future. In fact, under a federal-provincial agreement signed October 31, 1985, it was agreed that the export flowback system will be completely eliminated on November 1, 1986.[75] In the new regime, to be fully in place on November 1, 1986, where export prices are negotiated new sellers would be expected to be permitted to retain all the revenues they generate from new export sales. It could be argued that this would be one of the best ways to give them the needed incentives for negotiations with importers.

---

75. _Agreement Among the Governments of Canada, Alberta, British Columbia and Saskatchewan on Natural Gas Markets and Prices_, October 31, 1985, paragraph 19.

Petro-Canada

Turning now to the third major development of the period 1970 to 1980, the creation of Petro-Canada marked a new era as the federal government took a much more active role in the petroleum industry.

Petro-Canada was established in 1975 by the Petro-Canada Act.[76] It commenced operations in 1976 as a proprietary Crown corporation, that is, a public enterprise expected to operate in a commercial environment, and ultimately, to be self-financing. In spite of this commercial orientation, Petro-Canada was created to act as a policy tool for improving Canada's long-term energy supply. It was to improve supply by accelerating the timing of higher-risk exploration and development in the geological and technological frontiers, that is in the Arctic, the eastern offshore basins, and the heavy oils and tar sands of the Canadian prairie region.[77]

Petro-Canada's mandate was quite broad, and authorized the company to: import petroleum and petroleum products to assure a continuity of supply for Canadians; develop and exploit hydrocarbon deposits in Canada and abroad; carry out research and development projects in relation to hydrocarbons and other fuels; and engage in petroleum exploration, production, distribution, refining and marketing.[78]

---

76. Petro-Canada Act, S.C. 1974-75-76, c. 61.

77. For an account of the history of Petro-Canada's establishment, see L. Pratt (1981).

78. Petro-Canada Act, s.l. More specifically, the objects of the Corporation, as set out in section 6 of the Act are:

(a) to engage in exploration for and the development of hydrocarbons and other types of fuel or energy;

(b) to engage in research and development projects relating to fuel and energy resources;

(c) to import, produce, transport, distribute, refine and market hydrocarbons of all descriptions;

(d) to produce, distribute, transport and market other fuels and energy; and

Once it commenced operations, Petro-Canada quickly became a major actor in the petroleum sector. It was used by the federal government to inject hundreds of millions of dollars into non-conventional oil projects and frontier exploration. Between 1976 and 1981, Petro-Canada participated in two-thirds of the wells drilled off Canada's east coast and in the high Arctic.[79] The intent of the federal government was that by encouraging these long-term and higher-risk ventures, Petro-Canada would serve as a catalyst to promote a continuing search for commercial frontier petroleum resources.

Over this period, Petro-Canada became a leader in oil and gas research and development. The Company has been committed to developing new and improved exploration, production and heavy oil upgrading technology for application in Canada and abroad.[80] On the technological frontier, Petro-Canada quickly became involved in mining the oil sands and undertook a comprehensive evaluation of the Athabasca bitumen reserves that could be recoverable through mining techniques. It also undertook a test project to develop technology for recovering oil from Athabasca using in-situ recovery methods. In addition, Petro-Canada became involved in a program with private interests and the government of the province of Saskatchewan to accelerate heavy oil developments in that province.

Since 1975, Petro-Canada has become established as one of Canada's top petroleum producers through its acquisitions of Atlantic Richfield Canada Ltd. and Pacific Petroleum Ltd. A third acquisition, Petrofina Canada, took place in 1981. In 1983, the Canadian refineries and gas outlets of British Petroleum in Canada were purchased. In 1985, additional gas outlets and facilities in western Canada were acquired from Gulf Canada.

Regarding its import mandate, in the late 1970s, Petro-Canada established working relationships with state-owned companies in Venezuela and Mexico and negotiated state-to-state oil purchases which served to

---

(e) to engage or invest in ventures or enterprises related to the exploration, production, importation, distribution, refining and marketing of fuel, energy and related resources."

79. Petro-Canada (1982) p. 2.

80. Ibid., p. 20.

increase security of Canada's supply through diversification of import sources. Also, Petro-Canada undertook exploration in the North Sea and Indonesia and provided China with technical assistance related to petroleum activity in that country. As an active Crown corporation in the petroleum sector, Petro-Canada provided the federal government with a "window on the industry." That is, the government gained a new, inside perspective on such issues as taxation, prices, supply, land management, oil and gas production and marketing and exports.

In 1979, however, the government of Pierre Trudeau was replaced by a minority government, headed by Joe Clark. Although the Clark government remained in power less than one year, Petro-Canada was looked at very carefully. The Clark government wished to reduce the activities of Crown corporations in the private sector and examined the possibilities of winding down, breaking up, selling all or part of, or "privatizing" by some other means, several Crown corporations, including Petro-Canada. A key consideration was whether Petro-Canada was undertaking activities that industry would or could have undertaken as well or better in any case (or at lower cost), and whether the Crown corporation was making efficient use of public (taxpayers') funds. The Clark government never had time to take any significant actions towards privatizing Petro-Canada as it was defeated on a vote of non-confidence less than one year after taking office and Mr. Trudeau's government was returned to power.

With the return of Mr. Trudeau, over the years 1981 to 1984, Petro-Canada's strategic role was increased. Its role was not only to increase security of energy supply, but also to implement the government's programs to reduce foreign ownership and control of the sector. In November 1984, Brian Mulroney came to power. Again, decisions were taken to sell off Crown corporations such as Canadair and Dehaviland (aircraft companies), Eldorado Nuclear (a uranium mining and refining company) and Teleglobe (a telecommunications company). The philosophy behind these decisions was similar to that set out in the paragraph above. These were commercially-oriented corporations which, in 1984, were seen as serving only a very minimal policy role, if any. Mr. Mulroney's government announced that, while there were no immediate plans to sell Petro-Canada itself, certain parts of the corporation could well be sold off to private sector interests. Alternatively, shares could be issued and sold to the public. These sales would be a way of financing Petro-Canada's exploration and research operations, reducing required continuing equity contributions from the federal government.

5

Canada's Natural Gas Export Policy

This short chapter summarizes the main features of Canada's natural gas export policies. Each of these is then addressed in detail in the chapters which follow.

In general, Canadian natural gas exports have been encouraged in an environment dominated by private sector actors, a large portion of which were owned and controlled by non-residents. The private sector actors' activities in the matter of natural gas exports were regulated, first by government directly, through a Minister of the Crown, and after 1959, through a quasi-judicial regulatory agency, the National Energy Board, reporting to Governor-in-Council through a Minister.

Regulation at the federal level[1] consisted of reviewing export contracts and licensing export volumes and prices on a case-by-case basis; later, setting a uniform border price; and, as is the case at present, approving negotiated contracts, provided certain minimum conditions are met. In addition, fiscal policy was used to increase the attractiveness of investment in petroleum exploration and additional incentives were provided for investment in natural gas transmission systems.

Through direct intervention, and by withholding export authorizations, the federal government, in collaboration with the provincial government of Alberta, had an east-west transmission line put in place to serve markets east of Alberta as far as Montreal. In the 1980s this line was extended farther eastward to Quebec City. Again, federal incentives and subsidies were used to have the line extended.

---

1. Similar regulation occurred at the provincial level. Direct provincial control and regulation, however, extended to the production and exploration stages.

In 1975, the federal government took direct action in the exploration and development of Canada's petroleum resources through the establishment of a Crown corporation, Petro-Canada. This direct policy instrument was considered superior to the fiscal measures being used to encourage or stimulate private exploration and development in the petroleum sector. Creation of a Crown corporation with the mandate given to Petro-Canada is evidence that the federal government placed a higher value on (or perceived a variety of increased benefits to society from) obtaining information and knowledge about the extent of Canada's resource base and the timing and cost at which additional supplies of oil and natural gas would become available than did the private sector. Also, in view of the expectation that "strategic" energy resources would be in short supply worldwide, the government took the position that it made good sense to reduce the financial and profit-motivated pressures which tie commercially-timed exploration and development programs to production and, in the case of natural gas, to exports which are required for production to occur.

Of course, theoretically it would be possible for the government, through a Crown corporation or through providing incentives (such as fiscal stimulants, grants or "preferred" export licenses) to accelerate exploration activities, and once reserves were known, to defer development and production of the known reserves until this was perceived as being in the public interest. However, it is certainly not clear that government in Canada, at the federal (as well as at the provincial) level, can first encourage and stimulate a successful exploration effort, and then in fact defer allowing the successful explorers an opportunity to earn a rate of return on their investment in exploration.[2]

---

2. For example, Petro-Canada and its associates were successful in finding gas reserves in the High Arctic. Although they are not expected to be required in the near future in Canada, once discovered, there are immense pressures to develop the reserves and export the natural gas as LNG. Indeed there are convincing trade and energy security arguments that can be made for immediate development and export to the United States (through displacement) or to Europe or Japan. The arguments made by Petro-Canada in support of development for export bear a striking similarity to arguments made by private sector export proponents (cf. Application and arguments made by Petro-Canada, Dome Petroleum and associates to the National Energy Board

Whether the actors are private, public or entirely owned by the Crown, it appears totally reasonable to expect pressures to be exerted at many points in the political and regulatory system to allow successful efforts to be rewarded and to allow successful participants to grow and continue to expand and carry out more successful activities. In the case of oil companies, be they Crown corporations or private sector, foreign-owned and controlled or domestic, they can only be expected to pursue their interests and favor federal and provincial policies and strategies that allow them to prosper, give them an edge over some other firm, lower their costs, and increase their profits, power and prestige.

In the case of Petro-Canada in particular, and the high ideals under which it was established, it is difficult to imagine that its staff and managers, and others responsible for, or interested in, its activities and success, would not want to do all in their power to make the company grow and to make it more independent through internally-generated cash flow. Certainly, there are arguments which could be put forward by these officials to show why what they want is coincident with the public interest. Analysts of such firms outside North America have found that there are few national oil companies that have not been able to interpret the public interest according to the company's own needs and priorities.

There are a variety of policy tools that could have been used towards the achievement of the government's objectives for petroleum industry development and natural gas exports. For example, rather than create a Crown corporation, an existing company, domestic or foreign-owned, could have been purchased. Rather than deferring a given firm's production through regulation, natural gas could be purchased in the ground or produced, transported and stored in depleted reservoirs near markets. Loans against established reserves, at market or subsidized rates, could be made to all or some selected,[3] successful explorers to

---

in 1982). At different hearings, held in November 1985, Petro-Canada asked that natural gas exports be put on the free market and that all regulatory requirements to protect the future requirements of domestic gas customers be dropped (<u>Globe and Mail</u>, November 25, 1985, p. B.2).

3. For example, selections could be made according to a variety of criteria ranging from cash requirements of the firm, the ownership of the firm, the firm's success record, or a firm's investment intentions.

provide them with cash flow and a return on their investment. Cash flow for exploration could also be provided through direct grants or other subsidies for exploration in key areas. Drilling rights and leases could also be adjusted in line with government wishes.[4] Another method of allocating exports between producers would be to issue and sell export rights, perhaps using an auction, and to allow the highest bidder to export the gas (or sell his rights to another exporter).

An important set of issues arises from the federal government setting both export prices[5] and maximum exportable volumes, as well as issuing non-transferable, export-point and customer-specific export licences. A major question is whether the rigidities in the licencing system itself are inhibiting the attainment of higher net benefits from exports in that there may be little opportunity for the market to signal where the most valued markets for the exports are. As regards the dual set of constraints on total sales revenues, that is both prices and volumes being set or approved by a regulator, the major question is how do both of these, together, affect revenue maximization to Canadians. The analysis below examines the impact of maintaining dual controls rather than allowing one or the other to determine the volumes importers would bid for at a given price, or alternatively, the prices importers would bid to buy a given exportable volume. Alternative regulatory mechanisms are also examined.

---

4. These were, in fact, features of the National Energy Program announced in October 1980, and actually passed into legislation in 1982.

5. The case at the time of writing (since November 1984) is that the government "authorizes" rather than "sets" export prices. Authorization is given when certain minimum conditions are met, one being that export prices should not be below domestic prices. From November 1984 to November 1985 this floor price was the Toronto city-gate price (which included transportation costs to Toronto). In November 1985, the domestic price against which exports were considered became the price in the domestic markets adjacent to the export point. At that time, it was announced that after November 1986, domestic sales of natural gas will be freely negotiated between buyers and sellers and prices will no longer be prescribed (<u>Agreement Among the Governments of Canada, Alberta, British Columbia and Saskatchewan on Natural Gas Markets and Prices</u>, October 31, 1985, paragraph 3).

Domestic requirements could be protected by stockpiling as outlined above or by changing the economics of export sales and, therefore, the relative attractiveness of the domestic market. For example, this could be achieved by an export tax, or by creating a marketing board for natural gas sales into the export (and if desired, the domestic) market. Future requirements could also be provided through commercial undertakings such as swap arrangements that could be encouraged among private sector actors, or be arranged, undertaken, or guaranteed by government. Such swaps could be on a time basis (gas now for gas later), on a geographic basis (gas delivered at point X in return for gas delivered at point Y), on a commodity basis (gas for coal or some other commodity) or on some combination of these.

Within this overall context, the key goals in Canada's natural gas export policy were: to ensure adequate and secure energy supplies to Canadians by ascertaining that sufficient supplies were available to protect domestic requirements and to ensure that the price of these exports was "fair and reasonable." The questions of whether the timing of development was right and what constitutes a "fair and reasonable" price were either not explicitly addressed or left imprecise.

6

Uncertainty

In economic decision making related to the development and sale of natural resources there are no certainties, only probabilities that a given event will occur at a given point in time. Some events are or may be perceived as being more probable than others, but no one ever has the security of absolute certainty that a given event will in fact take place as expected.

One of the most difficult factors that must be addressed in policy making related to the management of natural resources in general and their development and sale, is "uncertainty". The issue is further amplified in the case of a non-renewable commodity being sold on the export market. This is an important component of the environment within which Canadian policies related to natural gas exports have been formulated.

Dealing with the issue of uncertainty has been one of the key factors in the elaboration of Canada's natural gas export policies. In order to judge the appropriateness of a given action or policy, one must rely on a forecast, or an expected future state (in terms of a given state of affairs, being more likely than a different state of affairs). However, history has demonstrated the difficulties of projecting supply and demand of the various energy sources. Past estimates have varied widely; few have turned out to be very accurate. It is not realistic to assume that more sophisticated forecasting techniques can resolve the problem of uncertainty. As regards current forecasts, uncertainty remains as to future oil and natural gas discoveries, new energy sources, economic growth, energy conservation, energy imports and their costs and availability, environmental and social effects of energy activities, and advances in energy supply and energy use technology, to name only the most important factors.

Although uncertainty creates difficulties for forecasting, and therefore, for policy formulation, in general, resource management policies, in the case of Canada and other countries, must be based on these projections. In the case of formulating energy policies for Canada, and in particular for regulating Canada's natural gas exports, uncertainty has been recognized as a central factor. Consequently, policies have been designed to deal with the costs of uncertainty. These policies include measures to reduce uncertainty, to insure against it, to establish contingency plans, and to keep options open as long as possible.

The protection of the reasonably foreseeable requirements for natural gas within Canada is one such policy designed to deal with the costs of uncertainty. Judgement as to what constitutes appropriate export prices, and at what rate Canada's natural gas reserves should be developed must depend upon forecasts of the supply and demand for natural gas and other energy sources, domestically and internationally. Accurate short-term and long-term forecasts are also required in order to prudently plan for future gas transportation systems. The consideration of many of the major transmission projects requires dependable forecasts of future conditions before any assessment can be made. For example, a large investment in a natural gas pipeline from a remote producing region may look attractive under certain assumptions about future gas prices but turn out to be commercially uneconomic if less-expensive supplies from conventional areas become available.

While forecasts are sometimes used improperly because of a user's failure to recognize that they may be imprecise, they do provide a basis or a framework for decision making. As long as the major assumptions are stated explicitly and/or well understood by the person using the forecast, that individual is in a more-informed position with the forecast than he would be without it.

Examples from History of Forecasting Difficulties

Difficulties in anticipating future events and making appropriate policy judgements in light of such expectations have existed throughout time, but most notably in the energy field since the industrial revolution.

Current arguments and discussions focusing on oil and natural gas problems are very similar to those of the past which were concerned with the use of wood and coal in western Europe, during the time when they were the chief sources of energy. As new technology was developed requiring different fuel characteristics, and as the lower cost supplies of wood were depleted, substitution occurred whereby wood was replaced largely by coal, and later coal was replaced by oil and gas. The cases of wood and coal demonstrate the economic mechanisms which come into play as an energy source becomes more costly and is replaced by another. The histories of these fuels illustrate that while such development of substitutes may well be expected, the precise timing and extent of substitution is difficult to forecast.[1] Also, the transition may take a number of generations. The concept of substitution is developed more fully in the next chapter. Is is useful at this point, however, to introduce the basic concept by way of example, and to discuss it as it relates to uncertainty and to forecasting how substitution will take place.

The Case of Wood[2]

If and when wood consumption in a particular area rises to a level that exceeds the rate of growth of new wood from economically accessible forests, a time is bound to come when forests start to disappear, wood prices rise, and shortages begin to occur. England experienced such a "National Timber Crisis" in the seventeenth and eighteenth centuries when wood fuel prices rose three times as fast as prices generally and laws were passed to conserve this resource. Wood shortages spurred more efficient use of timber in Europe, both as a fuel, and as a construction material. Wood shortages, and higher prices also led to the development of technology for the use of coal as a substitute. The industrial revolution in Britain essentially substituted cheap coal for wood as a source of fuel and power, and cheap and abundant iron for vanishing timber resources.[3]

Timber was more plentiful in North America, and the European experience of shortages and rising prices occurred much later there. In the absence of these higher relative prices, North Americans lagged behind Europeans in their efforts in both efficiency of timber use and in the timing of conversion to coal as an energy source. About a hundred years ago, wood was still the principal source of energy in North America, but

---

1. See, for example, Dasgupta and Heal (1974); Dasgupta and Stiglitz (1976); Hoel (1978).

2. Source for the factual content of the case is Rosenberg (1973).

3. See for example, Ashworth (1962), especially pp. 20-31; Boiteux (1982).

use of coal was increasing rapidly. As seen in Figure 6-1, coal overtook wood as the principle energy source in Canada at the turn of the century.

Figure 6-1[4]
Energy Consumption in Canada as Fuel Equivalent

(10^{15} Btu -- Logarithmic Scale)

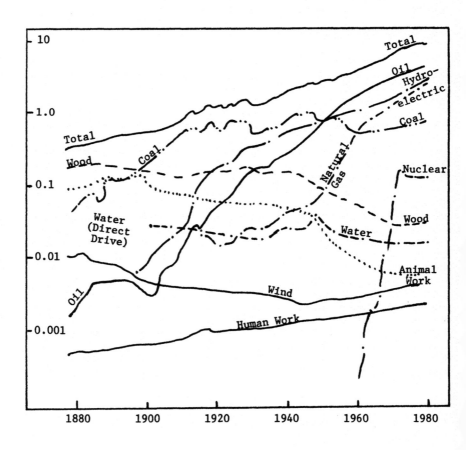

---

4. Steward (1978) p. 242; See also, Walsh and Overend (1981).

The Case of Coal

The history of coal as an energy source bears several similarities to that of wood. Just as wood was displaced by coal as a main energy source in the second half of the nineteenth century, so coal was largely displaced by oil and natural gas in the years after the Second World War. History has shown that as traditional resources become more costly, market mechanisms come into play to create incentives for change and technology is gradually devised to exploit a new set of more abundant resources which drastically reduce dependence upon the traditional, scarcer ones. No matter how refined forecasting techniques have become, the extent of these transitions and the rate at which they occur continues to present forecasters with great difficulty.

The British economist William Stanley Jevons, was perhaps one of the first to use statistical analysis to undertake energy supply and demand forecasting. There are many striking similarities between the problems considered by Jevons (with regard to coal) and those faced by policy makers during the late 1970s (with regard to petroleum resources). Jevons forecast British coal consumption and production in the late nineteenth century.[5] Writing in 1865, he projected historical rates of increase of coal consumption and concluded that Britain could not maintain such rates, as limits to production growth would be reached. He said that unless consumption were slowed down, a coal crisis could be expected to occur as early as the end of the nineteenth century, rendering Britain's industry uncompetitive with manufacturing in other countries. His advice to the British government was to stop coal exports from Britain, to institute measures to reduce the waste of coal and to put a damper on increased industrial activity and consequent increases in coal consumption.

This advice given over a century ago, is very similar to suggestions recently advocated by some parties before Canada's National Energy Board. At numerous public hearings, at which the Board considered energy supply and demand, or specific export applications, there has been testimony that natural gas is such a valuable resource that it cannot be considered "surplus" to future Canadian needs regardless of the level of reserves. By this reasoning, it would follow

---

5. Jevons (1906).

that it should all be retained in Canada to serve the requirements of future generations.[6]

Although Jevons was an extremely capable economist and statistician, when he attempted to forecast British supply and demand in the longer term he was not able to foresee economic substitutes for coal in Britain's industrial future.[7] He did not foresee the rise of oil or natural gas because he did not think there was sufficient natural supply. However, he did foresee the advantages of petroleum as a fuel, but believed that petroleum in quantity would have to be manufactured from coal. None of this is very surprising. How was he to forecast that there would be adequate supplies of oil or natural gas when there was little evidence at that time to support this contention? Also, he had no way of foreseeing the oil-based technological advances such as the development of the internal combustion engine or natural gas-based technological advances such as the thin-walled, high pressure, long distance pipeline.

As well as demonstrating some of the hazards of energy forecasting, Jevon's work expressed well the difficulties of formulating national energy policies. In the short term, Jevons was correctly concerned about the British coal supply situation. But his mind was too closed to the concept of substitution, and he failed to advocate that the British invest in research and development of coal substitutes, such as petroleum.

In his summary, Jevons wrote that allowing continued growth in coal production and exports, while it did contribute to the immediate expansion of Britain's wealth and power, could only lead to Britain's ultimate

---

6. See, for example, testimony and interventions made by Canada Wildlife Foundation, B. Willson at National Energy Board Hearings on Canadian Natural Gas Supply and Requirements, Fall, 1978. See also the testimony of the British Columbia Hydro and Power Authority and of the province of Ontario to National Energy Board hearings held in November 1985 (reported in Globe and Mail, November 21, 1985, p. B4; November 25, 1985, p. B2).

7. Jevons dismissed all possible substitutes to coal and steam power as either technologically or economically unsound. He further argued that increased efficiency in coal use (and consequent increases in profitability) would tend to encourage even greater consumption rather than a lower rate of growth of demand for coal. See Jevons (1906).

downfall, and therefore was like killing the goose that laid the golden egg.

The Case of Oil and Natural Gas

Ironically, Jevon's study was published just as the present petroleum age was beginning. By the time of Jevons' death in 1882, the United States had already witnessed its first Congressional investigation to consider how the United States could cope with an impending oil shortage. The shortage was feared due to the prospects of the exhaustion of the oil reserves at Drake's Well in Pennsylvania, discovered only about a decade earlier.

In 1922 a committee of oil experts appointed by the United States federal government warned of a shortage of oil reserves in the United States that could require imports that it believed could threaten the independence of the country.[8] These experts noted that oil reserves estimates made then were "fortunately" made with "far greater completeness than ever before"[9] and were "undoubtedly" the best ever made for the United States, and vastly superior to any estimates that had been prepared elsewhere in the world.[10] Of course, these experts vastly underestimated United States oil reserves, as have successive groups of experts commissioned to undertake similar studies over the years.

Accommodating Forecasting Uncertainty

Lessons from the past have much to offer users of forecasts. The history of the changing use of different energy supplies indicates several important points which must be borne in mind when attempting to assess possible scenarios for the future. These are:

1) Higher prices and supply constraints affecting a traditional fuel spur the use of substitutes.[11]

---

8. U.S. Geological Survey (1922) pp. 42-46.

9. Ibid., p. 42.

10. Ibid., p. 44.

11. See for example, Gordon (1973) pp. 106-110; Hotelling (1931); Nordhaus (1973); Odell (1975) pp. 226-230; Pearce and Grace (1976); Solow (1974).

2) Through research and development, technology will be developed for the economic use of such substitutes.[12]
3) The higher the price and the more constrained the supply, the faster and more efficiently consumers move to improve energy consumption patterns.[13]
4) Higher prices (netbacks) for producers will result in intensified exploration and development of traditional energy sources.[14]
5) In response to market-induced or politically-induced stimuli, technology will be developed for recovery of resources in more inaccessible locations in the world and for exploitation of lower grade resources.[15]
6) Where it is perceived to be in the public interest, government activities and programs and other social action can be expected to come into play to enhance the interplay of price and market mechanisms which produce the effects listed above.[16]

A forecaster must combine his knowledge of the past with his expectations for the future to provide a scenario of what he believes most likely to occur. In an era of rapid transition, such as occurred in the two and one-half decades since 1960, in the energy sector, this can be exceedingly difficult.

Forecast of Supply

As regards oil and natural gas supply, the forecaster can anticipate that higher prices and perceived

---

12. Odell (1975) p. 227; Roberts (1973).

13. See, for example, McKean (1973); Ross and Williams (1982); Roberts (1973); Stobaugh and Yergin (1979); Uri (1982).

14. See for example, Hotelling (1931); MacAvoy (1974); Solow (1974); Uhler (1976), (1979).

15. See for example, Goeller and Weinberg (1978); Grenon (1977).

16. See, for example, Canada, Energy Mines and Resources (1977); Frank, H. (1974); Hirst et al. (1982); Mansfield (1968); Miller (1974); Odell and Rosing (1980); Stuart (1981).

future shortages will stimulate increased activity in exploration and development of conventional resources. However, attempts to pin down the exact increase will not be possible because of commercial, geological, technical and political uncertainties that exist.[17]

Increased development of lower grade forms of conventional oil and gas will also be encouraged. However, such developments as the use of tertiary oil recovery methods, heavy oil upgrading and recovery of low permeability gas resources are subject to varying combinations of technical, commercial and political uncertainties and cannot be forecast exactly.

Higher prices and perceived shortages also stimulate the development of alternative energy resources such as solar, geothermal, wind, biomass and tidal energy. As was seen in the case of wood, higher prices of one energy resource can stimulate increased output of an alternative resource, with the degree and speed of the resultant substitution being difficult to quantify.

Forecast of Demand

As regards energy demand, forecasters can anticipate a number of similar areas of uncertainty. For example, rising prices and perceived possible shortages of a given fuel type will lead to interfuel substitution, but the degree and timing are hard to estimate. While forecasters can anticipate that demand for new competitive energy resources will increase, especially as these sources become more economically attractive, it is hard to judge the extent of such new demand until delivered costs of energy from these sources become known,[18] and a range of consumer tastes and preferences has been established.

Rising prices would be expected to lead to adoption of more-efficient energy use, but specific savings cannot be precisely estimated. For example, the commercial development of an efficient, economic electric

---

17. Adelman (1972a); Boiteux (1982); Grenon (1977); Odell and Rosing (1980).

18. See, for example, Ross and Williams (1982) who discuss various practical applications of a variety of new technologies, including solar energy, all of which have great potential for replacing current fuels and reducing energy consumption. However, as these authors point out, the relative prices of each source are of prime importance.

car would have a very significant impact on oil demand, but given the technical and commercial uncertainties, it is clearly most difficult to try to take such an event into account in a longer term forecast. Just as Jevons noted the advantages of petroleum as a coal substitute, one can only note this interesting possibility, rather than build it into a forecast.

The tables which follow illustrate dramatically these difficulties. Table 6-1 sets out the growth in consumption of natural gas in Canada over the period 1960 to 1980. Table 6-2 shows weighted average revenues from natural gas sales. From Table 6-2, it is observed that average nominal revenues from 1960 to 1973 were steady, ranging from 61 to 65 cents. In the last seven years of this period, however, average nominal revenues increased almost fourfold, from $0.65 per Mcf to $2.36 per Mcf.

Table 6-1 shows the expected relationships between increases in price and per capita consumption. Coincident with the nominal average revenue numbers, trends in per capita consumption of both total energy and natural gas were dramatically changed by the price changes for international oil that occurred in 1973-74 and 1979-80.

Sensitivity in Forecasts

To manage uncertainty, forecasters have developed various techniques that make their estimates more useful to the policy maker. One such technique is the development of a range of forecasts, or a series of forecast scenarios, which enables the forecaster to make allowances for certain areas of uncertainty. The chief advantage here is that the assumptions are made explicitly, and the user of a given scenario is able to evaluate the parameters upon which he is relying, and make allowances which attempt to balance the risks and uncertainties with the costs of risk reduction.[19]

In addition to the development of scenarios, forecasters can constantly monitor energy developments and make appropriate revisions to forecasts and to the methodology they have used. This allows the forecasters to incorporate knowledge gained with the passage of time.

In the natural gas transportation and transmission sector for example, at present, one may observe what previously would have been considered highly unlikely

---

19. See, for example, Lucas and Papaconstantinou (1982); Odell and Rosing (1980).

Table 6-1

CONSUMPTION OF ENERGY AND NATURAL GAS IN CANADA[20]

YEAR	Total Energy Consumed (Trillions of BTU)	Natural Gas Consumed (Trillions of BTU)	Natural Gas Consumed as % of total Canadian Consumption	Population June 1ST (Thousands)	Per Capita Consumption of Total Energy (Millions of BTU)	Per Capita Consumption of Natural Gas (Millions of BTU)
1960	2,951	382	12.9	17,870	165.1	21.4
1961	3,044	440	14.5	18,238	166.9	24.1
1962	3,234	506	15.7	18,583	174.0	27.2
1963	3,443	569	16.5	18,931	181.9	30.1
1964	3,699	658	17.8	19,291	191.8	34.1
1965	4,009	747	18.9	19,644	204.1	38.0
1966	4,231	828	19.6	20,015	211.4	41.4
1967	4,464	896	20.1	20,378	219.1	44.0
1968	4,766	1,005	21.1	20,701	230.2	48.5
1969	4,992	1,129	22.6	21,001	237.7	53.8
1970	5,329	1,250	23.4	21,297	250.2	58.7
1971	5,506	1,345	24.4	21,568	255.3	62.4
1972	5,932	1,528	25.7	21,802	272.1	70.1
1973	6,232	1,633	26.2	22,043	282.7	74.1
1974	6,354	1,666	26.2	22,364	284.1	74.5
1975	6,714	1,715	25.5	22,697	295.8	75.6
1976	6,558	1,760	26.8	22,993	285.2	76.5
1977	6,677	1,837	27.5	23,258	287.1	79.0
1978	6,859	1,877	27.4	23,476	292.2	80.0
1979	7,050	1,869	26.5	23,671	297.9	79.0
1980	7,167	1,873	26.1	24,058	297.9	77.9
1981	6,919	1,832	26.5	24,342	284.2	75.3
1982	6,705	1,869	27.9	24,616	272.4	75.9
1983	6,572	1,879	28.6	24,890	264.0	75.5
1984(p)	6,905	2,002	29.0	25,146	274.6	79.6

---

20. Canadian Gas Association (1982) pp. 3, 7. 1975 to 1984 from <u>Canadian Gas Facts 1985</u>, pp. 8, 42. Conversion factor (GJ) 93203 = MMBTu.

Table 6-2

REVENUES FROM NATURAL GAS SALES

BY CLASS OF SERVICE[21]

(Dollars per thousand cubic feet)

Year	Residential	Commercial	Industrial	Weighted Average
1960	0.99	0.69	0.33	0.61
1961	1.02	0.71	0.33	0.61
1962	1.03	0.72	0.35	0.63
1963	1.04	0.72	0.36	0.64
1964	1.04	0.72	0.38	0.65
1965	1.01	0.71	0.38	0.64
1966	1.04	0.73	0.40	0.65
1967	1.02	0.75	0.40	0.65
1968	1.03	0.73	0.39	0.63
1969	1.01	0.71	0.40	0.63
1970	1.01	0.71	0.41	0.63
1971	1.03	0.72	0.43	0.64
1972	1.02	0.73	0.45	0.65
1973	1.04	0.75	0.47	0.65
1974	1.12	0.84	0.57	0.75
1975	1.36	1.08	0.80	0.99
1976	1.79	1.50	1.17	1.38
1977	2.11	1.76	1.37	1.61
1978	2.41	2.06	1.62	1.89
1979	2.60	2.22	1.76	2.05
1980	2.99	2.49	2.05	2.36
1981	3.74	3.18	2.71	3.06
1982	4.36	3.77	3.22	3.67
1983	5.11	4.34	3.55	4.12
1984	5.23	4.47	3.56	4.18

---

21. Ibid., p. 34; <u>Canadian Natural Gas Facts 1985</u>, p. 23; Statistics Canada, Publication 55-002.

projects involving the transport of gas in liquid form across the world's oceans.[22] This particular technological development may prove to be especially important to Canada for the development of its natural gas reserves in the high Arctic. Also, export markets for liquid natural gas would extend to countries other than the United States, thus reducing the dependence of Canadian exporters on their traditional U.S. markets.

Use of Forecasts for Policy Making

Whether government policy makers are concerned with a specific company's transmission system, or that of the nation as a whole, when evaluating various energy scenarios, they must take into consideration the uncertainties that exist, and arrive at an understanding of the implications of alternative outcomes.[23]

Long-Term and Short-Term

Decisions made by policy makers will have both short and long-term effects on the elements of forecast supply/demand. Over the period under study, forecasts by Canada's National Energy Board emphasized the importance of the short-term, that is, the period over the following ten years. However, its energy forecasts usually covered a twenty-five-year period. Furthermore, in its published forecasting, the National Energy Board, in 1977, adopted the practice of providing three scenarios each of supply and demand -- thus explicitly

---

22. Mankabady (1975) describes the economic potential as well as the hazards to be overcome in future LNG transportation. See also Tussing and Barlow (1984) pp. 63-65.

23. See, for example, a statement made by S. Ostry, then head of the economics and statistics department of the Organization for Economic Cooperation and Development, quoted in the Toronto Globe and Mail, November 3, 1982 (p.6): "I'd be astonished if the forecasts worked out. We are not gazing into crystal balls. Anyone who believes a forecast is a novice who misunderstands the purpose of forecasting. It is an informational tool. It allows you to say what will happen if the present circumstances continue. But the circumstances rarely continue. The price of oil or the value of the dollar changes. What is important is to learn why the forecast went wrong..."

acknowledging a range of possibilities.[24] Also, forecasters must rely intensively on the process of revision, through regular updating on a regular basis, the frequency of which would depend on the purposes for which the forecasts are being used.

In the chapters that follow, specific elements of Canada's policies including export price regulation, domestic market protection, contract terms and conditions and the regulatory procedures are examined. The appropriateness of Canada's export policy can only be measured against this backdrop of uncertainty and the probability of occurrence of any given set of events.

Uncertainty Within the Context of Dependency

How do these features of uncertainty relate to dependency theory? In general, one would expect that the greater the level of dependency of a given peripheral state on a particular central state (or on a particular sector within a state)[25] the less capable will be that peripheral state (or sector) to maintain a broad range of options or to maintain contingency plans for unexpected events. This situation would be contrasted with the central state which, due to diversified sources of raw materials and access to a wide range of markets, is able to keep options open for longer periods of time and maintain contingency plans. In contrast to the dependent state, these contingency plans could include reducing production and moving into a different product line or different market, or building inventories in periods of low prices or slackened demand or a combination of these.[26]

---

24. Canada, National Energy Board (1977c), (1978), (1979).

25. For example a single commodity exporter, selling its product in one geographic market area.

26. In some cases, a dependent state could actually have an incentive to increase production and export volumes in a period of falling prices. This would occur if the dependent exporter had to maintain export revenues to meet short-term obligations. See for example Ashworth (1962) pp. 233-237. Ashworth provides examples of this phenomenon for wheat, sugar, coffee, rubber, copper and nitrates in the late 1920's. Some members of OPEC face this problem at the time of this writing. Some analysts have attributed Saudi Arabia's December 1985 change of policy to increase output to a

In short, in spite of the uncertainties, the dependent state would be expected to be less able than the central states to put in place policies to deal with uncertainties. A principle reason for this is that measures which address uncertainties all have various costs associated with them. Dependency theory would argue that the dependent state cannot bear these costs to the same extent as can the central states. The costs may be viewed as a kind of insurance premium against known and unknown risks. As dependent states cannot afford the "premium", they are forced to gamble, that is to be exposed to these risks. The result of course is that at any given point in time in the periphery there will be states facing very difficult and costly problems (against which they could not afford to take the prudent and/or necessary precautions) and other states which are managing quite well. Over time, as the fortunes of a peripheral state ebb and flow, it is likely that they will become vulnerable from time to time to a huge problem (or loss) which they cannot face without the assistance of a central state. As the central state may find it advantageous to assist a given peripheral state over a temporary difficulty, this would likely occur with the ultimate effect being an indebtedness which entails larger costs (including all negative effects) that would have been entailed in the "insurance premium" that could have avoided or reduced the difficulty in the first place. This, of course, may become a vicious circle of increasing indebtedness of the periphery to the center.[27]

There are of course arguments to show that after a certain point of indebtedness has been reached, the creditor may become dependent on the debtor. At the least, a state of interdependence comes into being, where the central state, or specific, vital groups in the central state (such as the banks), acquire an interest in the success, well-being, growth and development of the debtor, so that the debt can be repaid.[28] At the time of this writing, commodity

---

combination of economic and political necessities. These require that Saudi Arabia maintain revenues in spite of the fall in oil prices that increased Saudi production will precipitate (<u>Business Week</u>, December 30, 1985, p. 65).

27. See for example, Payer (1975).

28. See for example the comments by the majority of speakers at the meeting of the International Monetary Fund and the World Bank in Toronto, Canada, September 1982.

prices have fallen by about 10 percent over 1985, severely impacting the economies of developing exporters. Because of the international interdependencies now in place the only apparent way out of these difficulties will be for continued investment in developing countries to allow them to service their debts and to pursue promising development opportunities. In addition, lower deficits are required in the industrial countries, particularly the United States, in order to reduce the cost of money worldwide. Finally, it seems almost certain that it will be necessary to write off a portion of the debt now overhanging some Third World countries that have not any real prospects for repaying those loans.[29]

---

29. See, for example, the thoughtful editorial in The Economist, November 30, 1985, pp. 15-16; Makin (1985).

7

Substitution

Bearing in mind the "uncertainty" factor which was developed in the preceding chapter, the concept of "substitution", which was briefly introduced at that time, is now addressed more directly. Canada's natural gas exports, and the regulation of export prices and export volumes over the period under study were intimately related to the demand for other forms of energy in North America. This demand is, in turn, related to the overall demand for energy outside North America. Natural gas use is but one component of total energy demand. The prices of available substitutes in various markets such as various heavy fuel oils, various coals, electricity and other fuel sources contribute to determining demand for natural gas in general and Canadian exports in particular. This chapter examines the matter of substitution in general and how this bears on Canadian natural gas exports. In addition, comparative observations are made regarding the policies pursued by the Netherlands government and by the government of Norway, and also, at the sub-national level, by the state of Texas.

The key questions that must be faced by an exporter or regulatory authority are: what are the present and expected future costs and availability of alternative fuel supplies in a given export market; with what ease can an importer obtain them, and how quickly; and how does this affect his fixed and variable costs? The answers to these questions are required in order to assess the attractiveness of a given export, including the export price, at a given point in time. The exporter would then compare the prices and terms available over time in various alternative export markets with prices and terms available in domestic markets and make his export (or non-export) decision with the timing of sales (or receipt of cash flow) a crucial factor.

The role of the exporting government and its regulatory authority, if any, would be to balance the private considerations of a given exporter with the public interest and, where appropriate, take measures to encourage or discourage exports from taking place.[1]

Within these considerations, substitution -- the ability of current or potential users to obtain alternative supplies of gas or other fuel, or more broadly, to substitute other resources (such as labour or more-efficient plant and equipment) for fuel -- takes a central place. It should be kept in mind that timeframe is an important feature which impacts on the concept of substitution. In general, the shorter the timeframe of a given set of sales, the less the potential impact of substitution. The longer the purchaser's or seller's timeframe for a given transaction or series of transactions, the more important the substitution factor becomes.

In a short timeframe, natural gas users may have very little flexibility in using substitutes. In longer timeframes, it may be possible to put in place the necessary plant to use other energy sources. Similar conditions would hold true for the initial decision to install a natural-gas burning facility. As the capital costs are relatively high compared with substitutes, the purchaser (and the distributor) must look to some period of sales over which to amortize the initial costs, and compare this with the costs of using some substitute over a similar period.

In general, different categories of natural gas users would be influenced by different factors in purchase decisions (or decisions to install natural-gas burning facilities). For example, an industrial user's demand for natural gas in the short run is influenced by the advantages and disadvantages of natural gas over potential substitutes in terms of quality of fuel, the current price of natural gas, the current and expected future availability of natural gas, the price and availability of close substitutes, the user's price expectations for the short term and the longer term for both natural gas and substitute fuels, the purchaser's ability to efficiently and economically burn (and/or store) natural gas and/or the available substitute(s),

---

1. By the same token, an importer (or government of an importing country) could consider import prices and volumes, and other factors such as security of supply, cost and availability of substitutes and encourage the development of substitutes or alternative fuel supplies as appropriate.

the user's actual and expected level of economic activity and resultant fuel requirements. Residential users, on the other hand, would be more influenced by weather conditions and price expectations for natural gas and alternative fuels. This variety of factors and differences between users must be borne in mind when assessing the value of natural gas in terms of volumes deliverable over time, deliverability being a key consideration as both the actual gas and the ability to produce and deliver a given volume of gas both contribute to the value of natural gas in a given market at a given point in time.

There is a relatively long list of energy fuels and resources, all of which can be substituted for each other in some applications. As pointed out earlier, oil, coal and wood are potential substitutes for natural gas, as is electricity. Renewables such as solar energy, wind, water,[2] and tidal power are also potentially profitable substitutes for natural gas in some cases. In addition to substitution between fuels, substitutes to a particular source of natural gas will also include different sources of natural gas, produced and transported from different geographic areas or different geological structures.

The motivation of a user to choose between substitutes will be largely a function of relative prices, relative supply availability and relative desirable and undesirable technical features of each potential substitute. Industry structure, and other factors such as foreign ownership may also impact on a user's selections between substitutes, although these could also be seen as extensions of the factors just listed. For example, looking at a potential purchaser's perception of supply availability, the fact that natural gas distribution and pricing is regulated, may encourage or discourage particular users from selecting natural gas largely because of the fact that it is regulated. For example, this factor may cause a residential customer (favored by regulation) to select natural gas (because he feels the future is more easily predictable) while an industrial user might select an alternative fuel or buy gas but install the capability to burn alternatives in view of the uncertain possibility that a regulator may discriminate against his purchases (regardless of the prices he may be willing to bid in order to purchase required supplies).

---

2. For an interesting account of the use of wind and water power as the major non-human power sources in the Middle Ages, see Gimple (1976).

In view of the many potential substitutes for natural gas, and the possibility of new discoveries of these substitutes or new technologies for using these substitutes being developed, any regulation of export sales by the federal government of Canada which serves to reduce export opportunities in order to preserve supplies for future generations entails a substantial amount of risk. Canadians are betting that indeed, the regulator has accurately foreseen the future relative value of natural gas compared with alternatives that will be available at that point in time. Here, the concept of uncertainty joins with the substitution concept to present very difficult choices for policy makers. Do they allow sales to occur for all gas that is discovered or do they force the Canadian exporter to defer or to forego a sales opportunity? There is no definitive answer. Answers must only be based on the best estimates available of future supply and demand, for natural gas and substitute fuels.

The main point of this section has been to emphasize that Canada's natural gas exports are but one component of energy supply in a given export market whose value is closely related to the value of substitutes in the specific importing market. By the same token, the value of a specific flow of natural gas in a given export market must be compared with possible alternative uses of all or part of this resource in a specific domestic market at the time of export or at some other time in the future. The value of the natural gas in each case would reflect an estimation and a comparison of the cost of substitutes in the specific market in question.

Within the dependency framework, this discussion would apply to all traded commodities and attempts to restructure markets, prices and trading arrangements. For any given commodity, one would expect that there exist similar possibilities of substitution. If, therefore, the price of a given commodity were to be shifted upwards (or downwards) by some producer agreement or commodity agreement involving both sellers and buyers, one would expect this would impact on supply and demand for the substitutes. The length of time over which adjustments would occur is uncertain, but that these adjustments would eventually occur has to be expected.

What this says in terms of dependency is that there is little that can be done to restructure a given commodity market on a permanent basis, and that the most a single-resource exporter can realistically hope for is relatively short-term gains. Realistically, using short term gains to diversify production appears to be the best way to overcome the problems presented by the above analysis. It also serves to explain the advantage of the agent performing the value-added components of producing a given product. In the production of a composite commodity, the producer has the ability to select ingredients from a variety of sources, and to select the most beneficial combination of ingredients from among the possible substitutes. While this may be an advantage (as compared with the primary product exporter), it is also a factor which means that constant forecasting and adapting to changing conditions is required in order to perform in a manner superior to others engaged in a similar type of value-added activity. This translates into continuous competition between core countries, and means that individual arrangements between a select number of producers and consumers[3] are unlikely to have any significant major impact on broader markets in the longer term. However, it is true that the potential short-term benefits, including spin-off or linkage effects throughout the economies of the trading partners, may be substantial.

Strategic Commodities

Building upon the discussion above, the concept of a "strategic" commodity bears further examination. As occurred with coal, arguments have been advanced that natural gas is a "strategic" commodity; this argument concludes, therefore, that exports are imprudent. Given the analysis of the concepts of uncertainty and substitution however, the idea of a strategic commodity must be amplified. It must include an element of time and a specific quantity of that commodity such that the availability of less than this strategic quantity over some strategic time period would be disastrous. Because of the forces which come into play, and because of man's inherent adaptability and inventiveness, there are extremely few, if any, strategic commodities. There are, however, strategic quantities of given commodities, which relate to essential demand over a given time period. The strategic time period would relate to the amount of time required to change consumption patterns, change production patterns and increase use of substitutes to the commodity in question.

Having looked at the concepts of uncertainty and substitution, it is useful to consider the policies pursued by other major producers and exporters of natural gas such as Holland and Norway, and, at the sub-national level, by the state of Texas.

---

3. For example, the Lomé Convention.

The Case of Holland[4]

The large natural gas field of Groningen in the northeast of Holland was discovered in 1959. By 1963, its potential as a major fuel source was recognized, and a company formed, N.V. Netherlands Gasunie, to purchase and transport the natural gas to distribution companies, utilities and industrial users within Holland and to pursue export markets. This company was part-owned by the Dutch government.[5]

Following the discovery of the Groningen field, Holland experienced a rapid growth of energy-intensive industries based on natural gas.[6] Also, export contracts were entered into with customers in France, Belgium, West Germany and Italy.[7]

Gas prices in Holland were indexed to the oil price, and thus remained relatively constant over the period 1960 to 1973. As a result, most Dutch industry changed over to natural gas in view of its premium qualities as a fuel. (In addition to any price advantages, there are non-price factors which also contribute to demand for natural gas. As a "clean" fuel, there is a savings on maintenance and equipment, also there is a savings on storage costs which would be incurred for solid or liquid fuels.) Residential natural gas use too grew dramatically as coal and oil were displaced for residential space heating. In addition,

---

4. General background information on natural gas use in Holland was provided to the author by J.H.R.D. van Roijen, Counsellor, Royal Nederlands Embassy, Ottawa on several occasions in June 1979. His kind assistance is appreciated. Additional information was provided by J. Phillipson, Counsellor, Royal Nederlands Embassy, Ottawa, in November 1982.

5. N.V. Nederlands Gasunie (1977; 1978b). Shareholders are: Dutch Government 50 percent; Shell Nederlands B.V. 25 percent; Esso Holding Company Holland, Inc. 25 percent.

6. OECD. International Energy Agency (I.E.A.) (1979) p. 3; Odell (1975) p. 109.

7. N.V. Nederlands Gasunie. Facts. (1978).

virtually all of Holland's electrical generation stations were converted to natural gas in the 1960s.[8]

Over the 1960s, export contracts were concluded for about half of Hollands natural gas production. This was a period of constant or falling energy prices and abundant supply, and this was reflected in export prices.[9]

The situation started to turn in late 1970 and early 1971. At that time, people began to realize that the sharp rise in demand for Dutch gas, as well as the limited production capacity of the Groningen field, would soon result in an excess of demand over supply (at a given (desired and contracted for) price level). 1971 was a turning point at which holland's natural gas marketing was curtailed and imports were sought.[10] This change in direction was greatly amplified after the oil crisis of 1973.

The energy crisis of 1973, and the Club of Rome report cited earlier in this study,[11] had a significant impact on the Dutch government. Decisions were taken to further limit production from the Groningen gasfield in order to protect domestic natural gas requirements into the late 1990s.[12]

All fixed export prices were abandoned, and the price of natural gas was linked to the price of oil. In 1976, natural gas export prices were adjusted upwards again, and a mechanism put in place to ensure export prices would reflect future movements in the oil price. In addition, export customers were encouraged

---

8. N.V. Nederlands Gasunie (1977) pp. 1-2. By 1979, however, in view of Holland's limited natural gas resource, plans were made to eliminate gas utilization in electricity generation by 1988 (OECD, I.E.A. (1979) p. 5).

9. Odell notes that "orderly" marketing of Dutch natural gas, by maintaining a high price for the gas in relation to oil so that it did not back out oil sales was probably in the best short-term interest of the Dutch government and the two private sector partners marketing the Groningen natural gas. Odell (1970) p. 112.

10. N.V. Nederlands Gasunie (1977) pp. 2-4 (1978a), (1978b); O.E.C.D., I.E.A. (1979) p. 6.

11. Meadows et al. (1972).

12. Odell (1975) p. 226.

to switch to alternate suppliers of natural gas, and in particular, Norwegian Ekofisk gas. In fact, to facilitate new supply contracts, swap arrangements were entered into whereby, Dutch natural gas was made available for export in 1976 and 1977, and was to be replaced by Norwegian Ekofisk gas when deliveries started from that field.[13]

In addition to the deferral of export sales, with the advent of rapidly increasing oil prices, extensive conservation measures to slow the depletion of Holland's natural gas were undertaken. Also, in the late 1970s, Holland contracted for increasing volumes of natural gas imports from Norway and Algeria. In addition, Holland established contracts with producers in the Soviet Union and Iran (overland pipe), and Nigeria and the Middle East (liquified gas by ship).[14]

The case of Holland's natural gas exports, is therefore important to this study from a number of viewpoints. First, it illustrates the tendencies of the owners of a resource to wish to achieve rapid delineation of a given find and to achieve the economic growth and development generated from these activities.

In addition, it illustrates how it is possible for an exporter to rapidly shift gears and modify policies as conditions (and perception of the environment) change. The Dutch experience shows how important are dependable forecasts and contingency plans which attempt to take into account inherent uncertainties.

Also, there are several other important factors that can be brought out. First, as was the case with Canada, natural gas exports are a useful means to accelerate development, and can serve to help amortize the relatively expensive (high capital cost) front-end costs of putting in place natural gas transmission facilities. In addition, it is seen that once fixed-price contracts are entered into for exports, it is still possible for prices to be readjusted upwards (but logically also downwards if circumstances warrant) if unforeseen circumstances arise.[15] Thus, because

---

13. These return swaps began in late 1977. N.V. Nederlands Gasunie (1977) pp. 12-13. Confirmed in interview with Mr. T. Hanevold, First Secretary, Embassy of Norway, Ottawa, November 12, 1982.

14. N.V. Nederlands Gasunie (1978b) pp. 6-13.

15. Both Dutch and Canadian export contracts contained a provision allowing for price redetermination (N.V. Nederlands Gasunie (1977) p. 12).

governments are involved to protect the public interest of the exporting and importing countries, an export contract for natural gas may be seen more as a firm statement of intent than as a strict, enforceable contract (i.e. unenforceable in the sense that the seller and buyer have not agreed on firm, definite sales and delivery schedules at a given price and have agreed that key points are subject to renegotiation or further approvals).

Holland, in the context of dependency theory, is a central state rather than a peripheral state. While closely tied in to the economies and societies of Europe, one could argue that the policies adopted by Holland for the export of natural gas were determined from the standpoint of what was best for the long-term Dutch public interest rather than from some systematic imperatives imposed on that country by some other particular country or countries upon which Holland was/is dependent.

Regarding the non-Dutch ownership aspects of the Dutch industry, Holland's actions related to exports and the pricing of its natural gas exports appear to have been influenced by its partnerships with Shell and Esso in the development and marketing of the Groningen natural gas. However, it is difficult to argue that the Dutch policies were not consistent with the interest of Holland, given the environment in which decisions were made in the 1960s and 1970s.

With regard to the question of substitution, through the discovery of natural gas, Holland was given a measure of independence from other states in terms of being able to substitute natural gas for energy imports. This made Holland less vulnerable to supply disruption of alternative fuels.

The Case of Norway[16]

After the discovery of Holland's Groningen natural gas deposit in 1958, geologists suggested that there was a relatively good probability that the oil and natural gas bearing strata continued out off the coast of Holland under the bed of the Channel. This was confirmed, and the question of whether these deposits extended northwards into the vast sedimentary basin of

---

16. General background information on the development of Norway's petroleum resources was provided to the author by Mr. T. Hanevold, First Secretary, Embassy of Norway, Ottawa, November 12, 1982. His kind assistance is appreciated.

the North Sea was thereby raised. In late 1962, Phillips Petroleum contacted Norwegian authorities for permission to carry out seismic surveys on the Norwegian side of the North Sea.[17] The first exploration licences were issued by Norway in 1963.[18]

The possibility of discovering petroleum resources in the North Sea led to a series of negotiations and agreements with States having coastlines on that body of water, and, as concerns Norway, to a system of rules being put in place to govern exploration and development of Norwegian resources[19]. These Norwegian rules were quite standard to the oil industry at the time. Licences were required to carry out exploration. These exploration licences were quite liberal and encouraged many firms to engage in this activity. Norwegian production licences, on the other hand, were more stringent.

Production licences allow the licencee the exclusive right to production within a specific delimited area. For this purpose, the Norwegian shelf was mapped out into blocks, each with an area of 500 square km. In return for a production licence, the licencee pays an area fee which increases each year. Royalties of 8 percent to 16 percent of the total production value are paid on all oil produced, depending on the amount of oil produced. In addition, licencees are subject to an income tax and to a tax on total capital. In order to ensure that the allocated areas are exhaustively explored in a reasonable period of time, licencees must undertake to carry out a work program, negotiated in each licence. Each work program would specify, for example, that a minimum number of wells must be drilled at specific depths according to a predetermined schedule.[20]

---

17. Norway (1977) pp. 1-2. The American oil firm, Phillips Petroleum, based in Oklahoma, was the first oil firm to apply for an exploration licence from Norway.

18. Norway (1979) p. 1.

19. Norway (1977) pp. 2-6. These rules were instituted by <u>Royal Decree of 9 April 1965</u> and revised by <u>Royal Decree of 8 December 1972</u>. Although revised thoroughly in 1972, the main features of the 1965 system of rules were retained (Norway (1977) p. 4).

20. Norway (1977) pp. 4-5.

As drilling was carried out and commercial discoveries made, such as the Ecofisk discovery in 1970, the increased attractiveness (greater probability of success, reduced geological risk due to better and more geological information) of the Norwegian shelf allowed Norway to tighten the rules and conditions of new production licences. Licences granted under the <u>Royal Decree of 9 April, 1965</u> were granted for a period of 46 years with the condition that half the area had to be relinquished after nine years. In 1972, this was revised, and rights were limited in duration to 36 years, with half of the area to be relinquished after six years.[21]

In addition to these tighter provisions, terms and conditions concerning the right of the government of Norway to participate as co-owner in discovered fields also became new features of Norwegian production licences. With increasing oil prices worldwide, improved geological information of the North Sea resources and, therefore, increased likelihood of successful exploration activities, and higher levels of profitability, these terms and conditions became more stringent over time. This continued to the point that by 1977, Norway reserved the right to step in as co-owner with a share of at least 50 percent, and this without any requirement to pay any share of what it may have cost to find the relevant deposit. However, Norway would have to contribute its proportionate share of the cost of further developing that particular field.[22]

Drilling operations started on the Norwegian continental shelf in 1966. Ten exploratory wells were

---

21. Norway (1977) p. 5.

22. Norway (1977) pp. 5-6. Norway, in 1977 noted that the production licences contained "strict" terms as concerned royalties and participation by the state, but noted that these terms did not lead "to the companies losing interest in conducting operations on the Norwegian continental shelf" Norway (1977) p. 6). It is worth noting that in 1978, a group of senior Canadian officials visited Norway and were most impressed by these terms in the Norwegian production licences. When Canada's National Energy Program was announced in November 1980, such provisions were included as regards production licences for Canada lands although the interest reserved to the Crown was 25 percent, rather than Norway's 50 percent (Canada (1980) p. 47). There is little doubt that these Canadian rules were influenced by the Norwegian policies.

drilled before any significant discovery was made (Cod field in 1968), and it was the thirty-fourth well which provided the first proof of a discovery of definite commercial significance (Ecofisk in 1970).[23]

When the commercial viability of Norway's gas deposits became apparent, a corporation was established, 100 percent owned by Norway, to act as co-owner of the various discoveries. The company was called Den norske stats oljeselskap a/s, which is abbreviated to "Statoil". A second Norwegian firm, in which the government holds the majority of the shares, Norsk Hydro a/s, is also a participant in a number of licences, as is Saga Petroleum a/s and Co., a private Norwegian firm. However, most of the production licences have been issued to consortia in which non-Norwegian companies predominate, the largest being Esso, Shell, Phillips, Amoco, Conoco, Elf, Fina and Agip.[24]

Finding the Norwegian deposits was one thing, but producing the oil and natural gas in a difficult environment, and transporting them to markets was an equally difficult task. While production started in 1971 from Ekofisk, only very limited amounts of oil could be loaded and delivered until an oil pipeline was laid down and brought on stream from Ekofisk to Teesside in U.K. in October 1975. No natural gas was delivered from Norway until 1977 when a natural gas pipeline from Ekofisk to Emmen in the Federal Republic of Germany came on stream. Until a natural gas pipeline was in place, most natural gas which was produced with the oil was flared at the wellhead, while some was pumped back into the reservoirs.[25]

The map below shows the location of the petroleum deposits on the Norwegian Continental Shelf.[26] Gas pipelines to U.K. and Germany are indicated by a solid black line.

---

23. Norway (1977) p. 7.

24. Norway (1977) p. 6.

25. Norway (1977) p. 8; (1979) pp. 6-7.

26. Norway (1979) p. 8; Bergen Bank (1982) p. 12; Petroleum Economist (April 1985) pp. 119-124.

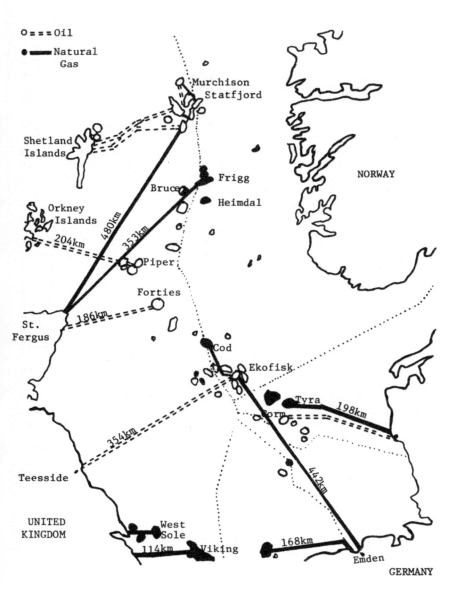
Oil and Gas in the North Sea

The general thrust of Norway's approach to petroleum development was to proceed slowly, and try to avoid any major and/or abrupt disruptions to the Norwegian economy and society. The Norwegian concerns were those of a country with full employment, wishing to avoid major dislocations by an oil industry boom.[27]

As regards exports in particular, Norway itself could not make use of its oil and natural gas resources domestically. Nor was it economically feasible to land natural gas in Norway by pipeline. Because of rising, attractive oil prices, and the needs of Western Europe and Norway's Scandinavian neighbors, and Norway's close interrelationships with these countries, as well as the obvious economic advantages of a successful, well-managed, Norwegian petroleum sector (with a high level of Norwegian participation), exports have been pursued vigorously. However, as much as possible, Norway has attempted to use its energy exports to obtain greater industrial cooperation and joint venture projects with its trading partners. Norway's objective has been to "impact a greater breadth to Norwegian industry, especially within activities where [Norway] ... can expect to be competitive".[28]

In approaching the question of natural gas exports, Norway has evaluated the desirability of exports in terms of the value of the gas if it could be landed in Norway, either as natural gas, or in some other form, such as LNG or (converted to) electricity. Using gas for electricity production on the field and then bringing the power to shore by means of ocean cables was rejected because of the uncertainties that made the economics too risky. As the ultimate size of available gas resources is uncertain, more information (through exploratory and delineation drilling) is vital,[29] before the various alternatives can be assessed with an acceptable degree of reliability.

As an example of Norwegian success in landing Norwegian gas in Norway where possible, one notes that in 1973 Norway concluded an agreement with the Phillips Group to the effect that the natural gas liquids (NGL) from the Ekofisk field would be brought, free of transport charges, back to Norway from the U.K. The NGL serve as the raw material for a new petrochemical industry in Norway. Norwegian working plants produce

---

27. Norway (1974); (1977); (1978a and b).

28. Norway (1978a) pp. 5-6, 9.

29. Himle (1978) p. 4.

ethylene and progylene which are further processed into polypropylene and polythylene (plastic raw materials).[30] Of course, one could assume that had there been no "free" transport of the NGL to Norway from U.K., Norway could have extracted a like monetary concession from the Phillips Group, which may or may not have been more attractive and beneficial than what came about in this matter.

Norway's policies related to the development of the North Sea petroleum resources and the export of natural gas shed light on a number of issues addressed in this study. As was the case of Holland, the Norwegian experience demonstrates again the tendency of resource owners to wish to achieve rapid delineation of specific resource discoveries. Although Norway got off to a relatively slow start, once commercial finds had been made, decision makers were quickly caught up in a need to reduce uncertainties relative to the size of the find (and its "exploitability") by speeding up the exploration and development process. Norway also rapidly felt a need to take quicker advantage of the economic spinoffs and growth that could be generated by development of its petroleum resources.

As was seen in the case of Holland, the Norwegian case again points out that policies can be modified rapidly in order to fit changing conditions and perceptions of the marketplace. In the case of Holland, exports were scaled down as the perceived limits of Holland's resource base were reduced in size. In Norway, on the other hand, as finds were made and perceived risks and profitability became more attractive, production licence terms and conditions were made more stringent in favor of the state,[31] and at the same time, exports continuously pursued.

Norway, in terms of dependency theory, cannot easily be classed as a central state (as it has no satellite states) or as a peripheral state. Its small population of about four million, while closely tied to its Scandinavian neighbors and the states of Western Europe, is quite independent and enjoys a very high

---

30. Norway (1977) p. 11.

31. Of course, it is always possible to argue that this was a case where the original licences were a bit too generous, and once the Norwegians had more knowledge of the industry, negotiated terms became more realistic. Perhaps this does provide to some extent a partial explanation of Norway's success in securing more stringent production licences.

standard of living. While certainly closely tied to and very sensitive to the economies and societies of its European neighbors, the Norwegian petroleum development and export policies were determined from the standpoint of the long term Norwegian public interests (as was also the case of Holland), rather than from a set of systematic imperatives being imposed by some other country or countries upon which Norway was/is dependent.

As regards the question of substitution, the discovery of oil and natural gas and its development by Norway for use in the U.K. and Western Europe, would certainly be expected to back out oil in these countries.[32] This would serve to reduce oil's market share and thereby, tend to restrain price increases in the case of substitute fuels.

The Case of Texas

On the sub-national level, the case of Texas is worth looking at. Texas, of course, as a state within the U.S. federal system is limited by the American Constitution as to the extent to which it can regulate the sale of its petroleum and other resources for use outside Texas.[33] While the U.S. Constitution does not explicitly and specifically forbid states from taxing or regulating interstate commerce, the interpretation

---

32. See, for example, Odell (1975) pp. 221-229.

33. Citing Article I, section 10 of the U.S. Constitution:

"No state shall enter into any treaty, alliance, or confederation; grant letters of marque and reprisal; ...pass any bill of attainder, or post facto law, or law impairing the obligation of contracts...

No state shall, without the consent of Congress, lay any imposts or duties on imports or exports, except what may be absolutely necessary for executing its inspection laws; and the net produce of all duties and imposts, laid by any State on imports or exports, shall be for the use of the Treasury of the United States; and all such laws shall be subject to the revision and control of the Congress.

No state shall, without the consent of Congress, lay any duty of tonnage...enter into any agreement or compact with another State, or with a foreign power..."

of the courts has been that they may not do so if the tax or regulation is unfair to, or unduly burdensome on, interstate commerce.[34] Also, in general, no state may attempt taxation or regulation in a manner which would be inconsistent with the federal Constitution, federal laws and international treaties.[35]

As part of the United States, therefore, the Texas legislature has relatively very little say as to the terms of the interstate commerce of its natural gas, or to measures undertaken at the national level which could impact on interstate commerce in natural gas.

The situation of Texas vis-à-vis the U.S. federal government, is of course fundamentally different from a situation that could exist (in the dependency framework) between a central state and a peripheral one. The major difference is that representation from Texas is one of the components of the U.S. federal government and the interests of Texas (and all the other states) are considered and balanced against the interests of all other states as part of the U.S. federal decision-making process. In the energy area, the interests of Texas would be mirrored by other energy "exporting" states, and the whole myriad of interests inside and outside these states would be represented in the political process of setting a given policy in this area at the federal level. In short, while Texas interstate commerce is controlled at the federal level, Texas itself has considerable influence over and direct input into federal policies. In this context, one could say that there is a type of "interdependency" rather than a "dependency" relationship. In fact, to the extent that the "total pie" increases, Texas will generally benefit as one state of the union.

Given this overall context, at the state government level, the state of Texas had a major role in regulating various aspects of the natural gas

---

34. McClesky (1969) p. 18.

35. This is drawn from Article VI of the U.S. Constitution which states:

"This Constitution and the laws of the United States, which shall be made in pursuance thereof, and all treaties made, or which shall be made, under the authority of the United States, shall be the supreme law of the land; and the judges in every State shall be bound thereby, anything in the Constitution or laws of any State to the contrary notwithstanding".

industry, and has done so in order to protect the best interests of Texans and Texas industry.[36] In general, the type of state regulation that has taken place in virtually all states, including Texas, has occurred in two major areas:

1) regulation of distribution companies as public utilities; and
2) regulation of rates of production in order to promote conservation and protect property rights and thereby, (implicitly) maintain a given price structure.[37]

As regards the specific question of removal of natural gas for sale outside of Texas, there is virtually no state control on producers, and no "export" or removal permits are required.[38]

First, as concerns the regulation of natural gas distribution companies, in Texas this is the responsibility of the municipalities, although disputes on ratemaking may be adjudicated by the Railroad Commission of Texas which then has authority to review the evidence, undertake further investigation, and fix rates.[39] This is quite a different situation from most other states in the United States (and all provinces in Canada) where rate regulation is done by a body at the level of the state (often called a Public Service

---

36. At the federal level, of course, these same objectives would be held by Texas' representatives in the federal government.

37. Price maintenance through regulation of production is possible given Texas' major market share in the United States which represented about half of U.S. production in 1950, and gradually declined to about 35 percent of U.S. production in 1980. (Texas, Railroad Commission of Texas (1980) p. 14).

38. Although, while it was never required over the period under study, in some instances where, for example a school or hospital was unable to purchase its gas requirements, the state would have the power to require production <u>from state lands</u> to be diverted from being exported from the state in order to meet the requirements of these users. It should be pointed out that most production in Texas is from private lands rather than state lands.

39. McClesky (1969) p. 336.

Commission, Energy Board or Commission or Utility Commission).[40]

In order to appreciate the kinds of problems involved, it is worth going into some of the issues that must be considered related to ratemaking. Having ratemaking occur at the municipal level puts the municipality at a disadvantage to the regulated firms due to the complexity of rate regulation and the consequent requirement for (often expensive) technical and expert advice in order to assess the relevant variables. Based on a review of a large number of cases, it can be stated that it is highly unlikely that any two rates experts will agree on the criteria for how to determine the rate base nor on the appropriate rate of return to be applied in a specific instance.[41]

Ever since this type of regulation has been undertaken, experts have debated, with very convincing arguments on each side, whether the rate base should be based on book value (i.e. original cost less depreciation) or replacement cost. The questions of required capacity, whether (or the extent to which) an asset was prudently acquired, whether (or the extent to which) an asset is used and useful and the like have been debated over and over with no one answer being apparently more valid than the others. On the rate of return to be applied, there are an additional series of very difficult questions related to determining an appropriate nominal rate of return to apply to the rate base once it has been calculated. The rate of return has a number of components, each of which raise several very difficult, highly subjective questions. For example, the rate of return will comprise a return to each sub-component of a firm's capital structure usually including debt capital, equity capital and deferred taxes. Each of these components should reflect a given nominal rate of return which takes account of market requirements for raising each type of

---

40. McClesky (1969) points out that periodic proposals for such a commission in Texas have always met with strong and successful opposition from the public utilities which prefer the advantageous arrangement of dealing with municipal rate regulation (p. 337).

41. This statement is based on review of numerous rate making cases. Review examined rate-making by provincial boards in Canada, National Energy Board testimony and decisions over the period 1974 to 1979, and cases of the Federal Power Commission.

capital. Each of these nominal rates would, in turn, include a risk premium (related to the riskiness of running the particular venture and the probability of loss from failure of the business), a premium to cover expected rates of inflation, and a positive return to capital.

As it is possible for knowledgeable persons to argue about each of the above variables in any specific case, and as each one of these variables will generally impact upon the rates allowed to a gas distributor, the complexity of ratemaking becomes apparent. In general, there are always well-definable interests at stake, that is the interests of the utility owners and managers vis-à-vis the interests of the customers (represented in theory in Texas by the individual municipalities); therefore, the answers to these questions are far from being academic.

The municipalities, therefore, may be at a distinct disadvantage to the distribution companies in terms of their ability (both financial and technical) to attempt stringent regulation. Regulatory hearings which attempted to address all these issues (which cannot be resolved for all time, but rather which change over time and require constant monitoring and modification to suit a changing economic environment) would certainly require major expenditures. These expenditures would include significant professional fees for lawyers, accountants, advisors and rate experts. Doubtlessly, hearings would be very time consuming for municipal officials, requiring many hearing-days, and probably civil suits and legal appeals. The tendency therefore, even for the largest cities in Texas, has been for municipalities to set rates satisfactory to the utilities.[42]

The ultimate effect of all this is that prices for natural gas to customers within Texas, and the profitability of distribution companies in Texas, would both be expected to be generally higher than would otherwise be the case, were there an effective state public utility regulatory commission that handled ratemaking.[43]

---

42. Examples provided in McClesky (1969) pp. 336-337.

43. The assumptions here are that such a body could afford better advice and could better develop its own ratemaking expertise than could the municipalities, and furthermore, that this body would find the task of more strict regulation of the overall operations of the natural gas distributors less difficult and more rewarding than would the individual municipalities. In

Certain parallels can be drawn between this situation and that which is suggested by the dependency framework. The municipalities of Texas apparently have difficulty doing what they are mandated to perform due to lack of expertise, resources and public recognition of advantages that may be won for the general public, (for example, a seven percent rather than a nine percent increase may not be recognized as being all that significant a net benefit). So too, the governments of the states in the periphery may have similar difficulties dealing with multinationals (that is, dividing a share of economic rents as they are generated from time to time). As may be the case with the municipalities, the difficulties of these states may be due to the imbalance of financial and human resources that may be available to be allocated to a given resource issue and to the knowledge level and the "attention level" devoted to a specific issue by the citizens of a particular host state.

This analysis can be extended to the Canadian export policy for natural gas. The Canadian policies to regulate export sales in a manner that "protects future Canadian requirements" and ensures that export prices are "fair and reasonable" are attractive from a political standpoint; however, they are very vague, and require a high level of expertise, knowledge, forecasting ability and such to implement. While the general goals are laudable, the implementation depends on the technical details and analysis that the regulator applies. As will be examined in the following chapters, a major question to be asked is how the Canadian regulator assesses the technical information and thus injects all-important detail into the general policy. How do the resources at the disposal of the regulator compare with those of the regulated parties? In Canada, at both the provincial and federal levels, over the period under study, these were very small compared with industry resources; there was a very heavy reliance on information supplied to regulators by the industry.

Moreover, the ability of the general public or the elected decision makers to assess the evidence and "technical" judgements of the regulator is, to say the least, quite limited. Regulatory decisions which are supported by the affected parties are therefore easier for the government and the general public to accept

---

many cases where there are, in fact, operating state public utility regulatory commissions, these assumptions may not be valid.

than those which give rise to a good deal of criticism or public debate.

Turning now to the regulation of production of oil and natural gas, this was done by the Railroad Commission of Texas in order to promote conservation and protect property rights of landowners (and leaseholders) who were co-owners of reservoirs containing petroleum resources. As Texas supplied a large portion of U.S. market requirements, the regulation of production certainly had an impact on the price level of hydrocarbons in the United States over the period under study.[44] Table 7-1 summarizes the statistics of Texas natural gas production over the period 1950 to 1980.

Although promoting conservation and protecting property rights by assessing, setting and enforcing rules related to maximum efficient rates of recovery and well spacing allowances appear to be very technical, the economic component of containing production is most significant. In addition to these measures, the shutting in of oil production over the period under study (prorating) in order to balance oil supply and demand also had a significant impact on natural gas supply from Texas, as large amounts of associated natural gas and natural gas dissolved in the crude oil would thus not be produced.[45]

In view of the likely price effects of such regulation, it is not surprising therefore, that the oil industry has had a very favorable attitude towards regulation in Texas. In addition, in the opinion of some Texas analysts, it appears that the regulatory body administers the regulations sympathetically, and that the selection process for Commissioners is influenced to a large extent by the oil industry.[46]

---

44. McClesky (1969) pp. 354-355.

45. These types of natural gas, classified as "castinghead gas" by the Railroad Commission of Texas, accounted for roughly over one third to one fifth of Texas natural gas production over the period under study (Texas, Railroad Commission of Texas (1980) p. 27).

46. See for example, McClesky (1969) pp. 356-358 who states that industry domination of the selection process is "subtle and informal", and that the Commission "would properly be classified as a 'captive' of the oil industry" (p. 356).

Table 7-1

TEXAS NATURAL GAS STATISTICS[47]

Trillion cubic feet (tcf)

	Pro-duction	Reserves at Year End	% of U.S. Reserves	Reserves/Production Ratio [Years]	% of U.S. Production	% Exported to Other States	Producing Wells at Year End	U.S. Price ¢/Mcf
1950	4.02	101.85	55.2	25.3	49.8	42.8	7,310	6.5
1955	5.74	107.70	48.4	18.8	50.3	54.3	11,793	10.4
1960	6.68	118.84	45.3	17.8	46.1	55.1	18,612	14.0
1965	7.86	120.67	42.1	15.4	41.1	50.0	23,570	15.6
1970	9.45	106.35	36.6	11.3	38.1	47.1	23,417	17.1
1971	9.57	101.47	36.4	10.6	38.0	47.1	23,280	18.2
1972	9.60	95.04	35.7	9.9	38.4	43.9	23,373	18.6
1973	9.34	84.94	34.0	9.1	37.6	42.0	23,796	21.6
1974	8.91	78.54	33.1	8.8	37.8	39.5	24,646	30.4
1975	8.05	71.04	31.1	8.8	37.2	38.5	26,193	44.5
1976	7.71	64.65	29.9	8.4	36.0	36.7	28,026	58.0
1977	7.56	62.12	29.8	8.2	35.2	35.4	32,122	79.0
1978	7.08	54.60	27.3	7.7	32.8	34.1	33,157	90.5
1979	7.12	53.02	26.4	7.4	34.2	38.1	35,377	117.8
1980	7.00	50.29	25.3	7.2	34.8	39.2	38,579	149.1

---

47. Texas, Railroad Commission of Texas (1980) p. 14; (1982) p. 12. Any comparisons of Canadian export prices with the average U.S. price shown in this table must bear in mind that Canada's share of the U.S. market was always less than five percent over the period under study.

The conservation measures which were applied by the Railroad Commission of Texas were later mirrored by similar commissions in other producing states of the United States and, in Canada, by the Alberta regulator. In all cases, this regulation was eventually supported by industry. Thus, it is possible to argue that these measures were beneficial to the industry, and government power was brought to bear to correct a situation of wastefulness. However, on the other side of the coin, it may be that the consuming public as a whole, was not well-represented and that, had alternative technical considerations been made, the price of hydrocarbon fuels could have been lower. This would surely have been the case, had producers been allowed to compete more freely in certain areas. For example, if low-cost producers had been able to back out higher cost supplies, this could have reduced prices.

Taking one step back, and examining this from the viewpoint of the dependency literature, and the international dialogue on commodities, these supply-control activities, performed by state regulators are not all that unlike what is being sought overall via international commodity agreements, or taken as an integrated program for commodity trade, the proposed Common Fund for commodities. The main difference here, however, is that the major consumers, being for the most part the industrialized central states, are well able to organize and devote the financial and human resources to address the technical details that will make any eventual integrated program function. This leads one to the fundamental difference in this case, where the regulator of the proposed Fund will likely not be a "captive" of the regulatees, but rather strongly influenced by and closely observed by both the consumers and the producers. Thus, if such an institution ever commences actual operations, both groups will likely be heavily involved in the development of operational guidelines and also, most likely, in the selection of key personnel.

8

Foreign Ownership in Canada's Petroleum Sector

The question of control over resource development and trade is directly related to the question of ownership of development rights and control of foreign investment. Particularly since the mid-1970s, control of foreign participation in the energy sector has become a key part of national economic policy within states that are members of OPEC and also within states that are non-OPEC oil producers, such as Canada, Great Britain, Norway, Australia and Mexico. In this chapter, the issue of foreign ownership in Canada's petroleum sector and the evolution of the role played by the multinational oil companies is outlined. Generally speaking, foreign investment has been actively sought to develop Canada's energy resources, except for a three-year period in the early 1980s when measures were put in place to increase Canadian ownership and control in the sector. Concern about foreign control in the sector is highest when expected profitability is high. As the risks and uncertainties are better appreciated, public concern over foreign ownership tends to become reduced as is the case in Canada at the time of this writing.

Foreign capital was in many respects one of the key ingredients for the development of Canada's petroleum industry. Despite poor drilling results over an extended period of time, U.S. firms (primarily Imperial Oil) continued to risk the funds needed to drill for oil. These efforts eventually resulted in the discovery of the Leduc oil field in Canada's western sedimentary basin. The Leduc discovery marked the beginning of the development period of Canada's oil and gas industry.

During the 1950s and 1960s, the Canadian energy sector was characterized by a small number of foreign-controlled, vertically integrated companies (exploration, production, refining and marketing). A number of small Canadian firms were active in the industry, concentrating their efforts towards exploration. Because of the economics of the industry, the subsequent discoveries of these companies were often either sold off or developed jointly with larger firms.

In effect, once the geological information gained from the Leduc experience was understood, the probability of an exploration effort being successful was raised significantly. The exploration activity was one of high-risk and high-payoff for success. Many small Canadian exploration-oriented firms were attracted to the exploration activities that promised the opportunity to increase a firm's net worth dramatically in a relatively short period of time, rather than the slower (less risky) growth possible from developing a discovered reserve. In some cases, smaller Canadian firms may have had difficulty obtaining required financing (or found the terms to be too costly) for development activities. For these reasons, these firms often found sales to the foreign-controlled, integrated firms attractive. Sales were made on a competitive basis, and reflected market conditions. In such an environment, the multinationals, in effect, provided a type of capital market for smaller Canadian companies which facilitated a continuation of and indeed the growth of the petroleum exploration industry in Canada.

This process, of course, is not unique to the development of Canada's petroleum exploration industry. As with most economic activity, potential benefits are usually attached to potential costs, and the risks and uncertainties of the changing marketplace are everpresent. As would be expected from the dependency literature, although this external source of finance fostered exploration by small Canadian firms, the development-oriented efforts of foreign companies in Canada's resource sector resulted in increased concentration of ownership of discovered petroleum reserves in the hands of a relatively small number of competing large firms. As is observed in the theoretical dependency literature, the consequences of a concentration of ownership by non-Canadians are that this potentially (but not necessarily) inhibits the extent to which Canadians share in the economic rents which may (or may not) eventually accrue to owners from time to time from oil and natural gas production.[1] In addition, depend-

---

1. Rents derived from export sales can be appropriated to government through means such as an export tax, royalties, land bonuses and the taxation of income. For a thoughtful discussion of the nature of rents generated in the discovery and production process, see Waverman (1981).

ing on the degree of competition domestically and internationally and on the regulatory environment within which all firms are required to function, it is possible that foreign ownership or control of companies responsible for developing a natural resource may result in the pursuit of corporate goals and objectives which may not coincide with the Canadian national interest.[2]

Until the mid-1970s, petroleum was not considered a strategic resource in Canada, in the sense that pre-

---

2. For example, the Canadian news media gave wide coverage in 1979, at a time of tight worldwide oil supply conditions, to a decision by Exxon to cut back supplies of imported crude to its Canadian subsidiary, Imperial Oil. With a view to what sells newspapers or improves ratings, the risks involved were discussed much more thoroughly than any potential benefits which may be obtained by the presence of active foreign-controlled firms. While this case deals more directly with imports, rather than with domestic production facilities, this type of action does provide an example of the nature of the potential costs associated with foreign control in the dependency literature. In this case, Canadians were reliant on a foreign, private sector actor. As an internal, company decision, this firm decided to cut back a significant portion of its regular crude imports into Canada. Such a cutback, had it occurred, could have resulted in running Canadian production at a higher level than was economic or drawing down crude inventories in Canada. In effect, through this action, Exxon could have brought about an allocation to others of Canadian domestic supply and inventory of what was then perceived as being a strategic commodity. The public pressure put on Imperial and Exxon at the time caused Exxon to change its directive. Moral suasion worked well in this case as the firms involved saw the value of good "corporate citizenship". However, the case points out the type of risk to which a nation such as Canada becomes exposed from foreign ownership and control in what, during this period, was considered a strategic sector. On the other hand, if the importers were Canadian firms or even Crown firms, they could have been at a disadvantage purchasing offshore supplies in competition with subsidiaries of the large multinationals. The risks of foreign investment must be weighed against the very positive benefits to consider the extent to which they are acceptable and/or necessary.

cautions had to be taken to ensure security of supply. Overseas oil was cheaper than domestic oil (both in Canada and the United States) and overseas supplies at these prices were considered secure. Policies pursued in the energy sector in the 1950s and 1960s were designed to overcome the economic attractiveness of foreign petroleum supplies and thereby, to promote the growth and development of the domestic oil industry and to encourage economic growth in western Canada. These policies had the effect of imposing higher direct costs for fuel in central Canada, and reduced significantly the income tax revenue obtained from the petroleum sector. Over this period the Canadian government put in place generous tax incentives and, where applicable, pricing arrangements, in the resource sector in order to achieve these goals.

Success in attracting foreign investors to put their capital to work in Canada's resource sectors was a key building block. Numerous efforts were made to attract foreign investment, and offshore funding helped in the attainment of Canada's resource development objectives. During the 1950s and 1960s the capital provided by foreign direct investment in Canada resulted in increased industrial activity and was an important factor in raising Canadian standards of living. In addition, foreign direct investment created employment opportunities and brought to Canada technological and managerial expertise that otherwise would have been unavailable.[3]

However, reliance on foreign capital to develop a nation's resources, while providing important benefits, is often not without costs. Consistent with the theoretical literature, foreign investment in Canada's petroleum sector has generally been truncated[4] in nature as all the various types of activity in the areas of research and development, exploration, production and manufacture of final products have not generally been undertaken in Canada. On the other hand, there are often sound economic reasons why this is so.

---

3. See, for example, Greenwood (1974). For other views, cf. Clement (1975), (1977); Levitt (1970); Naylor (1975) especially pp. 67-68.

4. Here "truncated" is used to connote an absence of forward and backward linkages.

To require these firms to act otherwise, could leave Canadians far worse off in many circumstances.[5]

Access to offshore knowledge and skills are important potential benefits to the industry in Canada. Research and the development of technology, for example, may be undertaken elsewhere, but Canada may gain by having access to the results of an effort which could not have been undertaken in the more limited Canadian environment. Similarly, management skills may often be imported from abroad but this gives Canadians the benefits of greater expertise and an early chance to learn and acquire those skills through association. This was the case, in particular, in the development of the Alberta petroleum industry during the 1950s and 1960s.

Here it is of interest to note that some Canadian oil firms are vertically integrated within Canada[6] while others are not.[7] Those firms that are not vertically integrated within Canada are generally involved in the exploration and production of crude oil and natural gas, and generally sell their production either within Canada or on the export market. Based on general competition theory, increased numbers of strong firms in exploration and production would be expected to increase the likelihood of discoveries and increase the size of land bonuses paid. It would also permit more advantageous production licences to be developed. The presence of these firms, which could, if they wished move into the downstream activities, is a factor which would be expected to increase competitiveness in

---

5. The debate on foreign ownership in Canada is succinctly reviewed in Lumsden (1970), and in the chapter by Cy Gonick in particular (pp. 43-73). A thoughtful discussion of foreign ownership versus domestic public ownership in LDC's is provided in Onyemelukwe (1974) pp. 73-86.

6. Examples of such firms would include Imperial Oil, controlled by Exxon, Shell Canada, controlled by Royal Dutch Shell, and Gulf Canada until its purchase by Olympia and York Ltd. in November 1985.

7. Usually such firms are involved in exploration and production, often for export. Examples include Amoco Canada, Mobil Canada, Chevron, Canadian Occidental and Amerada Minerals. Gulf Canada moved into this category after December 1985 because of the success of its new owners in selling off the firm's refining and marketing operations.

the marketing sector. Restricting the activities of these firms, or forcing sales to existing "more Canadian" firms would be expected to impact negatively on the number of actors and thereby on competition within the industry. Ultimately, if this were to occur, this would reduce benefits to Canadian customers and all Canadians in general.

The most potentially costly aspect of foreign direct investment is that effective ownership of Canada's resources and the related potential future economic benefit becomes vested with non-residents. This is a potential cost because there are never any guarantees that future economic benefits will in fact materialize. Moreover stimulants to reinvestment and the fiscal regimes that were in place in Canada from the 1950s until the National Energy Program in 1980 had the effect of maintaining the importance of the foreign investor's position in the sector by favoring existing operating companies and raising barriers to possible Canadian entrants. In fact, the implicit subsidies built into the Canadian tax system over the period under study probably reinforced the situation by channelling Canadian tax deferrals to the benefit of foreign-owned companies' spending programs. Of course, in the case of most investments, there is not necessarily a one-way street to growth and profits. The risks of sluggish growth and losses are always there.[8]

The fiscal system put in place was biased towards resource companies that were in place and ongoing, and in particular, those companies that had taxable resource income. With any specific fiscal measures come both advantages and disadvantages. The ability of taxable resource companies to take immediate advantage of earned depletion allowance credits and relatively fast write offs associated with resource expenditures enabled these particular firms to enjoy investment costs which were about 30 to 40 percent below those of non-tax paying firms. This cost advantage applied both to new investments and property acquisitions. In this situation, the multinationals were in the best position to realize the incentives embodied in the tax system, thus conferring to them a competitive advantage over many of their Canadian counterparts. Because resource income was, for the most part, required to take fullest advantage of fiscal incentives, the tax system helped

---

8. Generally, however, there is not usually much of an outcry in Canada or public concern over high levels of foreign ownership in an unprofitable sector, be it in resources or the manufacturing or services sectors.

successful existing firms to expand but also served to raise barriers to entry to potential new entrants. Thus, it could be argued that while these fiscal incentives did encourage investment and resource development activities, they also protected the industry position of foreign-controlled companies.[9]

But if there are some unintended impacts of a set of tax rules, the foreign-owned companies should not be held responsible. It is the host government that is responsible for periodically evaluating its taxation programs, and, where appropriate making necessary adjustments to correct problems. Such adjustments are made on a continuous basis in Canada. As the situation changed due to the rapid price rises in the 1970s, the Canadian government reassessed the fiscal system in place, and, in 1980, revised the entire fiscal system related to the petroleum sector. The government deleted the then existing provisions including depletion allowances and other write offs. These provisions were replaced with cash inventive payments and grants which provided higher benefits to firms which had higher levels of Canadian ownership and control.[10] With deterioration of the profitability of the sector in the mid-1980s, the grants system established in 1980 was scrapped in favor of a more traditional tax regime in 1985.

Another factor which would serve to accentuate further the biases of the fiscal system is the dependency concept that the cash flow generation capability of the multinationals would be expected to broaden substantially their borrowing base. In such a case, Canadian capital markets, therefore, would likely be tapped to finance the bulk of new resource development with the equity requirements supplied by oil companies. In such a case, the Canadian capital markets would finance directly and indirectly the bulk of resource activity without the potential benefit of ownership or control. But capital markets, generally speaking, are highly competitive and international in nature. Here again the question of risk, and the value of a dollar of equity is a foremost consideration. The equity which is at risk in a Canadian petroleum development investment must be attracted and held by the potential

---

9. Of course, the fiscal system in place was there because governments wanted to spur additional growth and economic activity in this sector and in western Canada.

10. See Canada, Department of Finance (1980).

for gain which goes with ownership. For example, some of the funds taken from the Canadian capital markets may be secured by income-producing assets. The risk would thus be lower and the potential benefits to be expected consequently less than would be the case for the initial equity investment. It is essential, therefore to look to the margin, and examine a specific capital infusion, and in particular the nature of the risks and potential benefits from that specific capital investment. The key question is of course, whether the actual cost of this equity investment to Canadians is appropriate.

As the above discussion indicates, when the wide variety of important factors are taken into account, including those of both a short and long term nature, the ultimate impacts of foreign direct investment on the achievement of Canada's objectives have been mixed. There are entries on both sides of the balance sheet. By any measure, benefits have been substantial. In general, however, with the benefit of perfect hindsight, it is easy for some analysts to cry fowl. If it pleases them to do so, they can observe that in light of the excellent profitability and growth of the petroleum industry over the 1970s, and the way that the resource industries have been taxed in Canada, the size of the benefits associated with successful resource development which would flow to Canadians would, in many instances, have been greater if undertaken by Canadian rather than foreign-controlled firms.[11] Although this may have been true for the period from 1970 to say 1980, it is not by any means certain that this industry will continue to grow and prosper at the same rate for the next decade. In the case of slow or negative growth, costs will of course be borne by equity holders, whether they are foreign or domestic.

Within the dependency framework, one of the main features of the peripheral states is that they are seen as suppliers of raw materials for the central states. High levels of foreign ownership and control in Canada's petroleum sector could be seen, therefore, as a

---

11. In evaluating the effects of foreign investment in Canada one must also be aware that there is a great deal of investment outside Canada by Canadians. Any actions taken to reduce Canada's attractiveness to foreign investors could be mirrored in foreign countries, to the detriment of Canadian investors. In such a case it is possible that the sum of the benefits resulting from Canada's international investments could be reduced.

means of ensuring this source of raw materials. Certainly much of the search for Canada's petroleum and non-petroleum resources has been motivated by the prospect of exports and a large portion of production has been for the export market. Incentives are given by the different levels of government to carry on exploration in order to better gage the size of the resource base. Once found, of course, pressures are brought to bear to bring these discoveries to market, and in view of the limited domestic market, exports are sought.

The central objective of Canadian government policy during the entire twentieth century in the energy sector in general and the petroleum sector in particular, has been to provide an adequate, continuing supply of economically-priced energy to Canadians. In this context, exports have not been the prime focus of policy, and have been viewed from the vantage point of how export opportunities would facilitate achieving the primary objective.

It is worthwhile at this point, to briefly leave the foreign investment question in order to clarify this exportable surplus concept. The basic principle underlying Canadian resource export policy, embodied in the initial legislation to control exports of 1907, is that only those energy resources considered to be or expected to be surplus to Canadian requirements are to be made available for export. This basic principle puts the case of Canadian energy exports somewhat beyond the traditional dependency analysis of exports where a given set of commodity exports are seen as more or less essential to the economic viability of the peripheral state.

The fact remains, however, that even with this exportable surplus principle in place, Canadian exports of energy resources have been very significant and the Canadian economy does depend thereupon to a very high degree. Provided known reserves are sufficiently large in relation to domestic requirements, peripheral states could well adopt a similar exportable surplus policy for their raw material exports without having any significant effect on the actual export levels or terms of trade. For example, state X could declare that as a matter of policy, only copper which is surplus to domestic requirements is to be exported. This begs the question of whether Canada's exportable surplus policy really puts the case of Canada's petroleum exports into a different set of circumstances than would be expected within the dependency framework.

To be more specific as to the trading partners involved, one notes that the largest portion of Canada's energy exports goes to the United States. For example, in 1970, about 96 percent of Canada's energy exports by value went to the United States. This percentage fell in the late 1970s to about the 85 percent range due to increasing exports of coal and uranium to countries other than the United States. For coal, Canada's chief customer has become Japan. Uranium is shipped to a number of customers in Asia, South America and Europe as well as the United States. In Canada's largest market areas, the United States and Japan, Canadian supply is only a relatively small proportion of total available supply. It is true however, that there are several regions of the United States which depend to a very important extent on Canadian supplies of natural gas and oil for reasons of geography and transportation economics.[12] Overall, it is fair to say that Canada depends more heavily on the export sales to the United States and Japan than these countries do on their purchases from Canada. Consistent with the dependency literature, which refers to this as the asymmetry of dependant trade, this relationship often gives the importer substantial capacity to affect the Canadian energy supply industry, and through it, the overall economy.

Returning now to the immediate topic of why foreign investors were interested in Canada's petroleum sector, during the 1950s and 1960s the appeal of Canada's petroleum sector to foreign investors was more related to obtaining an attractive potential return to investment than to securing a reliable supply of petroleum. In fact, for most of this period, imports to the United States were restricted and many U.S. producing areas were regulated to shut in production (thereby maintaining a higher U.S. domestic price level for petroleum resources than would otherwise have been the case). Certainly, security of supply becomes a much more important factor in the 1970s (but less so in the 1980s as supply and demand begin to react to the market signals generated in the late 1970s and early 1980s).

The attractiveness of Canada was, thus, a function of the investor's expected payoff for success, his chances of success and the various risks associated with the business activities of exploring for, producing, refining, transporting and selling the petroleum resources. If one accepts the basic notion that capital markets do function according to rational economic criteria, one would expect that investment dollars, be they Canadian or foreign, would be allo-

---

12. The key areas over the period under study were: the U.S. Northern Tier states, California, Ohio and Illinois.

cated by investors in a manner that maximized their expected total payoff (rate of return). This calculation would take into account how risky a given investment opportunity was perceived to be in relation to all other available opportunities with which these investors are familiar at a point in time.[13]

In this regard, assessment of a given investment opportunity would include consideration of all factors affecting the expected cash stream to be derived from the opportunity. These factors would include how the investment is expected to generate cash over time, and the various levels of risk associated with a disruption or reduction in the stream of cash occurring. It is immediately apparent that what counts to an investor (foreign or Canadian) is how much cash he will eventually net back after all expenses (including all taxes and quasi-taxes). Here the assessment of risk would require an investor to develop an expected scenario of what resources he might discover, how markets for this resource will behave in the future, whether markets or production or taxation or other various governmental policies might stay the same or change in the future and how his expected cash stream would be affected.

In general, the cost of money at a given time, measured by an expected rate of return to equity, will be equal for projects with equal projected cash flows and equal risk that the projection will be realized. Where these variables are not perceived as being equivalent, the most likely return to equity, a function of risk and probable cash flow will be expected to govern an investor's decision. For a foreign investor, an additional concern may be the ability to convert cash flow to another currency, and in many cases, this will also be a factor for domestic investors. Where security of supply of the commodity in question (through diverse sources, for example) is an issue to a given investor, the value of this security will be added to actual project cash flow in his calculations in a manner similar to the value of a given insurance premium.

This means that any action taken by government that causes (foreign) investors to be less certain of the size of the expected cash stream could have the effect of increasing the cost of money in that sector (or in that economy in general). Put differently, in a higher risk environment, investors will require a higher expected return to equity to offset the in-

---

13. Van Meurs (1981) pp. 235-249.

creased risk before committing funds.[14] Alternatively, only relatively lower-risk (i.e. from a technical rather than a political standpoint) projects will be able to attract investors. The degree of political risk, therefore, affects the cost of investment funds to a given economy. Uncertainty has the effect of making an investment dollar more expensive -- a higher return is required in order for it to be committed.

The main conclusion to be drawn from the above analysis is that the question of foreign ownership in a given sector, and what level of foreign ownership is acceptable, is a matter to be given utmost consideration, and given the real cost of political uncertainty, is best decided before investment is sought or allowed. Strict rules that are perceived as being unlikely to be modified may therefore be less "costly" than easier rules perceived as being open to change at any time.

A clear rule, a firm political decision that is perceived as highly unlikely to be modified, is likely to reduce the cost of investment dollars. In a situation of changing rules, (higher political risk) in a given geographic area, investors would be expected to seek higher returns to their investment dollar in that area than elsewhere. In investment environments where there is a perceived risk that various classes of investors will be subjected to discriminatory or arbitrary measures, the cost of investment capital would be expected to increase substantially.[15]

In general, over the period under study, only very minimal risk was associated with holding capital in Canada. In November 1980, however, changes were made to ownership and fiscal policies which, coupled with changes in the world market for petroleum, have had a dramatic impact on the levels of foreign ownership in the Canadian petroleum sector. An objective of Canada's National Energy Program of 1980 was to increase

---

14. Mikdashi (1976) examined statements of a variety of business executives of multinational resource-oriented companies and concluded that "adequate" rates of return on private investments in developing countries are usually set above those found in developing countries, the difference representing a premium to cover perceived higher risks. (p. 33).

15. Based on observations and discussions with American financiers and investors at a conference organized by The Financial Post, entitled "Canada's Energy Wealth," New York, November 1980.

the aggregate level of Canadian ownership and control in the petroleum sector to 50 percent by 1990 (from a level of about 30 percent in 1980).

An expected impact of the program to increase Canadian ownership in the petroleum sector which was put in place in November 1980 was to shift a larger part of the income and wealth generated from (then forecast) rising oil prices to Canadian residents and away from foreign investors. The way chosen to achieve this was by increased public ownership and by a variety of fiscal and requlatory measures, some of which were reversed in 1985.[16] Neither the benefits nor the costs of this program can be estimated with certainty. The benefits depend on how world oil prices move in the future, and whether Canadian resources will be found, produced and sold profitably in the future. In view of the softness of world oil markets, expected to last into the 1990s, significant overall benefits will not likely materialize in the near term. The costs, on the other hand, will depend on the size and extent of capital outflows that occur under the program, the success and growth rate of Canadian-controlled firms, the way in which capital outflows are financed and the spillover effects of this program (and its capital requirements) in other economic sectors.

Whether the program will have any permanent impact on Canada's level of dependence on foreign investment or on the United States, only time will tell. What is gained (or lost) in the energy sector could be counterbalanced by equivalent or higher costs in other sectors. While no firm assessments can be made until a reasonably long period of time has passed, during the few years it was in place, it had a severe short-term impact on Canada's balance of payments and consequently the exchange rate for the Canadian dollar, short-term interest rates in Canada, and thereby, the level of inflation in Canada. Clearly, economic nationalism, as it was expressed in Canada's 1980 Budget, is costly in the short run; and the potential long-term benefits are not certain.

To a certain extent, this program contributed to a turnaround in 1981 of foreign direct investment in

---

16. In 1981 and 1982 as a result of these incentives the following three major takeovers occurred: Petro-Canada purchased Petrofina, Dome Petroleum purchased control of Hudson's Bay Oil and Gas (from Conoco) and the Ontario Energy Corporation, a provincial Crown Corporation, purchased control of Sunoco (from Sun Oil).

Canada from a traditional positive flow of funds to a large withdrawal of capital; at the same time, direct investment outside Canada by Canadians increased substantially. These two factors produced an outflow of about $10.2 billion in 1981.

Whether this outflow was due to the Canadianisation program in the petroleum sector, other government policies, relative economic conditions and investment opportunities in Canada and outside Canada is not possible to say. The main point is that Canada's past dependence on foreign investment and resulting industry structure presents decision makers with difficult choices, made even more complicated by uncertainties in the future. Just because a given sector has been profitable in the recent past is no guarantee that it will be profitable in the future. Political concern for domestic ownership and control is usually focussed on profitable sectors rather than those marginal or unprofitable sectors. Perhaps this macro view is already an important factor in investment decision-making in many corporate boardrooms, both as concerns domestic and foreign investment opportunities.

In the petroleum sector in Canada, and in countries with industries having similar characteristics to the Canadian petroleum sector, the actual ownership and control of the companies in the sector, while important, is not the determining factor regarding net economic benefit to Canadians from resource development and domestic and external trade. Investors can be counted upon to seek out competitive rates of return on dollars at risk in given projects. Netback to investors and benefits to the domestic economy, trade benefits, security of supply benefits, and other economic and social benefits are all "controllable" by the domestic government. In a democratic country like Canada, with an open economy and unrestricted flows of capital, concern over actual levels of ownership in a given sector must be seen more as politically important, rather than as an imperative economic consideration. The various levels of government in Canada have ultimate control of all aspects of the petroleum sector and the nationality of ownership of particular companies is important within this context to the extent that the various levels of government rely on the activities of private companies, working within a highly regulated marketplace, to achieve the results sought.

Of course there are limits on the extent to which various levels of government can be expected to exercise this ultimate control. In general, there are numerous factors which put limitations on the exercise of this control. These would include such matters as the political structure of the government, the mood of the citizenry and the extent to which government actions reflect this mood over time. Economic variables would also be important, including the strength of the economy, profitability in the sector, and the cost and increased uncertainty and risk which would be incurred if existing policies and rules were modified. Also significant is the international environment, including the extent of government control in the sector in other countries and how any proposed new rules or modifications would compare with the situation in other countries.

9

The National Energy Board

The key federal agency for advising on and implementing policy related to Canada's natural gas exports, over the period under study, was the National Energy Board, established by an Act of Parliament[1] in July 1959. The <u>National Energy Board Act</u> took much from the legislation it repealed, namely the <u>Pipe Lines Act</u> of 1949 and the <u>Electricity and Fluid Exportation Act</u> of 1907. Very few totally new policies or powers were created through the establishment of a National Energy Board in 1959. However, a new agency, which gave an institutional character to a number of diverse energy-related activities being carried on in a number of government departments, was created.

The Board was and remains the federal energy regulatory authority, a counterpart to the Federal Power Commission, and later, the Federal Energy Regulatory Commission, in the United States. Similar agencies exist in many jurisdictions outside of Canada. The decision to create the Board followed a recommendation of the Royal Commission on Energy.[2] A principal reason for its establishment was a perceived need for an independent source of information and policy advice on energy. Over the years, however, the Board's policy advisory functions have become rather less important than its regulatory functions. This has occurred as

---

1. <u>National Energy Board Act</u>, S.C. 1959, c. 46. The material presented in this chapter does not constitute and should not be relied upon as a substitute for professional legal analysis or opinion. Furthermore, the analysis does not represent the official views of the government of Canada or any of its departments or agencies.

2. Canada, Royal Commission on Energy (1958) pp. 43-48.

the policy advisory capacity of Canada's Department of Energy, Mines and Resources was built up to respond to the higher profile energy issues took on in the 1970s.

The creation of the Board was a response to a perceived political need for an over-all, integrated energy policy and regulatory agency. The political debate around the construction of the TransCanada pipeline certainly gave emphasis to this need. Since an election had just been fought on what later became known as the "Great Pipeline Debate," there was a strong political will to enact legislation in order to place future energy-related debates one step away from the floor of the House of Commons.[3]

Upon its creation, the Board had two key types of function, which were set out in the <u>National Energy Board Act</u>. The first was an advisory function to the government on energy issues generally. In its second, regulatory function, the Board was given the authority to regulate the construction, operation and tariffs of pipelines and electricity transmission lines and to regulate the export or import of oil, natural gas and electricity. In addition to these aspects of the Board which are set out in the act, to the extent that the American Federal Power Commission provided a "negotiating tool" to American importers of Canadian energy resources, the National Energy Board could serve as a similar tool for Canadian traders, and in some cases could improve negotiation results otherwise attainable by Canadian exporters.

---

3. From the viewpoint of the politicians, there are additional advantages to having an agency like the National Energy Board. Recalling the circumstances surrounding the creation of the Board, governments have found it useful to have an independent Board assess individual company proposals. Particularly when there are competing applications, there are political advantages in this quasi-judicial process. Moreover, past governments have also used the Board as a vehicle to insulate themselves from the political pressure of interest groups. See, for example, the comments made by a Board Member, Mr. Bryan Horner to a Parliamentary committee when he stated: "...the NEB is a quasi-judicial body, independent. Consequently, it can be politically very handy; a mistake made is not the government's: today it is the independent body that made the mistake." (Canada. House of Commons. Minutes of Proceedings and Evidence of the Special Committee on Regulatory Reform (September 23, 1980) pp. 5:56-5:57) (Cited hereafter as Canada, House of Commons. Minutes (1980)).

With regard to the Board's legal powers, the
National Energy Board Act sets out the legal responsibilities of the Board. In addition, the act sets out
the policy principles for the exercise of these legal
regulatory powers. These principles are rather vague,
however, and serve more as guides than as clear,
precise rules to the Board in carrying out its legal
regulatory functions.

In the first place, the Board is legally responsible for providing over-all advice on energy matters.
As an advisor to the Minister of Energy, Mines and
Resources, the National Energy Board may hold public
hearings into particular energy questions, such as oil
or natural gas supply and demand[4] and issue reports
which set out its findings and recommendations.
Second, the Board is a quasi-judicial body, responsible
(subject to the approval of Cabinet) for the issuance
of certificates of public convenience and necessity to
construct or operate interprovincial and international
oil, natural gas and petroleum products pipelines, and
international electric power lines.[5] The Board can, if
it deems this appropriate, incorporate terms and/or
conditions in certificates.[6] Furthermore, provided
that this is approved by the Cabinet, and provided the
holder of the certificate has been given an opportunity
to explain, the Board can suspend or revoke a certificate if it finds that any term or condition has not
been followed.[7] Another major responsibility of the
Board is, when appropriate, to issue orders and licences for the export and import of electricity, natural
gas, oil and petroleum products.[8]

In practice, the Board's regulatory activities are
largely reactive. In general, the Board responds to
applications placed before it. When the Board finds it
to be in the public interest to grant a pipeline or
power transmission line certificate or to issue an

---

4. National Energy Board Act, s. 22.

5. Ibid., Part III.

6. Ibid., s. 46.

7. Ibid., ss. 47-48.

8. Ibid., Part VI. The Board did not deal with imports or exports of coal or uranium. These commodities
were the responsibility of the Dominion Coal Board
(abolished in 1970) and the Atomic Energy Control
Board.

export or import licence for natural gas, oil (for terms exceeding one year) or electricity, it reports its finding to the Cabinet through the Minister of Energy, Mines and Resources. However, the government can veto the issuance of these licences and certificates as they require the approval of Cabinet.[9]

It is significant that when the Board refuses an application, the decision does not require Cabinet approval. Board decisions regarding the rates, tolls and tariffs of pipeline companies under federal jurisdiction are also issued by the Board itself, without review and approval by Cabinet.[10] In addition, the Board may issue orders for minor additions or modifications to pipeline transmission systems without holding any public hearing and without Cabinet review.[11]

Some other types of Board orders are implemented directly by the Board. Given the recent developments in the natural gas markets, it is noteworthy that limited exports of natural gas, electricity, liquified natural gas, and ethane may also be licensed by Board order without reference to the Cabinet.[12] At the time of this writing, it is the government's stated intention to provide more open access by Canadian producers to export markets. In November 1985, the government undertook to amend the NEB export regulations "to allow the export of natural gas by order without volume limitation for terms not exceeding 24 months."[13] As the current trends continue for increased volumes of natural gas exports into the U.S. "spot" market, these short-term export licences are likely to become even more significant than they are at present.

Thus, there are two key types of National Energy Board decisions: those subject to approval by the government and those that do not require approval. Although on paper, most major decisions would be subject to government review, in practice, the informal

---

9. Ibid., s. 44.

10. Ibid., Part IV.

11. Ibid., s. 49.

12. National Energy Board Part VI Regulations, established by P.C. 1959-1411 and later amendments, s. 6A, 6B.

13. Agreement Among the Governments of Canada, Alberta, British Columbia and Saskatchewan on Natural Gas Markets and Prices, October 31, 1985, paragraph 17.

authority of the Board is much stronger than what is implied by the legislation. An original purpose of the Board was to remove Parliament from the business of direct export regulation. Government isolated itself from directly influencing Board decisions on such matters as natural gas exports. While the Board's formal regulatory powers are constrained to construction and operation of transmission facilities and to international trade, through the exercise of these powers, the Board does influence other aspects of the energy sector such as exploration, production and marketing.

The Board is, therefore, a very important institution in the energy sector, and its decisions on matters such as natural gas exports can have potentially large impacts on the sector. A basic question thus arises as to the degree of isolation between the Board and the government of the day on matters such as natural gas exports. Under the National Energy Board Act, the government cannot alter the specifics of a Board licence or certificate. It has a veto. It can approve or reject a Board recommendation. But this legal veto may be very difficult or embarrassing to apply in practice. Politically, rejecting a Board decision would mean taking on a Board finding, based on months of public hearings that (a) an exportable surplus existed and that (b) proposed prices were fair and reasonable. On what basis, or on what secret advice or new evidence would the government base its rejection of a Board recommendation? Board reports are public documents. When it recommends something, expectations are created in the marketplace, and these are the real factors that must be dealt with by the government of the day in assessing them.

Because of these constraints, since the mid-1970s, in a wise and prudent manner, the government has given public signals in advance to the National Energy Board to guide the Board in its interpretation of what would be "in the national interest". Examples of such indications were the extension of the oil pipeline to Montreal in 1974; the expansion of domestic natural gas sales in 1978 and 1979; the export of nuclear-generated electric power in 1981; and directives to relax exportable surplus determination procedures and export contract criteria in 1985.[14] Here, guidance from the

---

14. See, for example, Agreement Among the Governments of Canada, Alberta, British Columbia and Saskatchewan on Natural Gas Markets and Prices, October 31, 1985, paragraphs 16, 18.

government is certainly appropriate. To discuss the "national" interest, as pointed out earlier, uncertain assumptions must be made about Canada's economic future. In many cases, the choice of assumptions may require much judgemental input and have the effect of conferring benefits and costs in specific ways to specific parties. Even though public signals may have these qualities, in order to preserve the Board's intended independence, when they have been transmitted to the Board, they have been communicated in a way that did not interfere, nor appear to interfere, with a quasi-judicial process in which the technical aspects of specific applications were being given consideration.[15]

If any changes from the status quo were considered appropriate, there are several ways that these questions could be approached. These alternatives would certainly merit consideration for any similar types of international agencies established with similar mandates for the regulation of other traded commodities. Three alternatives are here considered: 1) more comprehensive assessment by the Board of the desirability of exports in general and once a clear strategy is defined, how specific applications fit in; 2) concentration on specific aspects of proposed exports such as either prices or volumes, thus setting a general export strategy which leaves more of the details of specific exports to the workings of the marketplace for resolution; 3) Board reports which present viable options and which set out confidence intervals for government consideration and decision rather than take-it-or-leave-it decisions and recommendations.

Looking at natural gas exports in particular, applied for export volumes, or pricing, depending on the specific terms, conditions and timing may or may not be appropriate and in the best interests of all Canadians. Some sectors, depending on terms and conditions, could certainly benefit. These questions could be addressed more fully, however, if the criteria used by the National Energy Board were made somewhat broader. Over the period 1970 to 1984, the Board was really only concerned with the narrow question of an exportable surplus determination, export prices being set at the border. After the pricing rules were relaxed in November 1984, the Board had to apply more judgement to consider whether pricing arrangements met

---

15. See, for example, Canada. House of Commons. Minutes (1980) pp. 5:50-5:64.

certain minimum criteria.[16] As an additional option to continuing in this manner, under the first approach listed above, the Board could examine exports in general, and consider specific applications in terms of Canada's overall strategy as to how its natural gas resources should be used in Canada and abroad. Alternatively, there are strong arguments that once a general framework for exports is elaborated, solutions which would rely on the diversity of the actors in the marketplace could be used. For example, tradeable export licences could be issued in place of licencing specific exporters' exports at specific border points. In addition, as market conditions fluctuate, (and while not feasible in the near term), it may, at times, make sense to tie exports and decisions on pipeline construction, or the construction of LNG facilities, into trade packages with the potential to achieve gains in international trade negotiations.

These points are elaborated further in the following chapters. The question of Board reporting, however, can be addressed briefly. A key point about the Board decision making and reporting process is that the Board's reports have always been arrived at through consensus. That is, Board reports generally have presented one finding, one conclusion to be accepted or rejected by the government. Other formats for reports would present a variety of different advantages and disadvantages. Never have viable alternatives been set out with one preferred alternative being recommended. Nor have dissenting opinions been published; nor have the opinions of Board staff ever been presented as such in a Board decision. This is largely a management decision which was made by the first Chairman of the Board, and subsequently, never changed. If it were considered desirable, and if the government wished to increase its direct control and exposure in this area, a government direction to the Board to alter this aspect of Board reporting would, in itself, be expected to give a much greater latitude to the government in assessing Board reports. In addition, this would substantially reduce the degree of reliance by the government on the Chairman of the National Energy

---

16. In November 1984 export pricing regulation was relaxed to allow negotiated sales prices above a floor price. The floor was the price of gas for domestic use at the Toronto city-gate. As conditions continued to evolve, in November 1985, this was further relaxed to permit exports at prices no less than domestic prices in the area near the border point of export.

Board, who shoulders the responsibility for forging the required Board consensus on all decisions.[17] Under this way of reporting, the government would still be able to consider Board decisions and recommendations. However, other viable options, developed by the Board as a result of its hearings could also be selected by the government. On the other hand, the status quo does have a number of significant advantages and in many circumstances, the government of the day may prefer to have an agency like the Board take responsibility for controversial decisions.

Within the dependency context, however, this discussion of process may be reduced in importance considerably. The facts of geography and available technology over the period under study made it imperative that if Canada wanted to transform its natural gas raw material to achieve a wealth stream and regional development in western Canada, it had to sell its natural gas outside its limited domestic market. Such gas could be transported economically only to Canada's one customer to the south. As a result of these facts, the government came under strong pressure to allow and indeed to encourage exports from companies with a commercial interest to do so and from producing provinces. Depending on the geographic power base of the federal government, it appears that the benefits of export sales have been shared and directed to benefit Canadians in central and eastern Canada as well as the companies and natural gas exporting provinces (although due to this sharing of benefits, total benefits accruing from export sales to these specific recipients have been reduced). As the customer had in place a federal regulatory commission to approve imports (the Federal Power Commission) it made sense for Canada to set up a counterpart. This would permit consultation and negotiations to take place on an agency-to-agency basis rather than leaving Canadian firms on their own to deal with the U.S. agency, or for the Canadian government itself to deal with the U.S. agency.

Certainly, from a political vantage point, the Board has produced valuable results. During the 1970s through the National Energy Board, the government of Canada was able to resist the very strong pressures to allow additional exports from commercial interests and exporting provinces, during a time when such additional exports did not appear prudent. Here, the fact that a quasi-judicial body, such as the Board, was able to

---

17.   Similar Comments have been made from time to time.   See, for example, Fischer (1971) p. 561.

refuse export applications and offer advice purportedly based on technical data, enhanced the government's ability to resist the political pressures pushing in the other direction. However, on the other hand, a dependency-oriented argument countering this could point out that the industry used the perceived shortages and the Board's application and hearing process to influence public opinion and the Canadian government in order to obtain a much increased netback for their proven reserves (and future discoveries). In this manner, the industry would have benefited very well from the temporary postponement of additional natural gas export licences.

Indeed, regarding the aspect of control of information, from the point of view of the Canadian public, there is a perceived advantage in various key sectors to have information collected in a democratic, hearings-type process by a quasi-judicial agency such as the Board rather than by an anonymous analytical unit buried inside a large government department. By means of public submissions to the Board, such information is provided by large numbers of intervenors, including provincial governments, on all sorts of important energy matters. However, the large informational requirements that are met from industry sources,[18] has led to assertions by some analysts and members of the public that the National Energy Board (as with other regulatory bodies in other economic sectors) is strongly influenced by and often may tend to favor the industry it is set up to regulate. As most decisions do represent a delicate balancing act between the industry and the public, there are generally benefits as well as costs which are incurred by all parties affected by the decision. Arguments that one side or the other is being "favored" are, therefore, more easily advanced than they are proven.

---

18. The National Energy Board uses industry data, for example, to calculate reserves. In Canada, there is very little other than industry data. The Board and other government geologists can independently interpret this data, but it is industry that does all the seismic testing and all the drilling. This reliance on the industry is one of the major reasons behind the creation of Crown corporations in this sector which are meant to provide regulators with a "window on the industry". See Canada, House of Commons, Minutes (1980) pp. 5:55, 5:61-5:62.

10

Export Prices

A major concern in the export issue has always been the price obtained for natural gas delivered to the Canada-United States border. Governments in Canada and in the United States have taken action aimed at increasing the share of the benefits from natural gas trade obtained for citizens under their respective jurisdictions.

Within the context of trade dependency, theorists might expect that if a dependent relationship exists, export prices would tend to be lower than they would be in a situation of non-dependency. It should, however, be cautioned that while important, export prices cannot be viewed in isolation from another crucial element - export volumes - which together with price determine gross export revenues. Indeed, a relatively high export price may be less attractive than some lower price combined with higher volumes, especially in the case of natural gas.

The regulation of export prices has a direct bearing on contracted for volumes and subsequent deliveries, as an importer's willingness to contract for specific minimum volumes and the incentives for producers to enter export contracts will certainly be a function of export prices. In this sense, regulation of export prices works hand in hand with the regulation of export volumes. It is likely, that as Canada supplies only a small portion[1] of the U.S. natural gas market, up to a certain point, for any given increase

---

1. Ranging from approximately 3 to 5 percent of total U.S. requirements over the period under study (American Gas Association **Annual Statistics**).

or decrease in export prices less or more exports would follow.[2]

An additional variable which must be considered in assessing export prices and government regulation is the portion of that price that flows to the specific exporter and to other producers, and that part that flows to governments, to domestic gas consumers[3] and to the public-at-large.[4] Non-price benefits may also be achieved by a given export that must also be valued and assessed in terms of the total value of an export sale to Canadians.

However, within the context of trade dependency, the whole area of the composition of trade rather than the export terms and conditions of a single commodity, has been the focus of theory. That is, the literature tends to be much more at a macro-level of an entire country[5] or set of countries than at the micro level of one specific commodity or sector within a country. In this context, examination of trade composition looks at the difficulties of trade in raw materials and argues that less should be exported in a non-processed form. Given Canada's relatively balanced mix of manufacturers, semi-processed and raw exports, and the wide variety of commodities and goods that are exported, this study, examining the case of Canada's natural gas exports, does not lend itself to addressing this type of issue, apart from considering whether natural gas exports might not be able to serve as a lever to obtain trade and other concessions outside the petroleum sector.

Turning to the objectives of government intervention in the area of export prices, stated generally, a basic theoretical commercial objective of government

---

2. This assumes also, that alternatives to Canadian natural gas imports are available to the importer over a given timeframe. The extent to which the U.S. spot market becomes developed, and the extent to which there is unused capacity in the natural gas transmission network are additional key factors.

3. As a subsidy, if any.

4. For example, the Province of Alberta created a "Heritage Fund," based on revenues from the petroleum sector, to benefit future generations of Albertans.

5. Although some work has been done which focuses on single commodity exporters, see for example, Moran (1974) on copper in Chile.

intervention on natural gas exports, and on the production and sale of a basic commodity in general, is to maximize the net present value to Canadians of the stream of revenues generated over the lifetime of production from Canada's total natural gas reserves, net of the cost to Canadians of discovering the natural gas, developing the reserves, gathering and processing the natural gas, and delivering it for sale.[6] An additional goal, related to security of supply, has been to ensure that sufficient supplies are available to meet domestic requirements before export volumes are committed.[7] In addition to these commercial objectives, more politically and socially-oriented goals such as building east-west ties or accelerating economic growth and development in a specific geographic region, also figure into the overall attractiveness of an export opportunity.

From the private firm's perspective, the general objective of the firm is to maximize the after-tax net present values of cash streams generated over the lifetime of all the reserves and potential reserves (to which it holds rights), net of the firm's own private costs, including a rate of return to capital employed in producing the revenue stream.[8]

As concerns the particular case of natural gas exports from Canada over the period under study, these objectives were pursued within the context of an export market in which the price level was directly influenced by an agency of the U.S. government, the Federal Power Commission (FPC), and later the Federal Energy Regulatory Commission (FERC), which determined wellhead prices for interstate natural gas. (Intrastate natural gas was not subject to wellhead price regulation by the FPC, but came under federal regulation in 1978 under the initiative of President Carter).

Canadian natural gas had to be competitive in the ultimate market being served with alternative natural gas supplies, as long as ample alternative supplies were available. Possible shortages of natural gas in the United States did not become an issue until the 1970s. Thus, until the 1970s, Canadian exporters of natural gas can be viewed essentially as price takers

---

6. Estimating this value requires an important judgement of the appropriate social rate of discount.

7. Of course, only a specific, limited timeframe is considered.

8. See, for example, Hotelling (1931); Solow (1974).

in the export market; after the oil price increases of the 1970s, and continuing until the weak market conditions after 1982, Canada's natural gas exports were priced in relation to an international oil reference price, which too was totally exogenous to Canadian control.

Within this environment, natural gas producers in Canada would be expected to pursue export sales to the extent that exports were consistent with their profit maximizing objective as stated above. In the standard theory of a firm's behavior, a producer would be expected to pursue exports to the point where the marginal unit of sales equated to his marginal costs of production, which in producing fields is very close to zero up to the point where facilities in place are being utilized at 100 percent capacity. In the case of a new reservoir, exploration costs are sunk and need not be figured into the exporter's evaluation of a specific marginal export contract. The extra costs of concern to the exporter are the costs of gathering, processing and transporting the natural gas to the point of sale to an importer.[9]

From the viewpoint of the private producer, timing of sales and resultant expected cash flow would be based on his judgement of how to maximize his after tax cash flow from his already-discovered reserves.[10]

From the point of view of a given producer, of course, the act of exploration, or the acquisition of reserves from a discoverer, is in itself an investment on which a firm must expect a given return equivalent to at least the private rate of discount. The commitment of a dollar to exploration implies that the in-

---

9. This discussion is discovery and reserve specific and relates to shut in gas. To the extent that development drilling is carried out on a field, and that gas production must be replaced through new exploration, production costs will rise, in the longer term, as a function of greater production. This is consistent with the arguments made by Adelman (1972b, pp. 16-24) to explain increasing production costs of crude oil over time.

10. Such a calculation would also be made by an "exploration-oriented" reserve holder who may prefer to realize a cash stream from the sale of reserves-in-the-ground in order to seek investment alternatives with a higher expected return (such as successful additional exploration). See, for example, Nordhaus (1973).

vestor expects a given cash flow over time on his investment. Natural gas, like all commodities, takes on real value only when produced, and the amount of funds a firm would choose to invest in natural gas reserves is directly related to price expectations and the potential timing of production, and the attractiveness of alternative investment vehicles that are available to the firm.

Financial considerations are also important. An initial decision to construct transmission facilities would usually require that a steady volume of natural gas for a relatively long term (traditionally 25 years) be contracted for. Wellhead prices for this "baseload" quantity, assuring a minimum throughput for a minimum period, when combined with transmission costs which covered the capital costs of the pipeline and distribution facilities, would have to be competitive in the ultimate markets with alternative fuel supplies. Pricing for additional volumes which did not require the construction of additional transmission facilities could be much more flexible.

Timing of deliveries over the course of a year would also affect the value of natural gas being exported. Usually demand for natural gas is lower in summer and higher in winter. The load factor, or degree of capacity utilization of the pipeline, is therefore an important consideration in evaluating contract prices. Depending on the nature of an importer's market, available storage facilities and the situation of other sellers of natural gas, real costs of natural gas to an importer may increase substantially if he contracts to maintain higher load factors.

A further consideration related to pricing in the export market is the purchaser's incentives to keep costs down. Under FPC (and later, FERC) rate regulation, pipeline companies would recover costs of service and a rate of return on "used and useful" investment. Cost of natural gas was recovered by the pipeline as a cost of service. Over the period in question, the pipelines were, in general allowed to "roll-in" the cost of natural gas purchased at various prices and recover an average cost per unit of natural gas sold. A marginal unit of higher-than-average cost natural gas would be sold at the (lower) average cost to the pipeline. Therefore, provided the pipeline company's "rolled in" price for gas was competitive with alternative fuels at the burner tip in the markets being served, and provided it was allowed to recover its cost for natural gas purchases, the firm's profits (return on investment) were relatively unaffected by the prices paid for any particular source of supply, including imports from Canada.

In fact, the apparent lack of commercial incentive for regulated pipelines to obtain gas at the lowest possible price was one of the major arguments used to support FPC regulation of wellhead prices. It is true, however, that in general the pipeline companies did and do have an incentive to keep prices as low as possible in order to penetrate as large a market as possible in their service areas. While they recover the cost of gas purchases as an expense, they earn a rate of return on prudently acquired, used and useful assets. The higher the utilization rate of their facilities, and the more facilities that can be justified, the larger the transmission company's rate base on which it earns a rate of return. Also, once transmission facilities of a certain capacity are constructed, their use at less than 100 percent capacity could be deemed wasteful or "imprudent" by the regulatory agency. This would usually translate into an ultimate reduction in allowed return to total investment, and consequently lower profits to equity holders.

The degree of ownership of reserves and production in Canada by U.S. transmission or distribution companies is another factor which would bear on the pricing arrangements for Canadian exports. If the U.S. purchaser has an equity interest in the Canadian production and/or transmission, then his decision on export volumes and prices would be expected to be based on the objective of maximizing the net present value of the after-tax (in all jurisdictions, i.e., both Canada and the United States) stream of cash from a given reserve.

Given that the export price is determined largely in relation to prices in the export market, and given that some private Canadian producers found exports at those prices to be attractive from their own points of view, under the institutional and legal framework in place over the period under study, the provincial and federal governments of Canada have been faced with a decision either to allow producers to make specific desired sales, or to refuse applications for export licences.

Of course, the fiscal incentives, royalty and leasing arrangements and other incentives to industry under governmental control could be used:

1) to accelerate or decelerate exploration for and development of reserves,
2) to change the attractiveness of exports at a given price level.

Government Regulation of Export Prices

The case of the exports of Westcoast Transmission provides some significant insights into the export pricing question. This case is set out and assessed below.

Before turning to that case, as an example of an attempt to capture economic rents, it is interesting to note that as early as 1899 discriminatory pricing, favoring domestic customers, was imposed by the Ontario government. In 1907, Ontario imposed a tax of two cents per Mcf on natural gas but provided that ninety percent of the tax would be remitted on gas consumed within the province.[11] The federal government, in its <u>Electricity and Fluid Exportation Act</u>[12] of 1907, specified that an export duty of up to ten cents per Mcf could be imposed on exports at the discretion of the federal government.[13] While these measures are interesting within the context of the history of federal-provincial relations in Canada, because these exports ended in 1909, and affected only a very small quantity of natural gas, the matter could be considered only marginal to the present study.[14]

Turning now to the case of Westcoast Transmission Company's exports, this example illustrates well the dilemmas facing Canadian policy makers and similar officials in other countries, in the pricing of natural gas exports. Canada's natural gas exports began to grow rapidly after 1950. Volumes grew quickly from 2,366 Mcf in 1950 to almost 8 million Mcf in 1952, over 10.5 million Mcf in 1956 and over 88 million in 1958. As export volumes grew, export prices became a matter of great public concern in Canada. In particular, the

---

11. Miller (1970) pp. 76-77. There were no exports of natural gas in the period 1909 to 1950. In fact, beginning in 1923, several Ontario companies imported natural gas to supplement domestic supplies (Miller, pp. 78-80).

12. <u>Electricity and Fluid Exportation Act</u>, S.C. 1907, c. 16.

13. Ibid., s. 10.

14. Canada's federal government has undoubted constitutional power to regulate external trade under subsection 91(2) of the <u>British North American Act</u>. See for example, <u>Citizen's Insurance Co. v. Parsons</u>, (1881), Vol. 7 appeal cases.

prices under which Westcoast Transmission delivered gas to the Canada-United States border came into the public spotlight. Westcoast's export prices were below the price of natural gas in the nearby Canadian market of Vancouver. To a large extent, this public concern over export prices was a driving force for the appointment in 1957 of the Royal Commission which examined energy export policy including natural gas export prices.[15]

Natural gas exports and pricing was perceived as being a hot political issue, and one that could not be left for resolution by market forces alone. The government perceived that people wanted their interests protected, and government responsibility in this area was well established.[16]

Regarding export prices, the Royal Commission recommended that when considering an export application, the federal government should be satisfied that the minimum export price is fair and reasonable. Furthermore, the Commission recommended that all future export contracts contain provisions for price adjustments during the term of the contract so that the exporter, and in turn the gas producers, could participate in any benefits accruing from price increases occurring in the export markets.[17]

Upon consideration of the Royal Commission's recommendations, the National Energy Board was created in 1959.[18] Among its powers were to issue, subject to Cabinet approval, licences for the export of natural gas,[19] and certificates for the construction and operation of international and interprovincial natural gas pipelines.[20] In considering an application for a licence to export natural gas, the **National Energy Board Act** specified that the Board had to satisfy itself, among other things, that "the price charged

---

15. Canada, *Order in Council*, P.C. 1957 - 1386.

16. As evidenced by the **Electricity and Fluid Exportation Act**, S.C. 1907, c. 16, and the **Pipeline Act**, S.C. 1949, Vol. 1, c. 20.

17. Canada, Royal Commission on Energy (1958) pp. 11-13.

18. **National Energy Board Act**, S.C. 1959, c. 46.

19. Ibid., s. 81; **National Energy Board Part VI Regulations**, Regulation 8.

20. Ibid., s. 26, 44.

by an applicant for gas exported by him is just and and reasonable in relation to the public interest."[21]

The difficult question of determining what constitutes a "just and reasonable" price in relation to the public interest was therefore put into the hands of a regulatory body, and removed by one level of decision from Canada's elected federal parliamentarians. However, ultimate control of exports remained with the federal Cabinet since all certificates to construct or operate pipelines and licences to export natural gas, issued by the Board, had to be approved by Cabinet.

The development of the Board's early pricing policies was primarily related to its regulation of natural gas exports by Westcoast Transmission Company Limited. Before the creation of the Board in 1959, Westcoast had received authority to export natural gas amounting to 200,000 Mcf per day. These volumes were sold at a price of 22 (U.S.) cents per Mcf, as specified in an agreement with its export customer, Pacific Northwest Pipeline Corporation, dated December 11, 1954. This price was subsequently called a "distress price" by the Board. Under the circumstances prevailing at the time of the agreement, however, accepting this price was the only alternative to abandoning the plan to build the Westcoast system.

The real question is, therefore, whether governments wished the Peace River district natural gas reserves to be developed over the time period in question.

In this author's opinion, the original Westcoast export proposal was deemed to be attractive since it:
1) allowed the development of the Peace River District reserves (considered to be "remote" and surplus to Alberta's requirements);

---

21. Ibid., s. 83. Section 83 reads as follows: "Upon an application for a licence the Board shall have regard to all considerations that appear to it to be relevant and, without limiting the generality of the foregoing, the Board shall satisfy itself that

a) the quantity of gas ... to be exported does not exceed the surplus remaining after due allowance has been made for the reasonably foreseeable requirements for use in Canada having regard to the trends in the discovery of gas in Canada; and
b) the price to be charged by an applicant for gas ... exported by him is just and reasonable in relation to the public interest."

2) would encourage exploration in northeastern British Columbia and northwestern Alberta;
3) would bring gas through British Columbia to Vancouver and would be competitive with alternate fuel supplies in these areas; and
4) would provide royalties and increased land bonuses to the government of Alberta and tax revenue and expected royalties and increased land bonuses to the province of British Columbia.

Implicit in these statements is the concept of the timing at that moment being appropriate for development of the Peace River District reserves, and increased exploration (which implies imminent or eventual development) of additional reserves in this region. Also implicit in this statement is the idea that bringing natural gas to Vancouver sooner rather than later (if ever) was appropriate, and that Peace River natural gas was more appropriate than imports from the pipeline to be built to Seattle by Pacific Northwest. Finally such an argument would also be based on the assumption that it was likely that the value of the cash stream of payments to the federal and provincial governments over the time period in question would be greater than or at least equal to the value of a cash stream generated at a later date.

But the export price criteria set out at the start of this section must be considered in the context of the political climate of the day. The question of the appropriate discount rate, or alternatively, of the length of time to be considered in an evaluation of benefits and the value of future benefits and costs is of course critical. General policies and strategies are always made keeping in mind the long term consequences. However, the realities of the political system and immediate benefit may well have a significant impact on the rates of discount and cause higher, rather than lower discount rates to be applied to assess the near and the longer term costs and benefits.

In the case of the Westcoast Transmission project, in spite of the statements which were subsequently made by regulatory bodies and politicians in Canada, there is no clearcut economic evidence that the deal was "bad" for Canadians or that revenues were not maximized over the timestream chosen for development. Essentially, the public concern arose because natural gas was sold at a price of 22 cents per Mcf at the border, but at about 32 cents per Mcf at the same time in Vancouver and other markets in southern British Columbia.

The Royal Commission on Energy reflected well the public arguments and concern over the contracts. Westcoast officials testified[22] that the export price was determined by reference to the laid down price of Texas gas in San Francisco. This price was 34 cents per Mcf and, as it was estimated it would cost 12 cents to transport gas from the Canadian border to San Francisco, the export price of 22 cents was thereby determined. Additional points confirmed in Westcoast testimony were:

1) None of the gas sold by Westcoast to Pacific Northwest was in fact laid down in San Francisco.
2) There would be some additional cost to be added to the 34 cent San Francisco laid down price to move Texas gas to the Pacific Northwest area.

At a later point in the hearings, Westcoast's chief promoter, Mr. F. McMahon, testified that the export price of 22 cents per Mcf and the price of 32 cents per Mcf charged by Westcoast to British Columbia Electric were determined by "fixing a common price for each of the distributing companies in the cities of Portland, Seattle and Vancouver, and deducting therefrom the estimated cost of delivering the gas to the United States cities from the Canadian border."[23] At the hearings, held in 1958, Mr. McMahon said he was not happy with the export price and agreed that Westcoast should be getting a better price. He added, however, that at the time the contract was negotiated, this was absolutely the best deal that could have been made.

In its report, the Commission dryly observed that in 1954 Westcoast was not in a position to bargain with Pacific Northwest on an equal footing. But how many business deals are struck between traders with equal power? Pacific Northwest held the natural gas sales franchise for that U.S. market area. Westcoast had under contract natural gas reserves in the Peace River district, but the Vancouver and southern B.C. markets were too small to support the costs of a transmission system. Thus, unless sales could be made in the Pacific Northwest franchise area, the Westcoast project could not proceed. The Commission concluded that under such conditions Westcoast would be "forced to take practically whatever terms Pacific northwest was prepared to offer".[24]

---

22. Canada, Royal Commission on Energy (1958) p. 22.

23. Loc. cit.

24. Ibid., p. 23.

Further, while it did not attempt to allocate costs between the export and domestic components of the Westcoast project, the Commission did state that there was a possibility that these costs were not fairly allocated. The Commission recommended that Canadian regulatory authorities should investigate the matter to ensure that Canadian consumers of natural gas were not subsidizing in any way the export sales.

While the Commission's way of thinking has a certain appeal from the point of view of justice and equity, the Company's and the public's benefits derived from the completion of the project were of course somewhat obscured. The workings of a market are usually independent of what politicians may define as justice or equity.

To be sure, the Commission and the public had every right to be upset. Something about the deal seemed suspicious. However, given the following conditions, which indeed, at the time of Westcoast's negotiating, were expected to hold true, there was nothing inherently wrong with the deal.

> Assumption 1: Natural gas in the Peace River district would have no domestic market in the reasonably foreseeable future. A pipeline to distant domestic markets in Alberta and British Columbia was not economic. Assumption 1 implies that if the Westcoast project did not proceed the net present value of the reserves would be close to zero.
> Assumption 2: Natural gas would compete with a variety of alternate fuel sources in potential market areas. The laid down cost of gas (i.e. wellhead price plus transmission) must be competitive with these alternatives for sales to occur. Without an export component, the transmission costs of Peace River gas to British Columbia markets would have been too high for natural gas to successfully compete with alternate fuels in these markets.
> Assumption 3: No significant changes in the relative or absolute prices or availability of alternative fuel supplies in potential markets was anticipated. This assumption implies that there is no economic or strategic advantage to pursuing sales later rather than sooner.

Within this context one can proceed to evaluate the initial Westcoast export.

First, it is reasonable to believe that the 22 cents per Mcf border price was the best Westcoast could do at the time of negotiations. There were certainly strong incentives for Westcoast to try for the highest price Pacific would pay. Pacific Northwest, on the other hand, had been awarded the franchise area, and was taking some gas from Westcoast simply so it could eliminate the possible court delays that would have been involved.

In order to get the line built (and the gas fields producing), a price of 22 cents per Mcf was acceptable to Westcoast, and allowed the company to get the required debt and equity financing. In the course of Westcoast becoming a viable operation, several parties which had been backing the company since 1949 saw the value of their equity holding increase hundreds of times from its (nominal) issue price.

As concerns the difference between the domestic and export sales prices, there is nothing surprising about the dual price system. If the best Westcoast could do in the export market was 22 cents per Mcf on a given volume (based on supply and demand for natural gas), then this must be taken as an exogenous price, outside the control of Westcoast or the Canadian government. By the same token, it appears that if Vancouver were to be supplied by imports from Pacific Northwest, the delivered wholesale price would have been slightly more than 32 cents per Mcf, Pacific Northwest's laid down price in Seattle, Washington.

As regards customers in southern British Columbia, regardless of where the natural gas originated, it is clear that compared with potential alternative fuels, they preferred natural gas at 32 cents per Mcf for its price advantage and other qualities as a fuel. It is hard to see why Westcoast, operating a natural monopoly, would voluntarily choose to sell into a given market at a discount to the 32 cents price that would have otherwise prevailed in the same market for similar volumes.

Westcoast was a monopolist, not subject to market pressure in domestic markets. However, if Westcoast were to be regulated on a traditional cost-of-service basis, it is unclear whether government regulators would have come to any alternative conclusions.

It is also useful to look one step past Westcoast, to the natural gas producers. The export and domestic prices of the natural gas, less the cost of transmission (including Westcoast's profits) is ultimately what determines the wellhead price of natural gas that Westcoast could pay to producers. As long as the Westcoast system was not in place, the potential producers would not be able to sell their gas.

If no sales or cash stream was expected in the foreseeable future, regardless of the rates at which producers normally would discount future revenues, the gas in the Peace River district would be of practically no value. Consequently, the cost of discovering these reserves would represent an investment with a very uncertain payback to these potential producers.[25]

The wellhead prices paid to producers, therefore, were also a key to the profitability of Westcoast, and to the profitability of domestic and export sales of natural gas. Related to wellhead prices, and profits of producers are the tax, royalty and bonus payments that would flow to the provincial and federal governments in Canada. In general, the higher the wellhead prices, the greater would be the value of the reserves and the higher would be the potential provincial royalty and bonus payments. Once a transmission system is in place, and producers can earn revenues from discovering and producing natural gas earlier, they would be expected to be prepared to bid higher at auctions for land, and land bonus payments to the provinces would consequently increase.

In general, therefore, under a given royalty and tax system the higher the wellhead price, the higher the netback (after-tax profit) to producers, the greater the incentive to find and develop more reserves, the higher the tax, royalty and land bonus payments that will be made to government. The provincial and federal governments would then allocate these revenues as required to meet policy objectives in various sectors, in various regions of the province or country.

If, on the other hand, domestic prices are reduced and wellhead prices reduced proportionately, assuming that there was still sufficient natural gas for sale by producers to fill the pipeline, then royalty payments and income taxes paid by producers could well fall. As the value of natural gas reserves would be reduced, and production profits smaller, land bonus payments would be smaller, and the incentive to explore in the area would also be reduced.

It is true that these lost revenues to government and producers are translated into lower cost natural gas for consumers in the residential, commercial and industrial sectors. (This assumes transmission company

---

25. It is true, however, that these reserves may have been discovered as the result of an oil-directed exploration effort. Such gas wells could therefore, be seen as a type of "no cost" consolation prize, one where there was at least a remote chance that some cash stream would be obtained eventually and thus one cut better than a dry hole.

charges are constant in both scenarios). The benefits of lower-than-otherwise natural gas prices would be distributed to customers in proportion to the amount consumed at lower prices.

Returning to the question of Westcoast's export and domestic prices, the following conclusions can be drawn:

1) At the time of negotiations, the 22 cents per Mcf export price was the best price Westcoast could obtain on sales to Pacific Northwest.
2) The Westcoast project held the promise of financial gain to its promoters, to the potential natural gas producers of the Peace River district and to the provincial and federal governments (and thereby to the Canadian public).
3) Benefits were derived by customers of both Westcoast in Vancouver and Pacific Northwest in Seattle by having natural gas available at 32 cents per Mcf wholesale rate, compared with alternative fuel sources.

Given the above conclusions:

If Westcoast were to provide natural gas at less than 32 cents per Mcf to domestic customers, this would imply that one or some combination of the following would have to occur:

1) If Westcoast required 32 cents on domestic sales to meet its cost of service related to domestic volumes, and 22 cents on export sales to meet its cost of service related to export volume, and if prices paid to producers (and hence governments) were left unchanged, then Westcoast would not earn required revenues to meet its domestic cost of service. The persons holding equity in Westcoast would not earn an adequate rate of return on invested capital, and a precedent would be set which would be somewhat unfavorable for further pipeline construction within British Columbia and/or Canada. At the very least, in such a case, potential pipeline investors would be expected to associate a higher risk with equity in Canadian pipeline companies, and require a higher expected rate of return before committing additional equity funds in this industry. The value of equity invested in Westcoast Transmission would decline.

2) If Westcoast equity holders were earning an economic rent (a higher than required rate of return to equity in relation to risk), and if prices paid to producers were left unchanged, then lower sales prices would cause return to equity to drop. This could lead to entrepreneurs, such as those which pursued the Westcoast venture, directing their talents to other types of ventures where potential economic rents could be earned. Further, the value of equity invested in Westcoast Transmission would drop, as would any rents being collected by governments through the fiscal system.
3) Payments to natural gas producers (and in consequence government receipts) would decline with consequences as discussed above.

Rather than suggest any changes to the existing contracts of Westcoast, the Royal Commission on Energy recommended (among other things):[26]

1) that Westcoast and other natural gas pipelines under federal jurisdiction be regulated as to their prices and rates, and that such companies be required, if necessary, to renegotiate the terms of any existing contracts for natural gas sold for consumption in Canada;
2) that the prices, tolls, rates or tariffs of oil and natural gas pipeline companies should be just and reasonable, non-discriminatory and calculated to yield a fair rate of return on the shareholders' equity, after making due allowance for reasonable and proper operating expenses, depreciation, interest, income taxes and other taxes;
3) that in the regulation of Westcoast Transmission, the regulator should take into account the prices at which gas is sold by Westcoast within Canada and for export from Canada, in order to ensure that the return on the shareholders' investment in the company does not result in Canadian consumers of natural gas contributing more than their fair, reasonable and proportionate share of the total return; and

---

26. Canada. Royal Commission on Energy (1958) pp. vii - x.

4) that if and when Westcoast makes application to the Government of Canada for a licence to export quantities of gas additional to those included in its existing export licence or for any variation in the quantities of natural gas now included in its licence, the Government of Canada before approving any such further licence or variation, ensure that the aggregate of natural gas to be exported by Westcoast, under all outstanding and proposed contracts for the sale of such gas, is sold at prices, which when averaged, are fair and reasonable after taking into account the price at which natural gas is sold to Pacific Northwest Pipeline Corporation under its contract with Westcoast dated December 11, 1954.

Evolution of Westcoast Exports and Government Policy on Prices

The economic viability of the Westcoast system improved during the early sixties, to the extent that, in 1966, it was able to reach a new agreement with its export customer. The new agreement provided for the revision of the prices of volumes exported under the 1954 agreement. Under the new agreement, total export volumes would increase to a maximum of 500,000 Mcf per day, and would be sold at a price of 27 (U.S.) cents per Mcf. Based on this agreement, Westcoast was granted a licence from Canada's National Energy Board to export the additional volumes in March 1967. However, government regulatory authorities quickly became deeply involved in additional negotiations on these contracts. The proposed Westcoast export application went back and forth like a ping pong ball between the two regulators, each attempting to outdo the other. The complementary U.S. import application was rejected by the FPC which did not approve of the redetermination of the price detailed in the 1954 agreement, nor of the price escalation clause of the 1966 agreement. Consequently, Westcoast applied to the National Energy Board in October 1967 to amend the export licence granted in March 1967 to reflect the FPC ruling.

After a public hearing in Vancouver during October 1967, the National Energy Board dismissed Westcoast's application to amend its export licence, primarily because it was not satisfied that the proposed export price was high enough, or in the terms used by the Board, "just and reasonable."

It was this December 1967 decision in which the Board first detailed the three tests for the determination of a "just and reasonable" export price. In an attempt to demonstrate to the industry and the U.S. regulatory authority that the Board's decision was not an arbitrary one, the Board stated that its consideration of the application as it related to export price rested on three main points:[27]

> 1) "the export price must recover its appropriate share of the cost incurred;
> 2) the export price should, under normal circumstances, not be less than the price to Canadians for similar deliveries in the same area;
> 3) the export price of gas should not result in prices in the United States market area materially less than the least cost alternative for energy from indigenous sources."

The Board's December 1967 decision concerning Westcoast's export application also outlined the interrelationship of the requirements detailed under section 83 of the National Energy Board Act. This section points out the interdependence of concerns related to (a) "having regard to the trends in the discovery of gas in Canada" and (b) an appropriate export price. This interdependence detracted from Westcoast's application. In its report, the Board noted the following:[28]

> "It is not so apparent to the Board that the export price ... will in fact provide an incentive to exploration work sufficient to maintain the trends in discovery of gas upon which the Board has replied in making its forecasts of future surplus of gas. Although both Pan American and Pacific Petroleum expressed confidence on this point, it seems fairly clear to the Board that, as the past low export price has had a stultifying effect upon exploration for gas in British Columbia as compared with Alberta, so will any failure of further exports to realize their fair market value be reflected back to prices available for new gas to the wellhead and to the budgeting of funds for exploration in British Columbia and the Northwest Territories."

---

27. Canada. National Energy Board (1967) p. 7-1.

28. Ibid., pp. 8-19.

In 1968 Westcoast reapplied for Board approval of additional exports at prices based on a Second Amendatory Agreement with El Paso. The Board viewed these prices as a satisfactory compromise between the initial application and the FPC decision. In February 1968, Westcoast's application was approved. In turn, the FPC looked favorably on these imports.

In 1969 Westcoast applied to the Board for a further increase in its authorized exports. As a result of this application, the Board issued Licence GL-41 which is Westcoast's present authority for exports at Huntingdon, British Columbia. Concern was expressed at the 1970 hearing of this application that, while future prices detailed in Westcoast's agreement with its export customer would be stable over time, prices to Westcoast's Canadian consumers could increase in the future. To deal with this concern, while ensuring that the Board's second price test continued to be satisfied, the Board ordered that the border price must at all times be at least 105 percent of the comparable Canadian rate in the general area of Huntingdon, British Columbia. This condition was written into Westcoast's export licence. This condition matched a price clause in an export agreement which formed part of an application, by Trans-Canada Pipeline Company, being heard simultaneously with Westcoast's application.

Price Revision of Existing Export Contracts

Accompanying the announcement of the granting of export Licence GL-41 to Westcoast, the then Minister of Energy, Mines and Resources, Mr. J.J. Greene, announced the addition of Regulation 11A to the National Energy Board's Part IV Regulations.[29] This regulation called for ongoing and systematic review of natural gas export prices.[30]

Subsequent to the promulgation of Regulation 11A[31] the Board undertook studies to formulate methods of collecting and evaluating data on energy prices in export markets. To assist it in determining the price

---

29. The exact wording of Regulation 11A is presented in Chapter 4, footnote 70.

30. Minister of Energy, Mines and Resources, Press Release, Ottawa: Department of Energy Mines and Resources, September 29, 1970.
190

31. Order in Council, P.C. 1970-1706.

of competing natural gas supplies and alternative energy sources in the export market, the Board held a public hearing in the spring of 1974.[32]

Starting in 1974, the Board issued reports on an annual basis which examined price increases for competing natural gas supplies and alternative energy sources in U.S. markets. In these reports, the Board made recommendations to increase the minimum export prices for natural gas based on what it called "commodity-value". "Commodity-value" referred to the maximum price at which natural gas would still be competitive with alternative energy sources available to an American importer.

As a result of the Board's calculations and recommendations, the export price of substantially all gas exported from Canada was raised from then current levels ranging from 23 to 60 cents per mcf in steps to a level of $1.94 per Mcf on January 1, 1977.

Substitution Cost

In its 1977 review of prices in Canadian natural gas export markets, the Board considered the commodity value of alternative energy sources, the costs to Canadians of foreign crude oil, the impact of natural gas shortages, that were then occurring on United States domestic prices and other factors. The Board recommended that the uniform border price of natural gas exports be denominated in United States dollars[33] and increased to $2.25 (U.S.) per Mcf. In the government's review of the Board's recommendation it decided that the concept of substitution value (based on the cost to Canadians of an equivalent fuel quantity (i.e. on a BTU basis) of oil purchased on the world market) or replacement cost was appropriate and set the new export price at $2.16 (U.S.) per Mcf (equivalent to $2.32 Canadian) effective September 21, 1977. Using this concept, border prices were steadily increased to a peak of $4.94 (U.S.) in 1981.

---

32. The Petroleum Administration Act, S.C. 1964-75-76, c. 47, was passed to provide further legislative authority for the National Energy Board to regulate the price of natural gas in interprovincial and export trade.

33. Over the period 1970 to 1977 the Canadian dollar traded at a rate close to par with the U.S. dollar. However, in 1977 the Canadian dollar depreciated significantly with respect to the U.S. dollar.

From a dependency viewpoint, the Westcoast case presents some contradictions. On the one hand, reserves in what was perceived as a "remote" area were developed and advantages were obtained and economic growth took place in Alberta and British Columbia. Consumers in British Columbia had natural gas made available to them at a price which was better than available substitutes. The importers obtained an attractive additional supply of natural gas at an attractive price. As a result of the export, exploration and development in the Peace River area became profitable and activity accelerated, resulting in more discoveries.

On the other side of the ledger, because of its strong negotiating position, the agreed upon export price favored the purchaser, although in the 1970s prices were readjusted to reflect the commodity and later the substitution value of the natural gas. It is noted that provided that royalties, taxes and bonuses are at appropriate levels, the actual export prices, arrived at by negotiation between traders, if it makes sense to the traders, may not be an issue for further government intervention (unless there is some very special strategic or political feature of the specific volume of the commodity in question at a specific point in time).

Other Considerations and Current Policy

To a certain extent, because there are so few U.S. buyers of Canadian natural gas, the setting of a uniform border price by the Canadian government may be seen as an appropriate way for Canadian producers to get the best possible price for their exports. As natural gas producers received the difference between the export price and the domestic price as an "export flowback" they were most supportive of this government intervention.

In order to keep peace with the Americans, who, via their government, negotiate[34] with other countries and state oil companies for natural gas purchases,[35] Canada based its mandated export price on a formula

---

34. That is, regulate imports and approve import applications according to negotiated agreements between governments.

35. For example, from Mexico by pipeline and (potentially) from Indonesia and Algeria by LNG vessels.

agreed upon with the American government[36]. Thus, although the price was in fact close to the maximum the market would bear, it was set with reference to its commodity or substitution value as defined above and this may have assisted the Americans in their negotiations on other imports. However technical- or scientific-looking the Canadian formula, the Canadian price was not set rigidly. In the early 1980s, U.S. natural gas demand fell due to a slowdown in economic activity, and increased U.S. gas production. This created a surplus of U.S. gas, and in response, the Canadian border price stopped increasing, and was no longer tied directly to comparative international oil prices. After November, 1984, a variety of border prices, tailored to the specifics of individual applications were authorized, provided certain minimum conditions were met.

Also, in the period 1980 to 1984, sales at non-peak times (such as over the summer months) virtually stopped or fell to absolute minimum levels, and Canadian imports were used as a peak supply, with baseload gas being purchased from (cheaper) United States sources. In these circumstances, the rigidities of the Canadian export regulation, while maintaining the relatively attractive export price, did not permit Canadian exporters to complete with American producers on price. Consequently, delivery volumes plummeted as did total export revenues.

Recognizing the need to react, on October 31, 1985, agreement was reached between the federal government and the producing provinces on how to achieve a market-oriented pricing system, appropriate for the market environment at the time of this writing. In this agreement the federal government agreed to amend its policy in regard to the conditions exporters of natural gas would have to meet for gas exported under licence. To obtain approval, in the future all licence holders will have to demonstrate that their negotiated contractual arrangements meet the following criteria:

"i) the price of exported gas must recover its appropriate share of costs incurred;
ii) the price of exported natural gas shall not be less than the price charged to Canadians for similar types of service in the area or zone adjacent to the export point;

---

36. The "substitution value" formula was agreed upon between the Canadian Energy Minister and the U.S. Secretary of Energy. The 1980 version came to be known as the Duncan-Lalonde formula.

iii) export contracts must contain provisions which permit adjustments to reflect changing market conditions over the life of the contract;
iv) exporters must demonstrate that export arrangements provide reasonable assurance that volumes contracted will be taken; and
v) exporters must demonstrate that producers supplying gas for an export project endorse the terms of the export arrangement and any subsequent revisions thereof."[37]

This new policy, is therefore a return to a modified version of the criteria announced in 1967. Its key difference with the 1967 criteria is that it recognizes the marketing difficulties that can be encountered and the potential volatility of North American natural gas markets. These new criteria are meant to carry the industry into an era of deregulated markets as all Canadian domestic prices are to be freely negotiated after November 1, 1986, and domestic prices will no longer be prescribed.

There are a wide number of options open to a government related to export prices in a context such as exists between Canada and the United States on natural gas trade. The main feature of any good alternative is that it must preserve flexibility as is the case with Canada's current policy. It must recognize that for trade in natural gas, as with all other commodities (and most manufacturers) there is no one way street where prices and revenues will continue to post real increases or even maintain real value over time. Flexibility is the key.

While this may be widely recognized, human nature is such that governments or regulators may still wish to gain the points that come from getting industry and the Canadian public what appears to be the best prices on exports and appearing to get benefits that would otherwise not be obtained from trade. In practice, it may be very difficult in traditionally regulated external and domestic environments as exist in the natural gas sector, to allow export sales to occur at prices below domestic levels (and this in spite of the subtle logic which indicates that maintaining a given level of deliveries over the entire year is a valuable feature in itself).

---

37. <u>Agreement Among the Governments of Canada, Alberta, British Columbia and Saskatchewan on Natural Gas Markets and Prices</u>, October 31, 1985, paragraph 18.

One way of maintaining flexibility, although it has never been tried in Canada, would be to have several identified components to an export price, a basic component, set by government in relation to a formula or concept such as commodity value or substitution value, and two others that could be set on a case-by-case basis, either by government or the contracting parties or by some combination of both. One of these would recognize the value of the gas in a specific market at a specific point in time; the other would reflect a given producer's valuation of making sales over a shorter or longer timeframe. This last component should be left much more in the hands of individual producers, as it is unclear how a government regulatory authority could second guess the specific needs and investment plans of individual producers.

Such a multi-tier pricing scheme would probably allow exports to occur in a manner that allows for variance of both prices and volumes, and therefore, would address maximizing revenues rather than merely price. The above discussion does introduce the importance of actual sales volumes and, in the next chapter, the regulation of export volumes is examined. Once these two components of export regulation are considered, the study will examine their overall effect and what alternative regulatory systems could look like. Potential elements such as export taxes, a marketing board, and other alternatives to the approval of specific contracts arrived at by specific export applicants are considered.

11

Protecting Domestic Requirements for Natural Gas

Apart from regulating export prices, the Canadian government has regulated the volumes of natural gas contracted for export. The purpose of regulating the exportable volumes was to ensure that reasonably foreseeable domestic requirements would be satisfied before natural gas was committed for export.[1]

Security of supply of natural gas has, therefore, been guaranteed in Canada by government fiat rather than by arrangements between private parties using available market mechanisms. For example, Canadian natural gas distribution companies could contract for reserves to meet the total expected future requirements plus some extra margin, if desired, in competition with purchasers in the export market. Protection of domestic requirements by the federal government in the manner chosen makes such forward purchase contracts unnecessary and shifts the costs of security of supply to be shared between importers and holders of natural gas reserves, with potential consequences for the value of established reserves, royalties, land bonus payments, profits, income taxes, and export and domestic prices.

---

1. As discussed, the political basis for instituting a policy to regulate exportable volumes was to have potential exporters agree to supply domestic markets as part of the "cost" of exporting. Thus, by the <u>Electricity and Fluid Exportation Act</u> of 1907, electricity exporters were, in fact, required to supply electric power to Canadian markets in southern Ontario before they could export electricity to the United States. Similarly, C.D. Howe's statements in 1953 required potential natural gas exporters to acquiesce to his demands that a Trans-Canada pipeline be put in place from Alberta to Montreal before additional natural gas exports were permitted.

The Exportable Surplus Mechanism

Until 1959, export licences were issued by the Minister of Trade and Commerce. No hearings were held, and there was no formal procedure, open to public scrutiny, that was applied to determine whether proposed exports were surplus to expected Canadian requirements. When the National Energy Board (NEB) was created in 1959, the <u>National Energy Board Act</u> empowered the Board to regulate natural gas exports and imports in a manner that reflected the policy recommendations made by the Borden Commission. Federal government policy was to allow exports for terms long enough to support the required investment in natural gas processing and transmission facilities, provided that the gas was surplus to domestic requirements and that the proposed export prices were judged appropriate. Policy regarding imports of natural gas was that imports would not be allowed to prevent the sale of Canadian natural gas to Canadian markets. However, imports would be permitted to supplement Canadian natural gas supplies or to encourage the development of markets to be made available later to Canadian supplies. These policies were basically consistent with the Borden Commission's optimism regarding the relative abundance of Canadian reserves of natural gas compared with foreseeable domestic requirements.

Over the period in question, there was no public, systematic examination of the total costs and benefits of exports in general or of a given specific export.[2] Rather, when presented with applications for exports, over the period until 1974, the NEB rather mechanically proceeded to estimate whether or not a surplus existed, and if so, whether the proposed export price was appropriate. Between 1974 and 1984, uniform export prices were set by the government, leaving only the volumes and other non-price terms and conditions to be considered. In assessing applications in the late 1970s and 1980s, the Board did examine a variety of non-price factors for a specific export such as rates of take, take-or-pay provisions, requirements for new transmis-

---

2. It must be pointed out, however, that omnibus export hearings which were conducted in two phases, one to determine whether a surplus exists and one to consider the merits of competing export applications, have been held in 1982 and 1983, a decision taken after the appointment of Mr. G. Edge as chairman of the NEB in 1979.

sion facilities, Canadian content, economic spin-offs, degree of Canadian ownership and the like.[3]

Looking at the manner in which Canada has calculated an "exportable surplus" of natural gas over the years, one is tempted to say that Canada has been an open, fair and predictable exporter whose procedures for determining surplus are at least explained to applicants and potential applicants. However, on close examination, one sees that the technical and scientific-looking formulae used by the NEB over the years have been varied very frequently. In fact, it could be argued by some that these formulae may have been used to justify a decision to permit or deny exports based on a number of other factors. In other words, despite the rhetoric, rather than being a constraint on the regulator, the procedures may have been adapted to support a desire to tighten or relax exports as market expectations change over time.

Going back to its origins, in March 1960, the NEB applied its first surplus calculations to carry out its responsibilities related to the protection of domestic requirements.[4] At that time the NEB calculated two surpluses to determine the volumes of natural gas that exceeded reasonably foreseeable domestic requirements -- a "current" surplus and a "future" surplus.[5]

The NEB's first step in calculating the current surplus was to estimate future requirements for Canadian natural gas by considering three factors. The first of these was future Canadian requirements. Natural gas requirements for a 21-year protection period were estimated by forecasting Canadian demand for four years and projecting the fourth year requirement over the remaining years of the 21-year term. The second factor to be considered was the commitments remaining under then existing export licences. The final consideration in the calculation was the amount of gas required under the export application then being considered by the NEB.

---

3. It is noted that as there was no surplus available (as then calculated) no new licences were issued after 1971 until 1980. A new surplus determination procedure was put in place in 1979 which indicated that a surplus existed, meaning that some new exports would be allowed (Canada, National Energy Board (1979)).

4. <u>National Energy Board Act</u>, R.S.C. 1970, S.83, sub (a).

5. Canada, National Energy Board (1960a).

The reserves necessary to support these requirements were calculated on the basis of a formula which considered in the first place, the volume of gas to be delivered to the pipeline over the period of projection; and, in the second place, the volume of pipeline gas required to be in place in the reservoir in the terminal year of the projection in order to supply peak-day deliverability.

To determine whether a current surplus existed, the NEB compared the required reserves thus calculated with the NEB's estimate of established reserves. Generally, the NEB relied on industry data, and interpreted this data to estimate the size of Canada's established reserves. Established reserves were defined to include all proven reserves plus a varying percentage, not exceeding fifty percent, of probable reserves. If this comparison did not indicate a current surplus, it was intended that the Board would reject the export application. If a current surplus did exist, then the NEB would do another calculation to determine whether a "future surplus" existed as well.

For the purpose of a future surplus calculation, Canadian requirements were estimated for a thirty-year period by forecasting total requirements over the full thirty-year term. (In the current surplus test, annual requirements were held constant at the fourth year level for the remaining years of the 21-year term.) Future export requirements and the determination of required reserves were estimated in the same manner as for the current surplus calculation. After determining required reserves, the NEB estimated available future gas reserves, which included the expected trend additions to reserves. If a comparison of NEB estimates of available and required future reserves indicated a surplus, an export application would be approved, subject to appropriate pricing.

Features of the above, apparently technical calculation of surplus, were changed and reinterpreted over the period under study. These modifications are now set out and how the procedures were applied is considered.

In July 1965, the NEB made four significant modifications to its method of determining current surplus.[6] The first three changes related to which

---

6. Canada, National Energy Board (1965b) pp. 4-28 to 4-38.

reserves could be included in the calculations.[7] The fourth modification related to natural gas reserved for use within Alberta.[8]

In its August 1966, decision on an export application by TransCanada Pipelines, the NEB modified the procedures again and set out the "principles" by which it intended to determine the exportable surplus.[9] These three principles became known as the 25A4 rule. They were as follows:

1) "Available reserves will include the remaining volumes under existing import licences, plus contractible reserves. The Board considers contractible reserves to be those established reserves which it believes a purchaser will be able to contract for, with delivery to begin within the next four years.

2) "Protection of Canadian gas requirements at an adequate level will be achieved if an amount of reserves equal to 25 times the estimated requirements level for the fourth year is set aside. The multiplier of 25 was selected not only because it appears to the Board to supply adequate protection under presently foreseeable circumstances, but also because it corresponds with the 25-year maximum term for export licences which can be granted by the

---

7. First, fifty percent of the Alberta and the B.C. reserves then considered to be beyond economic reach were considered as being available to meet Canadian requirements and export commitments. The Board's second modification was that reserves not expected to be available during the the period of protection for reasons of conservation by the Alberta Board were excluded from the calculation of available reserves. Thirdly, reserves which had been allocated for the protection of peak-day requirements in the terminal year of an export commitment and which would become available for other use after the termination of the licence were included in the surplus.

8. Following the practice of the Alberta Board, for the purpose of its calculation of a current surplus, the net Alberta requirements to be met from "reserves available" (Established Reserves as adjusted by the above factors) were taken as the full thirty-year requirements, less two years' growth in reserves.

9. Canada, National Energy Board (1966c).

Board. The fourth-year level was selected because it corresponds with the current policy of the pipeline companies in contracting for the purchase and sale of gas. These contracts provide for a time interval of not more than four years before acceptance and delivery of gas to meet forward requirements.
"In cases where authorization for removal of gas from the province in which it is produced is required by a statute of the province, the amount of protection provided for markets in the province will be the amount set by the province to be its requirement or the amount computed by the above rule, whichever is greater.

3) "Canadian market requirements, existing export licences, and those for which applications are under consideration, will not be given terminal year peak-day protection from established reserves provided that a surplus is indicated by calculating the difference between: (a) the the established reserves plus those indicated by the trends in the growth of reserves, and (b) the forecast Canadian requirements over a 30-year period, including terminal year peak-day protection plus export commitments and, further provided that in the opinion of the Board, the trend in the growth of reserves justifies continued confidence."

The application of these three principles significantly modified the current surplus calculation. By limiting its consideration to "contractible reserves", the NEB excluded reserves which were "beyond economic reach" from its estimate of available reserves. The period of protected Canadian requirements was also extended from 21 to 25 years and the requirement to meet the peak-day demand in the terminal year was dropped.

The future surplus calculation remained unchanged. However, its importance was significantly reduced since a future surplus was no longer a necessary condition for the approval of an export application. If no future surplus existed, the current surplus had to be recalculated to ensure that available reserves were adequate to provide terminal-year peak-day protection for Canadian requirements, and for exports committed or under consideration.

The details of the calculations were relaxed in August 1970. In a decision on seven simultaneous natural gas export applications,[10] (rather than modify its already relatively complex current surplus determination formulae) the NEB allowed fifty percent of reserves beyond economic reach and a part of the reserves deferred for supply conservation by Alberta to be included in its estimate of available reserves which was used to calculate the current surplus. (Even in the 1965 procedure, these Alberta reserves had been excluded.) At the same time, the NEB relaxed its method of calculating the future surplus. The period of calculation was reduced to twenty years from thirty, and peak-day requirements were no longer protected.

In addition, while not specifically part of the surplus determination procedure, in 1970, the NEB decided that because of possible future increases in price and lower expected deliverability, a fifteen-year limit should be placed on incremental licences to existing export systems. Export applications for 23-year periods applied for by Alberta and Southern, and Canadian-Montana were therefore granted for only fifteen years. TransCanada was granted an export licence for twenty years (it had applied for twenty-five years), but this was stated to be a special case. The NEB granted these export licences despite having calculated a small negative "Future Surplus". However, in its report, the Board emphasized the vital importance of an increased rate of discovery if substantial new exports were to be possible in the future.

Later in 1970 the NEB relaxed its tests further. In the matter of an Inter-City Gas application for an export of 200.9 Bcf, the Board granted its approval even though this resulted in a "current surplus" deficit of 55 Bcf. The NEB argued that this amount could be considered as being allocated from "trend" gas.[11]

In a November 1971, decision on additional gas export applications, the NEB estimated a deficiency of 1.1 Tcf from its current surplus calculation. As a result, the export applications were dismissed despite confidence at the time that new discoveries would augment existing reserves beyond the indicated deficiency. Thus, in this case, the NEB did not rely upon trend gas to offset deficits in current surplus calculations.[12] The surplus formula underwent significant modification in 1979 and again in 1982, as natural gas

---

10. Canada, National Energy Board (1970a).

11. Canada, National Energy Board (1970b).

12. Canada, National Energy Board (1971).

markets continued to evolve. In November 1985, the federal government and the producing provinces stated in an agreement that the "governments anticipate that reviews of surplus tests underway or shortly to be initiated by the National Energy Board and by the appropriate provincial authorities will result in significantly freer access to domestic and export markets and thus will contribute to the achievement of the market-oriented pricing system contemplated in this Agreement."[13] Thus, one would expect that a new technical procedure will be put in place in the near future.

Observations on the Application of the Surplus Formula

The "exportable surplus" policy for natural gas was originally used by the federal government to promote (or persuade industry into undertaking) the construction of the TransCanada Pipeline to bring western natural gas to eastern Canada. It was understood that only after eastern markets were connected, would additional natural gas exports be allowed. If the key short-term objective of the government in instituting a surplus determination procedure was to achieve the construction of this domestic pipeline, then the policy was successful. While this may be true, this short-term objective was never explicitly stated. Moreover, the policy remained in place after the TransCanada Pipeline was built. Indeed, it is doubtful whether any formal procedure was ever developed to meet the original objective.

Before the National Energy Board was created, and an explicit surplus determination procedure developed (1960), there was no public method for evaluating whether applied for exports were surplus to domestic needs. Rather, licences were issued by the Minister of Trade and Commerce, and no calculations of surplus were made public (if indeed any were formally carried out).

Although the immediate objective had been attained, the policy of protecting Canadian requirements remained intact and was incorporated into the <u>National Energy Board Act</u>. It is likely that this policy statement had considerable political appeal. Given this mandate and responsibility, the Board had to develop a procedure to make sure domestic requirements were protected for a reasonable period into the future.

---

13. <u>Agreement Among the Governments of Canada, Alberta, British Columbia and Saskatchewan on National Gas Markets and Prices</u>, October 31, 1985, paragraph 16.

However, as is observed from the above overview, although the NEB's surplus determination formulae appear to be precise and technical measures, in fact, over the years the procedures were applied in a very flexible manner. Also, the method of calculating surpluses underwent frequent change. Four key items have varied most in the surplus determination calculations. These are:

1) the definition of supply, that is, natural gas reserves eligible for inclusion in the calculations;
2) the method of calculating demand, that is, whether to use a best estimate of actual requirements or a "no-growth" scenario using a specific-year estimate as the base year;
3) the length of the protection period; and
4) the stated importance of protecting peak-day requirements.

In addition, when looked at over time, it looks like the NEB, as well as the government, used the surplus determination procedure much more as an informational tool than as a constraint on authorization of exports. This point is exemplified several times by the approval of export applications by the Board and subsequently by the Governor in Council even when the exportable surplus calculations then in use indicated that no surplus existed.

There is no evidence that the costs and benefits of the various procedures chosen and of possible alternatives were systematically considered until the end of the period under study. Only the NEB reports issued towards the end of the period give an indication that such analysis was systematically considered.[14]

The Value of Security of Supply

Although the variables in the numerous formulae that have been used (for example the 25A4 formulae used by the NEB after 1966) do not appear to have been fixed with reference to economic criteria, it is reasonable to suggest that various levels of domestic security of supply do have differing values to domestic consumers. In addition, they do imply differing levels of cost to those who must incur costs or forego or defer benefits in order to provide a secure supply.

---

14. Canada, National Energy Board (1977).

As is the case with other commodities used in society, if a secure supply of natural gas were not guaranteed, natural gas consumers would have to evaluate the costs and risk of supply disruption and/or curtailment, and, where they individually deem it appropriate:

1) install facilities to burn (more expensive or less desirable) alternative fuel sources that could be used if the natural gas supply were no longer available. A distribution system for the alternative supply and "stand-by" supply contracts would also be required. Both users and potential (stand-by) users would have to pay for these "stand-by" facilities, often as a "demand" charge. Also, sufficient delivery capacity would have to be put into place to meet potential demand in the event "stand-by" customers actually did draw on the available supply;
2) install storage facilities for natural gas or alternative fuels; and/or
3) make provision for lost output (industrial and commercial users) or a lower level of comfort (residential users) that would occur if natural gas supply were disrupted.

Transmission companies and distributors would have to evaluate the risk of supply disruption and/or curtailment, and where appropriate:

1) contract for future expected delivery requirements from proven reserves;
2) take the risk of supply disruption into account when making investment decisions. For example, pipeline investors could build in a higher than currently required return-to-equity on pipeline investments, or, alternatively require companies to amortize transmission facilities more quickly to ensure investment is recaptured while deliveries are more certain. In an industry regulated on a cost of service basis, this would likely result in a higher tariff and thus higher prices to natural gas customers. Depending on the regulatory environment, in combination with higher returns to equity, or more rapid amortization, transmission and distribution companies would be expected to demonstrate a preference to build lower capacity lines,

3) with a greater likelihood these smaller lines would be used to full capacity over the lifetime of contracted reserves; and/or construct storage facilities at appropriate locations along the transmission system to protect against temporary or short term disruption of service where this is perceived as a cost-effective measure.

The extent to which users, transporters and distributors engage in these activities is a function of the expected costs of supply disruption for a given period of time and how a given measure will impact on these costs; the costs of the measure itself, and the decision-makers perception of the likelihood of a disruption in supply occurring over time; and the expected costs and other effects of such disruptions.

To summarize, the value of supply security for a given known minimum period is largely related to the cost of converting to another energy source before the "plant" related to burning natural gas in a given geographic area has reached the end of its useful life, that is, the unexpected and accelerated obsolescence of pipelines, gas plants, and natural gas burning equipment. These costs would include the economic waste that would be obtained if a regional economy had to rapidly shift, without sufficient advance notice, from natural gas to other fuel sources.

The costs of a government regulation on exports whose purpose is to protect domestic natural gas requirements are related to the size of the inventory of natural gas that sellers are required to set aside specifically for the domestic market and the "quality" of that inventory. "Quality" would refer to the certainty that a given quantity of reserves actually exists and can be delivered to users in Canada.

From the point of view of trade dependency, putting in place a policy such as this may make sense for exporters of commodities that could be considered strategic. In such a case, particularly if the situation is one in which the sector is largely foreign-owned and controlled, potential exporters would have an interest in delineating additional reserves, thus reducing uncertainties in this respect to the level deemed to be required by the host country. The other side of the coin is that requiring the maintenance of larger than necessary inventories usually involves substantial costs which would reduce the size of potential rents and which reduction may be borne in full or in part by the host country in terms of reduced royalties, taxation of profits, and similar rent collection mechanisms. In addition, such a policy, to the extent it affects producers, is in many ways similar to a tax, and in this respect would be expected to reduce exploration and production, an effect that would be the opposite of that desired by the policy.

12

Alternative Regulatory Mechanisms

This chapter looks at alternative mechanisms by which the federal government of Canada could regulate trade in natural gas to achieve its policy objectives. The first set of alternatives to be set out, are those that would fit within the current regulatory framework as modifications or adjustments. A second set are discrete alternatives which could replace current mechanisms.

The first set would include:

1) price only or volume only regulation (that is to say, not both price and volume); and
2) the issuing of tradeable (transferable) export licences.

The second set would include:

1) no government regulation;
2) a marketing board for natural gas exports; and
3) a natural gas export tax.

Either Price or Volume

Although politically appealing, government regulation of both export prices and the volume of exports may well mean that revenues are not maximized at any given point in time. Whichever factor is constraining sales, the other may be reducing total sales revenue. For example, if exportable volumes are the constraint, it would be expected that in the absence of an export price or minimum price conditions set by the federal government, export prices would be bid up, up to the point that no volumes in excess of those deemed "surplus" would be desired. On the other hand, if price is the constraint, total volumes deemed "exportable" will not be exported and it is a matter for further case-by-case analysis as to whether revenues would be maximized or as to how much additional sales (and thus revenue) would be generated by a given decrease in price.[1]

Regulation of price only or of exportable volumes only would thus merit careful consideration. Looking first at regulation of price, there are numerous types of regulation that could be undertaken. As was the case for the period from 1950 to 1974, the government could examine and approve prices set by contracting parties on a contract-by-contract basis. Or, as was the case from 1974 to 1984, the government could set a uniform border price. Since 1984, negotiated prices have been allowed provided certain minimum conditions are met, namely that the sale will be of benefit to Canada and that the export price is not below the domestic price.[2] Variations on these two basic alternatives would be for the government:

1) to set a floor price for all exports and allow upwards variations to be negotiated between specific contracting parties;
2) to set different border prices for gas sold into different export markets;
3) to set a uniform floor price for natural gas sold at the wellhead, with transportation to the border point added to the wellhead price; and
4) to set a price for a given minimum volume of exports with additional volumes subject to a set or negotiated premium or, if warranted by market conditions, a discount.

Of course there are other variations and combinations that could be used. These variations could take account of the variance in the value of a specific

---

1. See comments by A. R. Tussing at a conference organized by the Financial Post entitled "Canada's Natural Gas Exports," Toronto, February 23, 24, 1983.

2. There is, of course, a large measure of judgement and subjectivity to these minimum conditions. There is also a fair amount of judgement required to compare border prices in say, British Columbia, with a "domestic price" which is set at the Toronto city-gate. In November 1985, this rule was relaxed to permit exports where the prices were not below domestic prices in Canada in markets near the border point. This served to remove the transportation charges from Alberta to the Toronto city gate from the previous "domestic price".

quantity of natural gas over the course of the year, and the value of a given level of deliverability (which could translate into a demand charge plus a commodity charge for natural gas sales).

The advantage of a government-set price or floor is that, due to the structure of the export market, this could serve to increase the negotiating strength of Canadian sellers, and thus the export prices that could be negotiated by any individual seller. This is expected because of the relatively small number of buyers of Canadian natural gas.[3] Certainly this could

---

3. There is a debate as to the extent to which sales could be made anywhere in the United States and delivered by displacement. On the one hand, it is argued that the entire market is linked and excess capacity in one transmission system could be used to transport gas for other transmission companies. Also, it is argued that sales through displacement should be possible everywhere in the system. On the other side of the coin, it is argued that transmission companies are in competition with each other, and are generally not interested in transporting some other company's gas. Rather, they want to move and sell their own gas. Also, state regulatory commissions, in general, appear to have removed a good deal of the incentives for geographic swaps in many cases. For example, in the case of an application for a sale of Indonesian LNG to New York City via displacement, and actually delivered in California, the ruling of the California regulatory commission killed the project as it would have caused the lion's share of the benefits to be passed on to natural gas customers in California through lower prices. The Commission was not really interested in seeing facilities paid for by Californian customers used for the benefit of customers in New York. The utilities that set up the deal, therefore, would only have been allowed to recover their costs and deliver the gas, which does not provide much incentive to look for more swap deals. However, leadership from the federal level of government, to encourage displacement sales by more significant financial incentives to the transmission companies, could make the U.S. marketplace much less fragmented (discrete regional markets) than it is at the present time. (Some facts based on presentations made at a conference organized by the Financial Post, held in Toronto Canada, February 23, 24, 1983 by J. E. Coventon, Vice-President Transcontinental Pipeline Company (Houston) and A. R. Tussing, an economist and consultant (Seattle, Washington)).

change over time as technological improvements in transporting LNG open new markets to Canadian natural gas.

On the other hand, given recent indications that a spot market for natural gas in North America is developing, and given the growth of new brokerage firms to sell natural gas to a large number of direct purchasers, there is no reason to believe that a government regulator will have a better feel for a specific market at a given point in time than an actual exporter or his sales agent. Similarly, there is much less reason to think that export prices will be higher due to governmental involvement.

The market for natural gas has changed, particularly of late. Until the 1980s, natural gas prices were held down in the United States and as such, natural gas was a bargain compared with alternative fuel supplies. Thus, over the period, marketing natural gas was not difficult. In the 1980s, however, energy prices, including the value of (deregulated U.S.) natural gas, will surely fluctuate,[4] and any regulated export prices must have this flexibility built into them so that exporters can respond to fluctuating conditions in the marketplace. The development of a spot market for natural gas in the United States will provide key signals for the pricing of incremental sales of natural gas into the U.S. system. Any regulated export prices would have to be consistent with spot sales or other current domestic U.S. contracts, against which Canadian natural gas imports would have to compete.

Turning now to regulation of exportable volumes, if, through a well-defined "exportable-surplus" calculation or "desired level of exports"[5] calculation, a given quantity of natural gas was designated to be available for exports over a specific period of time, exporters could then negotiate contracts for these volumes and compete for licences. Licences would be issued on the basis of net benefit to Canadians, and price would be one important consideration to distinguish differing applications.

---

4. See, for example, U.S. General Accounting Office (1982).

5. This would relate to a level of exports that could be greater or lesser than an exportable surplus, and would include additional considerations such as price expectations, desirability of increasing industry cash flow to fund exploration, spin-offs and forward and backward linkages generated by export sales, and such.

This would reduce the scope of the tasks to be undertaken by the regulator, and put more onus on each exporter to outdo the other. The regulator, while it could maintain contacts and undertake some market intelligence, would not have to actually define specific price levels. Competition between holders of natural gas reserves to seek out profitable export opportunities could be enhanced by requiring transmission companies to act as common carriers. That is, where capacity is available, they would be required to carry gas they do not own.

Transferable Export Licences

In addition to and apart from the above modifications to existing policies, once export licences are issued, be it through the current process in which maximum volumes are licenced to be exported at an approved export price, or through a modified pricing procedure as discussed above, licences to export volumes of natural gas could be made transferable.[6]

If exporters were allowed to transfer the right to export gas to any other exporter, a market would be expected to develop for these licences which, ultimately, would be expected to cause exports to take place in the most lucrative export market, at the best price available. Taking this concept one step further, government, rather than issuing transferable licences to specific export applicants could, once it has determined the desirable level of exports over time, issue export licences or certificates (that could expire after a given timeframe) to all holders of natural gas reserves. In addition, government could allow the marketplace to allocate these export rights, thus avoiding the (often substantial) costs of the hearing and application process. Variations of this option would include the government auctioning these rights or selling these rights to selected purchasers, using a variety of criteria. For example, rights could be distributed or sold only to exploration companies, on some basis such as their footage drilled, or extent of new discoveries. If desired, other factors such as the degree of foreign ownership of a purchaser or recipient of rights could be brought into the calculation. Sale of rights, by auction or other means, could be used as an alternative to export price regulation.

---

6. Over the period under study, and currently, licences to export gas are not transferable, and are for a specific exporter to deliver natural gas to a specific importer at a specific border point.

It is difficult to see why transferability of the right to export would not be a marked improvement over the export rights issued over the period under study. Such a system would allow the most useful and lucrative use of Canadian natural gas exports. Also, under a system of non-transferability, if a given exporter cannot sell his maximum allowable volume, this part of the total volume deemed "exportable" will not be sold, and this is a lost opportunity in terms of export sales foregone (or deferred) through an overly rigid "export rights" system. If given quantities of exports are desirable, a less rigid rights system increases the likelihood that they will in fact take place. Again, requiring natural gas transmission companies to act as common carriers would enhance export opportunities under a system of transferable licences.

In addition, it is possible that a North American natural gas spot or short term market could become established over the next few years and the issuance of transferable export licences could facilitate such a development. In particular, regional surpluses of natural gas in parts of the United States could make it advantageous for an Ontario distributor to import U.S. gas from Kansas or Oklahoma for example rather than buy it from Alberta producers.[7] This would reduce energy costs to Canadian customers but would not be welcomed by Alberta producers. With a system of transferable export licences, Canadian importers of U.S. gas could receive export licences to match their imports and trade these in the transferable licences market so that they could be used by western exporters. In such a case, exporters would avoid the need to go through an expensive and time consuming hearings process. If it were not considered desirable to allow importers to trade these licences, then export licences to offset imports could be put into the market directly by the government regulator using any of the methods cited earlier.

All of the above modifications could be adopted without a major new direction being adopted for natural gas exports from Canada. The ideas presented below are more distinct, and would constitute a significant shift in approach. The concepts of no government export regulation, the establishment of a marketing board for natural gas exports and a natural gas export tax are discussed below.

---

7. See, for example, "Union Gas makes deal for U.S. imports," Globe and Mail, December 20, 1985, p. B1.

No export regulation

Under this option, export contract terms and conditions would be set by contracting parties only. Government revenues would obtain from royalties, land bonuses and the fiscal system. The guiding principle here is that the appropriate minimum prices and share of economic rents would be set and captured through the royalty structure and expected future rents, captured through competitive land auctions. As such auctions could well under-value future rents, an actual share of taxable profits would be obtained through the fiscal system. Government regulatory activity related to "prices" therefore, would take place through these mechanisms rather than through regulating specific exports.[8]

Protection of the domestic market requirements would take place through the operation of the marketplace through which domestic utilities would be expected to contract for their "foreseeable" future requirements. If desired, in order to maintain the goal of protecting domestic requirements, as a type of minimum but indirect regulatory requirement for exports, all proposed export terms and conditions could first have to be offered by potential exporters to domestic purchasers; only where there is no interest expressed by Canadian buyers, could the exports take place. Domestic purchasers could have legal remedies in cases where they were not given first right of refusal. In such a situation, domestic customers would have to compete with export customers to obtain gas supplies. This could possibly, but not necessarily, push up domestic prices. In fact, if imports too were not restricted, it is possible that some Canadian distributors could purchase surplus U.S. gas more cheaply than gas from western Canada.

Removal of export controls would result in a variety of export prices being produced as has been the case since November, 1984, and as was the case prior to 1974. (A uniform border price was set from 1974 to 1984). While this scheme would allow producers to compete on price and to sell any and all gas they wished, it may not maximize revenues to Canada, nor control the timing of development. The various U.S. regional mar-

---

8. See Waverman (1981), who takes the position that the actual measurement of rent is most difficult and "designing fiscal instruments to efficiently and equitably collect rent [is] impossible" (p. 225).

ketplaces[9] are not truly competitive as there are really not that many buyers of Canadian gas. Selling into this type of market might produce lower prices as a small group of U.S. buyers plays off potential Canadian producers against one another. The situation could be quite different, however, if the numbers of importers were increased. This could occur through technological advance which allowed natural gas to be transported cheaply and in volume to markets outside North America, or through removal of the U.S. regulatory constraints that now prevent easy, profitable and rapid sale of Canadian natural gas by displacement to U.S. markets where it is most required.

On the other hand, if conditions change eventually, and the U.S. market becomes tight, with not much new supply available, as was the case for most of the period under the study,[10] purchasing transmission companies, which are regulated utilities and which can recover the cost of gas purchases as a cost of service, would have little incentive to bargain prices down. On the contrary, they would have an incentive to bid prices up so that they would have sufficient supplies to completely service their market areas. Their major constraint on what they could ultimately pay would be whether gas at that price would sell (in relation to competitive fuels). This would probably not be a major constraint to prices paid for imports which are a relatively small fraction of total purchases, provided of course, that the cost of these new marginal supplies was rolled-in with the cost of all other gas (including cheaper "old" gas, purchased under long term contracts) and sold at the average cost plus transmission charges.

An Export Marketing Board

A marketing board for natural gas exports could, in principle, be a good mechanism for securing maximum

---

9. Regional marketplaces exist because of the bottlenecks and regulatory constraints in place over the U.S. interstate natural gas transmission sector. These conditions are evolving, however, and as time passes, the U.S. marketplace may become more and more, a unitary, national marketplace.

10. But this is not the situation at the time of this writing, nor is it likely to be the case for the next several years.

revenues for gas exports.[11] Such a board could be owned completely by the federal government or in partnership with provincial governments and/or the private sector.[12] It could be set up to sell gas considered surplus to Canadian requirements. This could be achieved through a hearings process, or by a less expensive, less complex method such as setting the purchase price for marketing board purchases at some level below the domestic price of gas. This would ensure that no natural gas which was attractive to domestic purchasers and for which they were willing to contract would be diverted to the export market.

If it were considered desirable, the marketing board could give preferential treatment to various gas sources. For example, it could first offer to purchase all gas available from frontier areas (technological as well as geographic frontier gas), or could give preference to small Canadian exploration companies, or any other particular seller. Another way such a board could purchase natural gas would be to take offer bids from potential sellers and purchase the gas on the most favorable terms offered in the market.

Looking at the effect of such a board on export sales, the export sales prices would then be made by a monopolist seller, and in principle, competing U.S. purchasers could be played off against one another for the new supplies being offered on the market.[13]

---

11. See for example, Hamilton (1973(a), 1973(b)). As for addressing the question of how such a board, or, as discussed in the next section of this chapter, an export tax would increase the probability of capturing a larger share of any economic rents that may be generated through production and sale into the export market, or how such rents should best be shared, see the thoughtful, and intelligent treatments given in Waverman (1981) and Scott (1976).

12. Such a set up could require a change from current arrangements by which transmission firms own the natural gas they carry in their transmission system. Canadian natural gas transmission companies would become common carriers, carrying natural gas for others. Alternatively, marketing board ownership of the gas could occur once the gas is delivered to the Canadian border.

13. Subject, of course, to any U.S. regulatory approvals required for imports.

The marketing board could perhaps, regulate timing of sales better than a large number of independent, competing sellers, and could perhaps be more effective in arranging for geographic swapping arrangements to be made as importers would only have to deal with one sales entity. If it were set up as a well-financed government entity, the board could be used to smooth out fluctuations in gas prices, paying only an expected average price for purchases, but allowing export receipts to be higher or lower than the purchase price at various points in time.[14] This kind of flexibility would be less likely from independent producers.

Hopefully, in such circumstances the board would operate profitably, although there is always the possibility of difficulties due to the governmental nature of such a board. If it were not set up to be a profitable, self-financing entity, there could sometimes be temptations by the government of the day to enter non-commercial considerations into the board's management processes which may or may not be beneficial to the public at large. The accountability of management in such a case is made much more difficult.

From the dependency perspective, such a board might not be any improvement from the private, regulated seller scenario, if the marketing board itself were "captured" by the industry. As with some marketing boards, while potentially a powerful agent for change, what is actually achieved goes beyond the structure of the board and the simple fact that it is a public agent of the Crown, to its actual performance and accomplishments. From a political vantage point, given the uncertainties of the marketplace, the scope for decision-making, the political payoffs for successes compared with the flak that would be generated by the inevitable errors of judgment, the attractiveness of setting up such a board compared with regulating private sector players seems marginal. After all, when times are good, the current set up allows the industry to prosper and government receipts to increase through royalties and taxes; when times are hard, receipts to all fall, but the government is not necessarily to blame. If such a board were in place, there would surely be lobbying which pointed to the "profits" earned in good times to justify subsidies during the bad times. It is worth noting however, that such an

---

14. This approach, of course, relies on accurate price forecasts and due to the uncertainties of the marketplace would work best over short, rather than medium term periods.

agency, and such arguments might make good sense for other commodities, and other exporting countries, particularly as regards commodities subject to regular, cyclic swings in international prices.

An Export Tax

Turning now to the concept of levying a tax on all natural gas exported from Canada, this would be an additional tool to regulate trade and to capture, for the Canadian public, via government receipts, a share of the gains from trade, and this, in addition to or in combination with royalties and land bonuses.[15] Under such a system, the tax itself could be adjusted from time to time or "tailor calculated" to suit the circumstances of export deliveries. Thus, the tax would be a tool which could be used to increase or decrease the attractiveness of existing or additional exports over time.

The tax could be uniform, or adjusted to reflect timing of deliveries over the course of the year. Adjustments could also be made for the export point (and thus the market into which the gas is delivered, excluding the effects of geographic swaps or displacement sales), or source of supply or nature of the seller (e.g. small Canadian exploration companies). In addition, theoretically, the tax could be set at a level which would ensure that any sales made were in excess of Canadian requirements. In any case, it could be levied in a manner which guaranteed that the export price would always exceed the domestic price; although, this of course does not guarantee that export revenues

---

15. See Powrie (1975) who demonstrated that, like a royalty, an export tax would be expected to reduce the total amount of the commodity discovered and produced and showed that export taxes and royalties are both inferior (in terms of economic loss to society) to profit-related production levies and income taxes. This author agrees with Powrie's analysis, but the administrative attractiveness of export taxes (or other excise taxes) and royalties in terms of simplicity of application are such that some level of royalty or export tax would generally be a useful feature in any resource owner's set of regulatory tools; these tools are improved if they can in some way be related to the profitability of exploiting a given resource deposit. Powrie's analysis does not examine the administrative costs and advantages of actually applying the specific measures.

would be maximized. In one sense, the export tax could create a floor price for export sales as no sales would be made that did not cover the "tax portion" (i.e. royalties plus export tax) of the resource cost to the exporter.

An important consideration, in the Canadian context, however, would be how such a tax would be expected to impact on provincial revenues. There is likely to be a direct effect on the size of land bonuses which are received by the provinces. Thus, depending on whether and how the export tax was shared with the affected provinces, such a tax may meet with extremely strong opposition from the provinces.[16] Of course, such a tax would probably not be in the interests of any producers unless it were combined as a necessary component of a total package which contained net benefits for producers.

Other Considerations

Apart from the protection of domestic requirements and the revenue maximization arguments, there is a set of additional, related considerations which bear on export regulation. These would include security of supply; reduction of uncertainty (delineation of the resource base); economic spin-offs from exports; and regional development which may, at times, relate to a desire to maintain a given level of exploration in a given area. In these cases, government may wish to induce additional exploration activity. Options to stimulate exploration, other than the general regulation of overall export prices and/or volumes, would include:

1) to permit unregulated export of new finds for a specific period. If regional development were a main consideration, such authorization could be made region-specific;
2) a variant of (1) would be to regulate all exports, but to accord preferential treatment to "new" gas discoveries over "old" gas; and
3) to encourage natural gas time swaps whereby exports would be allowed to take place, but where an obligation would be incurred by the importer to return the natural gas at some definite time in the future.

---

16. This was indeed the case when the idea was "floated" by the federal government of Canada in 1980 (See Canada, Department of Finance (1980) pp. 7-8).

Options (1), (2) and (3) above would not involve any direct government expenditure, and could be viewed as a way of allocating the "exportable surplus". Moving to measures which would directly impact on government revenue or expenditure, the intended impact of the measures listed below would be to put cash in the hands of exploration firms:

4) to allow fiscal incentives[17] or cash grants[18] for exploration expenditures;
5) to make government loans or guarantee private loans made against gas-in-the-ground as collateral; and
6) to actually purchase shut-in natural gas and store it as a government stockpile. Storage could be in the producing reservoir or in depleted fields.

These measures in effect, change the after-tax cost of funds committed to exploration. In this sense, to the extent that market forces related to risk-reward optimization by entrepreneurs can efficiently allocate a given supply of investment capital to its most lucrative (highest value) use, then some distortion away from non-exploratory investment will of course take place. The rationalization for such distortion of the normal functioning of the capital markets would be with the concept that individual, risk-averse investors would tend to under-invest in exploration related to other potential investments. In contrast, society as a whole can accept the aggregate (lower) risks faced from the prospect of a wider base and more intense drilling activity which still allows investors to choose what they consider to be the most attractive prospects, within the restrictions and constraints established by the government intervention. Society may also be willing to pay the equivalent of an insurance premium to reduce the level of uncertainties related to security of supply and the size of the resource base.

Looking at these measures individually, it is observed that while here discussed in terms of natural gas, these would also be applicable in the case of many other traded commodities.

---

17. Fiscal incentives were put in place in Canada over the period under study, and considerably sweetened over the mid-1970s.

18. A grant system was put in place starting in 1980 to replace some of the fiscal incentives in the petroleum sector in Canada.

As for the fiscal incentives and cash grants to encourage exploration, these have both been used extensively in Canada. Fiscal incentives were used for the entire period under study with grants being used in the period from 1980 until 1986 to encourage exploration in certain preferred areas by non foreign-controlled firms. The move from fiscal incentives to grants was made as the fiscal incentives were of more value to existing firms with taxable income than to other potential exploration firms. Grants on the other hand, would be paid without regard to the tax position of the firm, but, as they were implemented, were affected by the degree of Canadian ownership of the applicant.

Turning now to the concept of guaranteeing private loans or making government loans against gas-in-the-ground, or acquiring a government stockpile, such measures are subject to a number of drawbacks.[19]

In the first place, within the Canadian petroleum sector, there is always a market for petroleum assets. In addition, the nature of the various activities related to petroleum exploration and production is such that very few companies would ever be 100 percent shut-in; rather, ongoing companies would generally find that they have a variety of revenue-producing assets. In short, the problem would be one of companies and individuals, in what they perceive as a relatively high-growth, profitable industry, having sufficient revenues to participate in all the activities they wish to pursue. Conversely, in times of slumps or depression, companies may lack cash to maintain their existing level of assets.

A market exists for petroleum properties. Successful exploration in Canada always requires a decision to hold or sell discovered reserves. The successful explorer must decide on a mix of current and future activities and investment in:

---

19. Such a scheme was suggested in the National Energy Program of 1980 (See Canada, Department of Energy Mines and Resources (1980)). In this regard, a fact-finding team conducted a series of interviews with the petroleum industry and the Canadian chartered banks in March and April 1981. To date, no such scheme has been put in place in Canada. However, the views expressed in this study are the views of the author alone and may not reflect the views of the government of Canada or any of its departments or agencies. Neither do the views expressed here necessarily represent the views of the fact-finding team or any official of any government, bank or private or public petroleum company that may have been interviewed by that team.

1) proving up, developing and producing reserves;
2) new exploration activities; and
3) other investment opportunities.

These decisions are based on the risks the owners of these companies are prepared to take in relation to the expected return to investment in each type of activity.

A wide variety of private vehicles exists to permit a reserve holder to obtain cash for currently shut-in reserves. The amount of cash obtained would depend on the quality of the reserves. "Quality" is here used not only to refer to the technical qualities of the natural gas itself but also to the probability of the gas actually being produced and sold in a given timeframe. Proven, contracted for natural gas, already connected to a transmission system would thus be much higher "quality" than gas which has just been discovered by one discovery well, remote from all other known wells, hundreds of miles from the nearest transmission system.

Another significant issue merits consideration. If measures such as these were taken by government, careful thought would have to be given to the extremely difficult and subjective task of identifying "excess" shut-in gas. This would relate to the requirement for surplus gas and deliverability in order to protect future Canadian requirements,[20] the extent to which exploration has taken place in areas which are beyond economic reach, and the fact that there is a willingness of firms with different sizes, capital structures and risk aversion to "bank" natural gas, in the expectation of future price appreciation. Thus, the fact that some gas is "shut-in," does not in itself mean that this gas is "excess."

The market for established reserves would be expected to clear at prices deemed attractive to buyer and seller, based on their valuation of expected future cash flows. Sales and purchases would be expected to take place between exploration firms and firms that prefer to hold reserves as each would use different discount rates.

Any interventions "to increase cash flow" via the tools discussed above would thus be intervening in a market that can and does provide "cash flow" to companies holding natural gas reserves. That is, government

---

20. If this were to continue to be a component of Canada's export policy. In this case, the "excess" referred to is as set out in formulae, from time to time by the National Energy Board.

could subsidize (Canadian) companies by paying more than market value for reserves or by guaranteeing loans by banks, thus permitting loans against low quality reserves, or by making attractive prepayments for future gas production (similar to higher risk loans).Seen in this light, the question is not one of merely providing an increased cash flow, but one of providing a subsidy for a given activity.

Within this context, an inconsistency exists. Through one or more of these measures, government would attempt to provide financing to explorers holding shut-in gas which they "cannot sell" in order to encourage exploration within Canada. Successful exploration would in turn compound the problem of shut-in gas, unless markets for natural gas were to expand considerably.

In sum, the solution to this type of problem (that is, where government wishes to continue exploration and delineation of the resource base in spite of market constraints) can only be to market the discovered reserves. The wisdom of accumulating inventories, or subsidizing or financing the accumulation of inventories, depends on a government's forecast regarding future markets (both export and domestic) for the commodity. Given a positive view concerning the future markets for the commodity, an additional benefit that could be had from undertaking these measures would be that they could reduce the often violent fluctuations in exploration activity by Canadian explorers. If a near-term or medium-term improvement were expected in the market, such measures could serve to flatten out the bottom of a market cycle or temporarily reduce the severity of a downturn. The question then becomes one of whether the estimated costs of the measures are justified by the value of these potential benefits.

13

Conclusions

Apart from the conclusions related specifically to Canada's natural gas export policies, the case of non-renewable resources is applicable to the more general problems related to international commodity trade and dependency theory. Canada's attempts to regulate natural gas trade shed light on a number of fundamental issues.

Reviewing the evolution of the Canadian petroleum sector, Canada's natural gas exports and the history of how trade has been regulated over the period under study, several major developments stand out as likely to be experienced time and again for a wide variety of commodities and a broad number of exporters. Once these patterns of experience are contemplated, a number of conclusions can be derived, conclusions which go beyond the regional specifics of natural gas exports to the broader and general aspects of resource development, international trade and international political economy.

There are four major developments over the period 1945 to 1985. These are related to:

1) price appreciation and fluctuation;
2) increasing involvement of governments;
3) changing rules under which trade occurs; and
4) technological developments affecting supply and demand.

Price Appreciation and Fluctuation

Looking back over the history of Canada's natural gas exports, one observes a steady appreciation in nominal field and border prices until the 1970s. At that time, in response to price shocks related to internationally traded crude oil, nominal prices shot dramatically upwards and then stabilized for a short period (1980 to 1982) after which they declined. In terms of real as opposed to nominal prices, at times, prices appreciated at a rate faster than the level of inflation, while at other times, appreciation occurred at a rate slower than the general rate of inflation. During these periods of slow appreciation, rapid and steady appreciation, and decline, general perception of price levels and price expectations underwent substantial modification and these affected the actions and reactions of all the major players in the marketplace for natural gas.

The general observation is that once a certain change has occurred, human nature is such that a large number of market participants expect a trend, once it is reasonably well established, to continue for a long time (if not forever). Changing trends, and slowness of recognition of the impact of the response generated by a new trend amplify the difficulties for actors in the marketplace, including producers, sellers, buyers and government regulators, out to protect the public interest. When there was slow price appreciation, continuation of this trend was generally expected well into the future by producers, and both domestic customers and potential importers. Only when potential shortages began to appear possible were expectations slowly altered. For example, throughout the 1960s, although no "exportable surplus" was found by National Energy Board tests, the tests were modified to permit new export authorizations. Price increases which exceeded the rate of inflation were not expected. Only in the early 1970s, as the possibility of shortages developing became more real (and more rapid price appreciation therefore more likely),[1] were new exports refused by the National Energy Board.

During this early period, the problem was marketing. As the market shifted from a buyers' market to a sellers' market, the concern turned less and less on marketing the Canadian gas to get maximum development in western Canada, and more and more to extracting greater gains from a commodity that was becoming "more and more scarce," as growth of deliverable reserves slowed.

The question of "negotiating strength" of buyer and seller tended to shift. Due to market conditions and perceptions of the future, the attractiveness of present as opposed to future sales shifted and negotiating power moved from the buyer to the seller.

Once accelerating prices became accepted, as occurred in the 1970s, perceptions of the future

---

1. The value of security of supply would rise in proportion to the risk of supply disruption.

changed. All of a sudden, expectations changed dramatically and natural gas took on special features as a commodity where expected price increases would exceed the rate of inflation for many years to come.[2] Saving the resource for the distant future thus made sense and any sales made earlier rather than later were seen as including a type of gift or subsidy to the purchaser.

On the other hand, when prices stabilized, and later declined in the early 1980s, at first this was seen as giving away resources at "fire sale" prices. As perceptions became used to the new, difficult, marketing scenario, however, forecasts shifted totally in the opposite direction, and gloom and doom prevailed as the conventional wisdom for the long term. In short, perceptions take a long time to change, and price fluctuations, in which trends change direction, although readily apparent for all commodities over time, is rarely expected at any given point in time.

Although producers, consumers and regulators may, from time to time, single out special commodities which, for a given period, are not expected to be subject to greater-than-expected fluctuation, because of the large number of factors that together influence the value and market price of a given traded commodity, the uncertainties related to the pricing of that commodity must be recognized. Although the statement may seem contradictory, the high probability that a dramatic revision of expectations will be necessary should be acknowledged and anticipated. In spite of the very human need for stability and the desire to know that the future will unfold in an orderly fashion, traders and governments where they are involved, should try to complement their desires to believe in orderliness and stability with a realistic "early warning system" built into their plans. Plans should acknowledge that the future is unknown and contingency plans should be established in the event changes take place. No policy or plan is complete without some explicit manner to monitor, recognize, and deal with alternative developments from those that were expected in the short, and medium terms. Decision-makers must accept the fact that action taken and plans made today may not be correct after the passage of time and rapid shifts to meet changing circumstances may become attractive.

---

2. For example, the pricing aspects of Canada's National Energy Program of 1980 assumed a 2 percent real increase in price for at least the entire decade of the 1980s.

Long term plans are necessary to provide short term direction, but they will likely require frequent and regular reassessment and revision if they are to remain viable and realistic.

In terms of broader application, these observations cast doubt on the price stabilization measures being contemplated as set out in the second chapter of this study. This analysis adds to the evidence which suggests that no price stabilization scheme will succeed over the long term, and the most any such scheme can expect to achieve is a smoothing out of price fluctuation. Due to the substitution factor and the market mechanisms and social and political actions which tend to come into play from time to time in specific commodity markets in response to these fluctuations, stabilization schemes which attempt more than this or which work in a different direction than these powerful forces, will require more resources than could possibly be assembled in the current environment, and will likely be relatively short-lived. Such schemes are further doomed to very limited effectiveness due to the real competition that is faced between exporters of a given commodity and its substitutes and between importers and users of the specific commodities in order to process the proper mix of raw products into a given, useable, valuable output. The importers too are in competition as they bet on the right mix of inputs in order to gain over their competitors. Even in areas were a specific technology may confer advantage on one player over another, within the international political economy of trade in natural resources, such advantage is likely to be very short-lived. It would be expected that competition between holders of competing technologies will take place with the expected effect that the value of the technologies in question will be subject to fluctuation over time.

Increasing Involvement of Governments

A second major development which is observed in this study is the ever-present and growing involvement of various levels of government at more and more stages of the discovery, production and distribution process. It is worth considering the extent to which this observation is generalizable over a broad range of internationally traded commodities.

At the beginning of the period under study, government involvement was minimal, with virtually all natural gas developments initiated and implemented by private sector actors, operating under the general scrutiny of government. Soon, ad hoc commissions were established and regulatory activity started to take shape. Much of the Canadian regulatory activity mirrored increasing government involvement in other countries, especially the United States. Apart from the trade specific protection of the public interest, the Canadian federal government quickly saw the potential contribution to its political objectives, such as reinforcing east-west ties within Canada, that could be had through increased regulation of exports. Consequently, government stepped in to force the building of an east-west transmission line through Canada to Montreal (and, later, to Quebec City) using export authorizations (or the withholding thereof) as a lever.

From the viewpoint of securing greater gains from trade, or appearing to protect the public interest through appearing to gain a greater share of the gains from trade for Canadians, governments in Canada eventually got involved in the specific details of prices and reserves estimation and comparison of the various terms and conditions of contracts of competing applicants. This ultimately resulted in the setting of border prices and conducting state-to-state negotiations to set the basic ground rules for contracts between traders. In general, the case study has shown that the federal regulatory body, the National Energy Board, carried out its regulatory duties by putting in place technical-looking formulae in order to assist in judging the various applications and regulatory questions in a manner based on "facts." However, on close examination, the study showed how difficult and expensive it is to assemble the "facts", and how the regulated parties can be expected to participate in providing regulators with their versions of the facts and their estimates of the situation in the industry. The study demonstrated how large a degree of interpretation is usually required in order to make a "technical" judgement, and that, upon reflection, regulatory decisions are likely to be much more judgmental (and thus open to various influences and interpretations) than they are purported to be.

The matter of price fluctuation and increased government involvement are interrelated. Once the perception took hold that indeed, prices were likely to follow a one-way street upwards (in real terms), governments became tempted to take a much more active role through outright ownership of firms in the industry. At first, in Canada, these firms were set up to complement the activities of private firms by undertaking socially desirable activities[3] which were not

---

3. Such as, frontier exploration and research.

commercially attractive in the short run (in terms of expected payoff in relation to the magnitude of the risk exposure); but, were attractive when the total costs and benefits were calculated. These economic but non-commercial benefits included gaining additional information about the resource base, developing new technologies and knowledge bases that could be used by industry with hopefully large spin-off effects, including both forward and backward linkages, and developing high-priority regions of the country that, it was expected, would likely have been neglected by the private sector. As these firms became established, however, their mandates tended to become broader and their activities tended to expand into areas which were being undertaken by private firms. Often, expansion of the Crown firms took place through acquisition of private firms in the sector. Eventually, these public firms were called on to play very active roles in the achievement of other goals in addition to their roles as agents to help correct market failures in the economic aspects of the sector.

The increasing involvement of governments in trade in primary commodities, if accepted as a trend, leads to the conclusion that more and more, market signals are likely to be distorted or amplified by political signals as economics and politics merge closer in the day-to-day operations of these markets. In attempting to plan for the future and manage the development, production and sale (for exporters) and the consumption and purchase of these commodities, both economic and political factors will have to be carefully evaluated for any given trade decision. In such a case, discrete markets for individual commodities may give way to more integrated trade packages where more than one commodity or manufacturer are considered together, or where strategic, military and political considerations override the specific economics of any given component of the traded goods being discussed.[4] Although this development may reduce the total economic wealth generated from the development and sale of a specific commodity, when measured in terms of both economic and socio-political benefits that may be obtained, the citizens of the states in question may well be better off as a result of this politicization of the trade

---

4. Using Soviet natural gas sales to European customers as an example, this deal involves a broad number of issues to the trading partners as well as other states which see their interests affected such as the United States.

process (Although in economic terms, some actors may be worse off individually. Redistribution of wealth and cross-subsidization are among the expected impacts of this politicization of trade).

Changing Rules for Trade

Related to the two developments that have been discussed above, another significant development demonstrated in the case of Canada's natural gas exports is that the agreed upon terms for trade underwent substantial revision. For example, often as a result of government fiat, the terms of contracts were not respected and in particular, price clauses were replaced. This development is in part related to the changing perceptions and expectations in response to a changing market as well as to the increasing involvement of governments and resulting politicization of trade. That such changes are or were warranted is a matter for philosophical debate. For any particular case, a specific export made sense for all parties concerned at a specific time under specific terms and conditions and was approved by government. Is it right and proper for the seller or buyer to insist that the contract terms and conditions be modified merely because unforeseen new circumstances have the effect that it is now a better deal for one of the parties involved? Does continual changing of the ground rules reduce the level of orderliness of society in general and thus result in vastly increased risks and therefore costs for trade in all sectors?

Such questions have been considered by jurists within countries, and questions of contract law and trading rights, obligations and remedies are generally well spelled out within an individual country's jurisdiction. As regards the international political economy however, this state of higher risk, higher uncertainty prevails. If the government of Canada believes its natural gas exporters are getting a poor deal for their export sales at any point in time, then by proclamation it can rectify the situation. Of course, such steps would only be taken after careful consideration of all the consequences, including any expected impacts on other trade arrangements for other commodities.

The conclusion that can be drawn from this is that there may be virtually no limits to what trading arrangements could change as politics continues to merge with economics in international affairs. Many contracts are likely to become only indicators of intent to transact, the precise (and often crucial) terms of specific transactions, left to be determined later.

What this does is increase the uncertainties and thereby heighten the levels of risk involved in trade. Higher returns to equity, or put differently, shorter payback periods become the norm. Fewer marginal projects would be likely to proceed. Current arrangements would tend to get frozen, and any problems, get resolved more politically than with regard to the economic forces that may be pushing in a different direction.

The above discussion is intimately linked to the question of an appropriate contract term for resource exploitation. The desirability of a long term, as opposed to a short term commitment is of course directly related to the contractors' perceptions of the future, amortization periods for the front-end costs of a project and the general "mix of perceptions" or current conventional wisdom of the marketplace. In the case of regulated commodities, the above discussion indicates that any hard-and-fast rule would be unwise and probably lead to backtracking and flip-flops in cases where sellers and buyers, with the backing of the regulators, move to react to unexpected changes in market conditions. Once an environment develops in which some long-term contract terms and conditions are not respected, all long-term contract terms and conditions become more likely to be altered. This will tend to increase commercial riskiness with consequent increase in the cost of capital and application of higher discount rates for cash streams which are expected in the future. Ultimately, this will reduce the size and the rate of development of the resources in question.

Although perhaps politically more difficult to achieve, respect for long term contracts would likely be highly beneficial to all parties in spite of any short term gains that might be had by any one party through refusing to respect a given term of a contract-in-place.

To achieve the maximum advantages from trade, parties should acknowledge that the stability of long term contracts is desirable and that once these are disrupted, then there will be few "stable" components to any trading relationship, but only one hectic roller coaster ride which follows the fluctuations of the rest of the market both up and down. But in view of the nature of the international political economy, perhaps this is the most realistic scenario. If the short term interests of individual, competing states are the major driving forces, then the concept of long-term economic contractual arrangements is really much like a deception in itself. In such a case, some would consider that it would make good sense to enter into long-term commitments, thus earning any concessions available, but bearing in mind that these commitments may not have to be honored if circumstances were to change significantly. In such a case, such long-term contractual arrangements, regardless of the technical details included in the contract, could be seen as little more than statements of intent, and treated as such.

Technological Change

The fourth major development over the period relates to technological advances and improvements in geological and engineering knowledge. These affected all aspects of trade in natural gas by increasing available supplies and the rate of appreciation of natural gas supply and by increasing the efficiency of use of natural gas and decreasing requirements in general. Looking at how technological change may impact on supply, the sub-components of supply may be broken up into exploration, development and production and transmission, while demand components would include burning efficiency as well as advances in conservation technology. While technological change may work to increase efficiency of use and thereby decrease existing demand as occurred in the case of natural gas, it may also work to increase demand for a given commodity. For example, the demand for gasoline and thereby crude oil increased dramatically with the introduction of the internal combustion engine and motor vehicles. Also, improved efficiency and conservation technology may attract new users who would select natural gas over alternative sources thus increasing overall demand.

With regard to supply, technological changes such as enhanced recovery techniques and various improved methods to stimulate reservoirs increased the actual supply of natural gas recoverable from known reserves as well as making new discoveries possible (such as deep natural gas wells or producing from "tight" natural gas bearing geological formations). Technological changes affecting the transmission sector of the industry, such as the introduction of larger diameter pipelines, lowered unit costs, which increased potential deliverability from frontier areas and opened new market possibilities. Improvements in the technical aspects of transporting natural gas as LNG allowed for increased markets as well as new markets to be served, as LNG terminals could be located near existing as well as new market areas. In this respect, the development of LNG technology would impact both on supply and demand. Demand would be increased in the sense of new, additional markets being made accessible. This would also serve to increase competition for markets and supplies between exporters and importers and would tend to "internationalize" the market for a commodity which was traditionally constrained by transportation economics and segregated into distinct regional markets, economically serviceable by pipeline.

One would expect that if technological advances were to continue to the point where a market was developed which involved a large number of countries which were significant traders (importers and exporters), then any attempts at regulation by specific countries would have to be co-ordinated internationally, rather than on a country-by-country basis as was the case for Canada's natural gas exports over the period under study.

Clearly, this development is closely tied in with the first three discussed. Technological developments, while their timing and impacts cannot be forecast with precision, must be expected over time and in particular, will likely be responsive to market incentives (which usually occur in conjunction with price fluctuations). In addition, in view of increasing involvement of governments, market incentives will likely be amplified by political incentives, creating very clear and strong signals for the development and application of new technologies. One observes here a dynamic, interrelated set of processes. As technology changes and is perceived to change, both for a specific commodity and for its substitutes, the negotiating position of exporters and importers of a given commodity will shift over time.

The conclusion to be drawn from this development is that traders and governments should plan for technological change, and where required (based on uncertain expectations) provide incentives for them to be used. Expenditure and programs used by any one actor to preserve the status quo or prevent or inhibit technological change are unlikely to meet with success over time. What this means is that management of resources should be change-oriented rather than clinging to old concepts and ways of operating. Long-term policy actions by traders and governments must be flexible and readily adaptable to quick changes in the short and medium terms.

A practical example will likely prove useful in illustrating this point. In applying its surplus determination procedures, over the period under study, the National Energy Board has prepared a number of forecasts of supply and compared them with various scenarios depicting expected demand. At times "trend gas" has been estimated and included in the expected supply, at times not. In light of this discussion, such forecasts of supply should make explicit expectations and/or possible scenarios for the future which relate to the impact of new technologies. For example, the regulator may or may not decide to include various known reserves which require new technological development to be economically produced. The Board's 1979 finding that an exportable surplus existed, and allocation of the entire surplus to export applicants in 1980, was based on a new exportable surplus procedure which was then put in place (under the then-existing "25A4" formula no surplus would have been found). While certain reserves from the "technological" frontier were not included in the forecast, surely these export approvals, to a certain extent, were approved due to the additional comfort of vast new "frontier" reserves discovered in the Elmworth area of Alberta (tight geological formation). These were not included in the Board's forecast because they depended on technological advance for their eventual development. The assumptions here could have been made more explicit for decision-makers. Surely it made good sense to approve these additional exports, but the probabilities related to technological advance and eventual production from these fields should have been carefully assessed and made explicit.

If such an analysis were undertaken within the context of export regulations, certain options could have been examined which were precluded from consideration due to the regulatory framework. For example, if the regulator is in fact saying that eventual development of these reserves is a good bet, then perhaps an "open" export authorization for production from these fields would make sense. That is, rather than the regulator insisting that existing reserves be proven and deliverable before an export licence will be delivered, it might make sense to remove all further regulatory uncertainty and cost by authorizing any and all exports that may be produced from certain reserves for a given period of time. This reduced uncertainty would then spur the efforts of that part of the industry concerned with the development of this technology.

A Market Cycle for Commodities

The four observed developments and the conclusions which can be derived therefrom are observed to be closely interrelated. As prices fluctuate over time, both during periods when the trend is up and when the trend is down, pressures mount for increasing government intervention. Such political intervention may result in replacing existing rules for trade as well as provide additional incentives which accelerate technological change. Rather than stabilize, these trends point up the fluctuations, and may further destabilize trading conditions as specific, influential or powerful actors are shielded from market downturn or profit more generously from upturns, and this at the expense of other participants.

As regards price fluctuation and uncertainty, these are identified as a major cause of dependency in the case of single-commodity exporters. One set of solutions to this problem of having all of one's eggs in the same basket is to spread the risks, through diversification of markets, traded commodities and trade partners. An additional remedy would be through the regulation, domestically where possible and otherwise internationally, of the commodity market in question to achieve greater stability (and equity). The above analysis suggests, however, that because of the wide range of non-controllable factors which influence trade, no price "stabilization" method will succeed in the long term. As the size and nature of people's needs and ways of meeting them change over time, so too will supplies of and requirements for (and therefore prices of) the various inputs to meet these needs.

Unlike the hypothesis that has been advanced that except for oil, which is a "special" commodity, terms of trade invariably favor the central states, this study suggests that no one trading partner is likely to be favored over time and that there are few (if any) "special" commodities. Although for various short periods it was viewed as being "unique," natural gas is a commodity like many others and prices of all such commodities will fluctuate over time. Negotiating strengths of both exporters and importers will shift over time. In the short run, the market for a given commodity may be dominated by either sellers or buyers, or for certain commodities, by transnational firms. Commodity markets are dynamic and as a result of both economic and political forces move through cycles.[5] The first market situation could be represented as "free," in which transnational firms may dominate, and such a market situation would likely experience rather volatile price fluctuations, accelerated and/or amplified by speculators and the transnationals. Any rents generated from time to time in these markets would generally be shared through negotiations between transnationals and individual host countries.

The market would eventually be expected to change as producing governments became more involved in the production and export of the commodity in question. The next stage of the market cycle would see the crea-

---

5. Winberg (1981) pp. 188-189.

tion of producer associations that attempt to co-ordinate price and production levels in an attempt to stabilize prices, or at least to reduce the size of price fluctuations around long term trends, and at the same time, to increase the host states' share of rents being captured by transnationals. The relative success of producers and any attempts they may make to extract monopoly rents will eventually lead to the next phase of the market cycle in which purchasers (importers) will associate to counter the monopoly powers exercised by the producer association. In the next phase of the market cycle, inherent weaknesses and conflicts of interest in both groups would likely eventually lead to a negotiated commodity agreement between producers and consumers which attempts to forecast and perhaps even regulate long term supply and demand. As discussed earlier in this study, how long such commodity agreements last depends on how well future trends in supply and demand are predicted and on how long all parties act in good faith. Eventually, because of the nature of the international political economy, the technical problems of predicting the future and making adjustments for change, and the incentives to cheat in most such agreements, the commodity agreement would be expected to break down, resulting in a situation similar to the first phase, except that each association, while perhaps not functioning well, would still have a nucleus in existence, ready to go into action more quickly as conditions change.

This analysis is readily applied against the dependency hypothesis that the terms of trade of commodity exporters tend to deteriorate over time. In support of this hypothesis, there is an argument that a group of central or core countries can systematically control markets and thereby, continuously exploit a group of resource exporters in what is called the "periphery." However, this study does not support the general "deteriorating terms of trade" hypothesis. Rather it suggests that terms of trade fluctuate and that markets are dynamic, at times favoring importers, at times exporters. It further suggests that the factors which determine the length of time over which one group of traders are dominated by another are very diverse and unpredictable and thus probably outside the control of any one specific actor or group of actors in the international political economy.

Bibliography

Adelman, Morris Albert. *Alaska Oil: Costs and Supply*. New York, Praeger, 1971.
_____. "American Import Policy and the World Oil Market." *Energy Policy* 1 (September 1973): 91-99.
_____. "Efficiency of Resource Use in Crude Petroleum." *Southern Economic Journal* 31 (October 1964a): 101-122).
_____. "Foreign Oil: A Political-Economic Problem." *Technology Review* 76 (March-April 1974b): 43-47.
_____. "International Oil." *Natural Resources Journal* 18 (October 1978): 725-730.
_____. "Is the Oil Shortage Real? Oil Companies as OPEC tax collectors." *Foreign Policy* (Spring 1972a): 67-109.
_____. "Oil Prices in the Long Run (1963-1975)." *Journal of Business of University of Chicago.* (April 1964): 143-161.
_____. "Politics, Economics, and World Oil." *American Economic Review* 64 (May 1974): 58-67.
_____. "The Supply and Price of Natural Gas." *(A Supplement to the Journal of Industrial Economics)* Oxford: Basil Blackwell, 1962.
_____. "The World Oil Cartel: Scarcity, Economics, and Politics." *Quarterly Review of Economics and Business* 16 (Summer 1976): 7-19.
_____. *The World Petroleum Market*. Baltimore: John Hopkins University Press, 1972b.
Ager-Hanssen, Herik. "The Exploitation of Norwegian Oil and Gas." *Energy Policy* 8 (June 1980): 153-164.
Ahern, William R. "Applying Principles of Policy Analysis to an Offshore Oil-Leasing Decision." *Policy Analysis* 1 (Winter 1975): 133-139.
Aitchison, J. *Choice Against Chance*. Reading, Mass.: Addison Wesley, 1970.
Alberta, Energy Resources Conservation Board of Alberta. *Report on Field Pricing of Gas in Alberta.* Calgary, August 1972.

_____. Energy Resources Conservation Board of Alberta. Reserves of Crude Oil, Gas, Natural Gas Liquids and Sulphur, Province of Alberta. Calgary: December 1972 and 1973 editions.

_____. Oil and Gas Conservation Board. Export and Decision on Review of Plan for Maximum Oil Production Rate Limitation in Alberta. Calgary: Oil and Gas Conservation Board Report 65-3, March 1965.

Aliber, Robert Z. "Oil and the Money Crunch." In Gary D. Eppen (ed.) Energy: The Policy Issues. pp. 82-95. Chicago: University of Chicago Press, 1975.

Alschuler, Lawrence R. Predicting Development, Dependency, and Conflict in Latin America: A Social Field Theory. Ottawa: University of Ottawa Press, 1978.

_____. "Satellization and Stagnation in Latin America." International Studies Quarterly 20 (March 1976): 39-82.

American Gas Association. Historical Statistics of the Gas Utility Industry 1966-1975. Arlington, Virginia: American Gas Association, 1977.

Amin, S. Neo-colonialism in West Africa. New York and London: Monthly Review Press, 1974.

Anthrop, Donald F. "The Need for a Long-Term Policy." Bulletin of the Atomic Scientists 30 (April 1974): 33-38.

Appleby, A. J. "Energy Costs and Society: The High Price of Future Energy." Energy Policy 4 (June 1976): 87-97.

Arrow, J. K. "Limited Knowledge and Economic Analysis." American Economic Review (May 1974): 1-10.

_____. "Some Ordinalist-Utilitarian Notes on Rawls' Theory of Justice." The Journal of Philosophy 70 (May 1973): 245-263.

_____, and M. Kurtz. Public Investment, The Rate of Return, and Optimal Fiscal Policy. Baltimore: John Hopkins Press, 1970.

Ashworth, William. A Short History of the International Economy since 1850. Second Edition. London: Longman, 1962.

Aspin, Les. "A Solution to the Energy Crisis: The Case for Increased Competition." Annals of the American Academy of Political and Social Science 410 (November 1973): 154-163.

Averch, H. and Johnson, H. L. "Behavior of the Firm under Regulatory Constraint." American Economic Review 52 (December 1962): 1062-67.

Bagge, Carl E. "The Federal Power Commission." Boston College Industrial and Commercial Law Review 11 (May 1970): 689-721.

Balestra, P. The Demand for Natural Gas in the United States: A Dynamic Approach for the Residential and Commercial Market. Amsterdam: North-Holland Publishing Company, 1967.

Barnet, R. and R. Muller. Global Reach: The Power of the Multinational Corporations. New York: Simon and Schuster, 1974.

Barnett, Harold J. and Chandler Morse. Scarcity and Growth: The Economics of Natural Resource Availability. Baltimore: Resources for the Future, 1963.

Barzel, Yoram and Christopher D. Hall. The Political Economy of the Oil Import Quota. Stanford, California: Hoover Institution Press of Stanford University, 1977.

Barnes, Robert. "International Oil Companies Confront Governments: A Half-Century of Experience." International Studies Quarterly 16 (December 1972): 454-471.

Beckman, M. J. "A Note on the Optimal Rates of Resources Exhaustion." Review of Economic Studies (1974): 121-122.

Beigie, Carl E. and Alfred O. Hero, Jr. (eds.). Natural Resources in U.S. - Canadian Relations. Three Volumes. Boulder, Colorado: Westview Press, 1980.

Bergen, Bank. Petroleum Activities in Norway. Bergen and Oslo: January, 1982.

Berner, Arthur S. and Sue Scoggins. "Oil and Gas Drilling Programs--Structure and Regulation." George Washington Law Review 41 (March 1973): 471-504.

Berry, Glyn R. "The Oil Lobby and the Energy Crisis." Canadian Public Administration 17 (Winter 1974): 600-635.

Berry, R. Stephen. "Crisis of Resource Scarcity." Bulletin of the Atomic Scientists 31 (January 1975): 31-35.

Berndt, Ernst R., Catherine J. Morrison and G. Campbell Watkins. Dynamic Models of Energy Demand: An Assessment and Comparison. Vancouver: University of British Columbia, Resources Paper No. 49. February, 1980.

Biersteker, Thomas. Distortion or Development? Cambridge, Mass.: MIT Press, 1978.

Blair, John M. The Control of Oil. New York: Pantheon, 1976.

Blissett, Marlan, Bob Davis and Harriet Hahn. "Energy Policy in Texas: State Problems and Responses." Public Affairs Commentary 21 (May 1975): 1-6.

Bockris, J. O. "Energy Sources in a Post-Industrial Society." Austrian Quarterly 45 (September 1973): 32-41.

Bodenheimer, Suzanne. "Dependency and Imperialism: The Roots of Latin American Underdevelopment." Politics and Society (May 1971): 327-357.
Bohi, Douglas R. U.S. Energy Policy: Alternatives for Security. Baltimore: John Hopkins University Press, 1975.
Boiteux, M. "Y a-t'il un problème de l'énergie?" Revue d'Economie politique 92 (May-June 1982): 281-290.
Bonar, J. Malthus and his Work. London: Frank Cass & Co.
Borch, K. H. The Economics of Uncertainty. Princeton, N.J.: Princeton University Press, 1968.
Boulding, Kenneth E. "The Economics of Energy." Annals of the American Academy of Political and Social Science 410 (November 1973): 120-126.
Boyd, F. C. "Nuclear Power in Canada: A Different Approach." Energy Policy 2 (June 1974): 126-135.
Boyer, M. "A Habit Forming Optimal Growth Model." International Economic Review 19 (October 1978): 585-609.
Bradley, Paul G. "Increasing Scarcity: The Case of Energy Resources." American Economic Review 63 (May 1973): 119-125.
Brannon, Gerard M. (ed.). Energy Taxes and Subsidies. Cambridge, Mass.: Ballinger, 1974a.
_____. "Prices and Income: The Dilemma of Energy Policy." Harvard Journal on Legislation 13 (April 1976): 445-477.
_____. (ed.). Studies in Energy Tax Policy. Cambridge, Mass.: Ballinger, 1975a.
_____. "The Social System and the Energy Crisis." Science 184 (April 1974b): 255-257.
_____. "U.S. Taxes on Energy Resources." American Economic Review 65 (May 1975b): 397-404.
Brenscheidt, M. H. "Petroleum Legislation in the North Sea Countries." Texas International Law Journal 11 (Spring 1976): 281-303.
Breyer, Steven G. and Paul W. MacAvoy. Energy Regulation by the F.P.C., Studies in the Regulation of Economic Activity. Washington D.C.: Brookings Institute, 1974.
_____. "The Natural Gas Shortage and the Regulation of Natural Gas Producers." Harvard Law Review 86 (April 1973): 941-987.
Britton, John N. H. and James M. Gilmore. The Weakest Link: A Technological Perspective on Canadian Industrial Underdevelopment. Ottawa: Economic Council of Canada, Background Study 43. 1978.
Brook, E. M. and Enzo Grilli. "Commodity Price Stabilization and the Developing World." Finance and Development 14 (March 1977): 8-11.

Brooks, David B. (ed.). Resource Economics: Selected Works of Orris C. Herfindal. Baltimore and London: Resources for the Future Inc., 1974.

Brooks, Gary H. "The Utility of Downs' Analysis of Bureau Territoriality for Policy Evaluation: The Case of Kansas Energy Policy." Midwest Review of Public Administration 8 (April 1974): 178-190.

Brown, Christopher P. Primary Commodity Control. London: Oxford University Press, 1975.

———. The Political and Social Economy of Commodity Control. New York: Praeger, 1980.

Brown, G. A. "The Evaluation of Risk in Mining Ventures." The Canadian Institute of Mining and Metallurgy Bulletin 63 (October 1970): 1165-1171.

Brown, Keith C. Regulation of the Natural Gas Producing Industry. Baltimore and London: Resources for the Future, 1972.

———. Federal Power Commission Control of Natural Gas Producer Prices. West Lafayette, Indiana: Purdue University, Krannect Graduate School of Industrial Administration, Report No. 494. February, 1975.

Browne Lynn E. and R. F. Syron, "The Deregulation of Natural Gas: Its Potential Impact on New England." New England Economic Review (September/October, 1976).

Brubaker, Sterling. "International Controls of Scarce Resources?" Current History 69 (July-August, 1975): 37-40.

Bryan, Ingrid. Economic Policies in Canada. Toronto: Butterworths, 1982.

Buckley, K. "The Role of Staple Industries in Canada's Economic Development." Journal of Economic History. 18 (December, 1958): 439-450.

Bucovetsky, M. The Taxation of Mineral Extraction. Ottawa: Queen's Printer, 1966.

Bullard, Clark W. III. "Energy Costs and Benefits: Net Energy." Energy Systems and Policy 1 (1976): 367-382.

Burness, H. Stuart "On the Taxation of Nonreplenishable Natural Resources." Journal of Environmental Economics and Management (1976): 289-311.

Burt, O. R. and R. G. Cummings. "Production and Investment in Natural Resource Industries." American Economic Review 60 (September 1970): 576-590.

Caldwell, Lynton K. "A National Policy for Energy?" Indiana University Law Review 47 (Summer 1972): 624-635.

Cameron, V. S. (ed.). Exploration and the Economics of the Petroleum Industry. New York: Mathew Bender, 1977.

Campbell, B. and L. K. Mytelka. "Petrodollars, Foreign Aid and International Statification." Journal of World Trade Law 9 (Nov.-Dec. 1975): 597-621.

Campbell, R. W. The Economics of Soviet Oil and Gas. Baltimore: John Hopkins Press, 1968.

Canada. Foreign Direct Investment in Canada. Ottawa: Information Canada, 1972.

―――. Petroleum in Canada. Ottawa: Minister of Supply and Services, 1977 and 1979 editions.

―――. Berger Report. Northern Frontier Northern Homeland. Vol. 1. Ottawa: Minister of Supply and Services, 1977.

―――. Department of Energy, Mines and Resources. Energy Conservation in Canada: Programs and Perspectives. Report EP77-7. Ottawa: Department of Energy, Mines and Resources, 1977.

―――. The National Energy Program, 1980. Ottawa: Department of Energy Mines and Resources, 1980.

―――. Department of Finance. The Budget. Ottawa: Department of Finance, October 28, 1980.

―――. Department of Industry, Trade and Commerce. Direct Investment in Canada by Non-Residents Since 1945. Ottawa: Department of Industry, Trade and Commerce, October 1973.

―――. U.S. Direct Investment In Canada as Reported by U.S. Sources' 1946 - 1967 AMENDMENT LIST NUMBER 1 March, 1971.

―――. Direct Investment In Canada By Non-Residents Since 1945 AMENDMENT NUMBER 2 June, 1974.

―――. House of Commons. Minutes of Proceedings and Evidence of the Special Committee on Regulatory Reform (Mr. James Peterson, M.P., Chairman). Ottawa: September 23, 1980. (Testimony of officials from the National Energy Board and the Department of Energy, Mines and Resources).

―――. National Energy Board. Annual Reports. Ottawa: 1959 to 1984.

―――. Canadian Natural Gas: Supply and Requirements. Ottawa: April, 1975.

―――. Canadian Natural Gas: Supply and Requirements. Ottawa: February, 1979.

―――. Canadian Oil: Supply and Requirements. Ottawa: February, 1977a.

―――. Canadian Oil: Supply and Requirements. Ottawa: September, 1978.

―――. Energy Supply and Demand in Canada and Export Demand for Canadian Energy, 1966 to 1980. Ottawa, Queen's Printers, 1969.

_____. National Energy Board Report to the Governor in Council in the matter of the applications under the National Energy Board Act of Trans-Canada Pipe Lines Limited, Alberta and Southern Gas Co. Ltd., Alberta Natural Gas Company, Westcoast Transmission Company Limited, Canadian-Montana Pipe Line Company, and Niagara Gas Transmission Limited. Ottawa: March, 1960a.

_____. National Energy Board Report to the Governor in Council regarding the application of Niagara Gas Transmission Ltd. Ottawa: May, 1960b.

_____. National Energy Board Report to the Governor in Council regarding the application of Westcoast Transmission Co. Ltd. Ottawa: July, 1964a.

_____. National Energy Board Report to the Governor in Council regarding the application of Union Gas Company of Canada Ltd. Ottawa: December, 1964b.

_____. National Energy Board Report to the Governor in Council regarding the application of Trans-Canada Pipe Lines Ltd. Ottawa: May, 1965a.

_____. National Energy Board Report to the Governor in Council regarding the applications, under the National Energy Board Act of Alberta and Southern, Alberta Natural Gas, Canadian Montana Pipeline, and Trans-Canada Pipeline. Ottawa: July, 1965b.

_____. National Energy Board Report to the Governor in Council regarding the application of Transmission Gas Storage Ltd. Ottawa: January, 1966a.

_____. National Energy Board Report to the Governor in Council regarding the application of Trans-Canada Pipe Lines Ltd. Ottawa: July, 1966b.

_____. National Energy Board Report to the Governor in Council in the matter of the application to transport natural gas to Central Ontario via the United States of America. Ottawa: August, 1966c.

_____. National Energy Report to the Governor in Council regarding the application of Westcoast Transmission Co. Ltd. Ottawa: March, 1967a.

_____. National Energy Board Report to the Governor in Council regarding the applications of Alberta and Southern Gas Co. Ltd., Alberta Natural Gas Co., and Canadian-Montana Pipe Line Co. Ottawa: May, 1967b.

_____. National Energy Board Report to the Governor in Council in the matter of an application by Westcoast Transmission Ltd. Ottawa: December, 1967c.

_____. National Energy Board Reasons for Decision regarding the application of Westcoast Transmission Co. Ltd. Ottawa: February, 1968a.

_____. National Energy Board Reasons for Decision regarding the application of Union Gas Company of Canada Ltd. Ottawa: December, 1968b.

———. National Energy Board Reasons for Decision regarding the application of Westcoast Transmission Co. Ltd. Ottawa: July, 1969a.

———. National Energy Board Report to the Governor in Council in the matter of the application of Westcoast Transmission Co. Ltd. Ottawa: August 1969b.

———. National Energy Board Report to the Governor in Council regarding the application of Canadian-Montana Pipe Line Co. Ottawa: April 18, 1969c.

———. National Energy Board Report to the Governor In Council in the matter of the applications of Alberta & Southern Gas Co. Ltd., Alberta Natural Gas Co., Canadian-Montana Pipe Line Co., Consolidated Natural Gas Ltd., Consolidated Pipe Lines Co. Ltd., and Westcoast Transmission Co. Ltd. Ottawa: August, 1970a.

———. National Energy Board Report to the Governor in Council regarding the application of Inter-City Gas Ltd. Ottawa: November, 1970b.

———. National Energy Board Report to the Governor in Council regarding the application of Trans-Canada Pipe Lines Ltd. Ottawa: April, 1971a.

———. National Energy Board Reasons for Decision regarding applications of Alberta & Southern Gas Co. Ltd., Alberta Natural Gas Co., Canadian-Montana Pipe Line Co., Consolidated Natural Gas Ltd., Consolidated Pipe Lines Co., and Trans-Canada Pipe Lines Ltd. Ottawa: November, 1971b.

———. National Energy Board Report to the Governor in Council regarding the application of Westcoast Transmission Co. Ltd. Ottawa: January, 1972a.

———. National Energy Board Report to the Governor in Council regarding the applications of Consolidated Natural Gas Ltd. and Consolidated Pipe Lines Company. Ottawa: April, 1972b.

———. National Energy Board Report to the Governor in Council regarding the application of Westcoast Transmission Co. Ltd. Ottawa: June, 1973.

———. National Energy Board Report to the Governor in Council in the matter of the pricing of natural gas being exported under existing licences. July, 1974.

———. National Energy Board Report to the Governor in Council regarding Canadian natural gas supply and requirements. Ottawa: April, 1975a.

———. National Energy Board Report to the Governor in Council in the matter of the pricing of natural gas being exported under existing licences. Ottawa: March, 1975b.

_____. National Energy Board Report to the Governor in Council in the matter of the pricing of natural gas being exported under existing licences. Ottawa: April 1976.

_____. National Energy Board Report to the Governor in Council in the matter of the pricing of natural gas being exported under existing licences. Ottawa: April, 1977b.

_____. Reasons for Decision: Northern Pipelines. Ottawa: June, 1977c.

_____. Reasons for Decisions in the matter of Phase II: The Licence Phase and Phase III: The Surplus Phase of the Gas Export Omnibus Hearing, 1982. Ottawa: January, 1983.

Canada. Royal Commission on Canada's Economic Prospects. Final Report. Ottawa: November, 1957.

_____. Royal Commission on Energy. First Report. Ottawa: November, 1958.

Canadian-American Committee. Wanted: A Working Environment More Conducive to Canadian-American Trade in Natural Gas. Washington: National Planning Association and Private Planning Association of Canada, 1959.

Canadian-American Committee. Keeping Options Open in Canada-US Oil and Natural Gas Trade. Montreal: C. D. Howe Research Institute, 1975.

Canadian-American Committee. A Time of Difficult Transitions: Canada-US Relations in 1976: A Staff Report. Montreal, Washington: 1976.

Canadian Gas Association. Historical Statistics of the Canadian Gas Industry. Toronto: Canadian Gas Association, 1982.

_____, Canadian Gas Facts 1985. Toronto: Canadian Gas Association, 1985.

Canadian Institute for Economic Policy. Out of Joint with the Times: An Overview of the Canadian Economic Dilemma. Ottawa: Canadian Institute for Economic Policy, 1979.

Canadian Petroleum Association. Statistical Year Books, 1946-1973. Calgary: Canadian Petroleum Association.

Caporaso, James A. "Dependence, dependency, and power in the global system: a structural and behavioral analysis." Internal Organization 32 (Winter 1978): 13-43.

Cardoso, Fernando Henrique. "Théorie de la dépendance ou analyses concrètes de situations de dépendance?". L'Homme et la Sociéte. 33-34 (juillet-décembre, 1974): 111-123.

_____, and Enzo Faletto. Dependency and Development in Latin America. (Marjory M. Urquidi, tr.). Los Angeles: University of California Press, 1979.

Carver, John A., Jr. "Federal Land Resource Utilization Policy." In Jack M. Hollander (ed.) Annual Review of Energy, pp. 727-741. Palo Alto, California: Annual Reviews, 1976.

Catawba Corporation. The Outlook for Natural Gas in the US. New York: Catawba Corporation, 1963.

Center for Governmental Responsibility. Energy: The Power of the States. Gainesville, Florida: Center for Governmental Responsibility, University of Florida, 1975.

Cetron, Marvin J. and Vary T. Coates. "Energy and Society." Proceedings of the Academy of Political Science 31 (December 1973): 33-40.

Cheney, Eric S. "U.S. Energy Resources: Limits and Future Outlook." American Scientist 62 (January-February 1974): 14-18.

Christiansen, Bill. "The Energy Crunch." State Government 47 (Autumn 1974): 204-208.

Clay, Herbert D. "The Natural Gas Industry and Project Independence: A Perspective on Energy Self-Sufficiency." Public Utilities Fortnightly 94 (October 24, 1974): 19-22.

Cleland, N. A. Evaluation of Canadian Oil and Gas Properties. Calgary: Sproule Associates Ltd., January, 1979.

Clement, Wallace. Continental Corporate Power: Economic Elite Linkages between Canada and the US. Toronto: McClelland and Stewart, 1977.

_____. The Canadian Corporate Elite: An Analysis of Economic Power. Toronto: McClelland and Stewart, 1975.

Chandler, Geoffrey. "The Myth of Oil Power: International Groups and National Sovereignty." International Affairs 46 (October 1970): 710-718.

Chevalier, J. M. "Elements Théoriques: l'introduction a l'économie du pétrole, l'analyse du rapport de force." Revue d'Economie Politique (March-April 1975): 231-256.

Cheng, Chu-yuan. China's Petroleum Industry. New York, Washington, London: Praeger, 1976.

Choucri, Nazli. International Politics of Energy Interdependence. Lexington, Mass.: D. C. Heath, 1976.

Chu, K. and T. H. Naylor. "A Dynamic Model of the Firm." Management Science (May 1965): 736-750.

Clawson, Marion (ed.). Natural Resources and International Development. Baltimore: John Hopkins Press, 1964.

Cole, H. D. S., Christopher Freeman, Marie Jahoda and K. L. R. Pavitt. Thinking About the Future: A Critique of the Limits to Growth. London: Chatto and Windus Ltd., 1973.

Commission of the European Communities. *Information: The Convention of Lomé* No. 129/76/X/E (July 1977).
Commoner, Barry. "Energy Crisis--All of a Piece." *Center Magazine* 8 (March 1975): 26-31.
_____. *The Closing Circle*. New York: Bantam, 1972.
_____. *The Poverty of Power: Energy and the Economic Crisis*. New York: Alfred A. Knopf, 1976.
Connelly, Philip and Robert Perlman. *The Politics of Scarcity: Resource Conflicts in International Relations*. London, New York, Toronto: Oxford University Press, 1975.
Cook, C. Sharp. "Energy: Planning for the Future." *American Scientist* 61 (January-February 1973): 61-65.
Copithorne, L. "International Corporate Transfer Prices and Government Policy." *Canadian Journal of Economics* 4 (August 1971): 324-41.
Council of State Governments. *State Responses to the Energy Crisis*. Lexington, Ky.: Council of State Governments, 1974.
Courchene, Thomas J. "Towards a protected society: The politicization of economic life." *The Canadian Journal of Economics* 13 (November 1980): 556-577.
Crane, David. "Canada's Energy Policies in a Global Context." *International Perspectives* (July-August 1973): 32-37.
Crawford, A. B. "Energy Crisis: A Blessing in Disguise?" *Futurist* 10 (August 1976): 198-201.
Creighton, Donald. *Canada's First Century*. Toronto: Macmillan, 1970.
Crommelin, Michael, Peter H. Pearse, and Anthony Scott. "Management of Oil and Gas Resources in Alberta: An Economic Evaluation of Public Policy." 18 *Natural Resources Journal* (April 1978): 337-389.
Crommelin, Michael and Andrew R. Thompson (eds.). *Mineral Leasing as an Instrument of Public Policy*. Vancouver: University of British Columbia Press, 1977.
Crowe, Marshall. "Canadian Energy Developments." *Natural Resources Lawyer* 9 (1976): 1-10.
Cummings, R. G. "Some Extensions of the Economic Theory of Exhaustible Resources." *Western Economic Journal* 7 (September 1969): 201-210.
Dales, John. *Pollution, Property and Prices*. Toronto and Buffalo: University of Toronto Press, 1968.
Daly, Herman E. "The Economics of the Steady State." *American Economic Review* 64 (May 1974): 15-21.
_____. (ed.). *Toward a Steady-State Economy*. San Francisco: W. H. Freeman, 1973.
Dam, Kenneth W. *Oil Resources: Who Gets What How?* Chicago: University of Chicago Press, 1976.

Darmstadter, Joel, Perry D. Tietlebaum, and Jaroslav Polach. Energy in the World's Economy: A Statistical Review of Trends in Output, Trade and Consumption Since 1925. Baltimore: Johns Hopkins University Press, 1971.

Dasgupta, P. and G. M. Heal. "The Optimal Depletion of Exhaustible Resources." Review of Economic Studies (Symposium on the Economics of Exhaustible Resources). (1974): 3-28.

_____, and J. E. Stiglitz. Uncertainty and the Rate of Extraction under Alternative Institutional Arrangements. (Technical Report No. 179). Stanford: Institute for Mathematical Studies in the Social Sciences, 1976.

David, Edward E., Jr. "Energy: A Strategy of Diversity." Technology Review 25 (June 1973): 26-31.

Davidson, Jeff. "Natural Gas and the Federal Power Commission." Indiana Law Journal 47 (Summer 1972): 725-741.

Davis, A. Canadian Energy Prospects. Ottawa: Royal Commission on Canada's Economic Prospects, 1957.

Davis, David H. Energy Politics. New York: St. Martin's Press, 1974.

Davis, Ralph E. Stories of Natural Gas. New York: R. E. Davis 1964.

deMontribal, T. "For a new world economic order." Foreign Affairs 54 (October 1975): 61-78.

Deutsch, J. J. et al (ed.). The Canadian Economy: Selected Readings. Revised Edition. Toronto: Macmillan, 1965.

DiBona, Charles J. "Administration Policies Affecting the Natural Gas Industry." Natural Resources Lawyer 6 (Fall 1973): 503-521.

Dobell, Peter C. Canada's Search for New Roles: Foreign Policy In The Trudeau Era. London, New York and Toronto: Oxford University Press, 1972.

Doran, Charles F. "Oil Politics and Rise of Codependence." In Marvin S. Sorros and David Orr (eds.) The Global Predicament: Ecological Perspective on World Order, pp. 195-208. Raleigh, North Carolina: University of North Carolina Press, 1979.

Dos Santos, Theotonio. "The Structure of Dependence." American Economic Review 60 (May 1970): 235-246.

Easterbrook, W. T. and M. H. Watkins (eds.). Approaches to Canadian Economic History. Toronto: McClelland and Stewart, 1967.

Eckbo, Paul Leo. The Future of World Oil. Cambridge, Mass.: Ballinger Publishing Co., 1976.

Eckstein, O. "Investment criteria for economic development and the theory of intertemporal welfare economics." *Quarterly Journal of Economics* 71 (1957): 56-85.

Economic Council of Canada. *Connections: An Energy Strategy for the Future.* Ottawa: Minister of Supply and Services, 1985.

Edwards, Anthony. *The Potential for New Commodity Cartels: Copying OPEC, or Improved International Agreements?* London: The Economist Intelligence Unit Ltd., 1975.

Eglington, Peter Cheston. *The Economics of Industry Petroleum Exploration.* Unpublished Ph.D. thesis. Vancouver: University of British Columbia, 1975.

Ellingen, Dana C. and William E. Towsey. *A Bibliography of Congressional Publications on Energy from the 89th Congress to July 1, 1971.* Washington, D. C.: Government Printing Office, 1971.

Engler, Robert. *The Brotherhood of Oil: Energy Policy and the Public Interest.* Chicago: University of Chicago Press, 1977.

Eppen, Gary D. (ed.). *Energy: The Policy Issues.* Chicago: University of Chicago Press, 1975.

Erickson, Edward W. "Crude Oil Prices, Drilling Incentives and the Supply of New Discoveries." *Natural Resources Journal* 10 (January 1970): 27-52.

____, and R. M. Spann. "Supply Response in a Regulated Industry: The Case of Natural Gas." *Bell Journal of Economics and Management Science* 2 (Spring 1971): 94-121.

____, and Leonard Waverman (eds.). *The Energy Question: An International Failure of Policy.* Vols. 1 and 2. Toronto: University of Toronto Press, 1974.

Evan, Harry Z. "The Multinational Oil Company and the Nation State." *Journal of World Trade Law* 4 (September-October 1970): 666-685.

Evans, Peter. *Dependent Development: The Alliance of Multinationals, State, and Local Capital in Brazil.* Princeton, N.J.: Princeton University Press, 1979.

Farrar, D. E. *The Investment Decision Under Uncertainty.* Englewood Cliffs, N.J.: Prentice Hall, 1962.

Fawcett, James. *International Economic Conflicts: Prevention and Resolution.* London: Europa Publications, 1977.

____, and Audrey Parry. *Law and International Resource Conflicts.* London: Oxford University Press, 1981.

Feehan, John G. "The Energy Crisis and the Consumer States." Natural Resources Lawyer 6 (Fall 1973): 495-502.
Feldstein, M. S. "The Social Time Preference Discount Rate in Cost-Benefit Analysis." Economic Journal 74 (1964): 360-79, republished with slight revisions as "The Social Time Preference Rate" in Richard Layard (ed.). Cost-Benefit Analysis. London: Penguin, 1972, pp. 245-269 (Cited in text footnotes as "Feldstein (1964)").
Finder, Alan. "State Responses to Energy Problems." State Government 49 (Summer 1976): 161-165.
Fisher, B. "The Role of the National Energy Board in Controlling the Export of Natural Gas From Canada." Osgoode Hall Law Journal. 9 (1971): 554-558.
Fisher, John C. Energy Crisis in Perspective. New York: John Wiley and Sons, 1974.
Forrester, J. W. Industrial Dynamics. Cambridge, Mass.: M.I.T. Press, 1961.
Frank, André Gunder. Capitalism and Underdevelopment in Latin America. New York: Monthly Review Press, 1967.
_____. "The Development of Underdevelopment." In A.G. Frank (ed.), Latin America: Underdevelopment or Revolution? New York and London: Monthly Review Press, 1969.
Frank, Helmut J. "Economic Strategy for Import-Export Controls on Energy Materials." Science 184 (April 19, 1974): 316-321.
Frankel, P. H. Oil, The Facts of Life. London: Weidenfeld and Nicolson, 1962.
Fraser, Lugg. Petroleum and Natural Gas Industry in Canada 1963-1968. Ottawa: Department of Energy Mines and Resources, Mineral Resources Branch, 1970.
Freeman, S. David. Energy: The New Era. New York: Random House, 1974.
_____. "Is There an Energy Crisis? An Overview." Annals of the American Academy of Political and Social Science 410 (November 1973): 1-10.
Freymond, J. "New Dimensions in International Relations." Review of Politics 37 (October 1975): 464-478.
Friedeberg, Alfred S. "The Lomé Agreement: Cooperation Rather than Confrontation." Journal of World Trade Law 9 (Nov.-Dec. 1975): 691-701.
Friedland, Edward, Paul Seabury and Aaron Wildavsky. "Oil and the Decline of Western Power." Political Science Quarterly I (Fall 1971): 749-772.
Furtado, Celso. Diagnosis of the Brazilian Crisis. (Suzette Macedo, tr.). Los Angeles: University of California Press, 1965.

_____. Economic Development of Latin America. 2nd ed. London: Cambridge University Press, 1977.
_____. La Formation Economique du Brasil de l'époque Coloniale Aux Temps Modernes. (Translated from Portugese by Janine Peffau). Paris: Mouton, 1973.
Gadda, David G. "Taxation as a Tool of Natural Resource Management: Oil as A Case Study." Ecology Law Quarterly 1 (Fall 1971): 749-772.
Gaffney, M. (ed.). Extractive Resources and Taxation. Milwaukee: University of Wisconsin Press, 1967.
Galtung, J. "A Structural Theory of Imperialism." Journal of Peace Research 8 (1971): 81-117.
_____. "Measuring World Development." Alternatives 1 (1975): 523-555.
Garner, C. R. and T. J. Campbell Jr., "Economic Evaluation and Planning of Exploration Programs." Oil and Gas Journal 71 (June 4, 1973): 94-96.
Georgescu-Roegen, Nicholas. Analytical Economics: Issues and Problems. Cambridge, Mass.: Harvard University Press, 1967.
_____. "Energy and Economic Myths." Southern Economic Journal 41 (January 1975): 347-381.
Getty, J. P. My Life and Fortune. London: G. Allen and Unwin, 1964.
Gilpin, Robert. U.S. Power and the Multinational Corporation: The Political Economy of Foreign Direct Investment. New York: Basic Books, 1975.
Gimpel, Jean. The Medieval Machine: The Industrial Revolution of the Middle Ages. New York: Holt, Rinehart and Winston, 1976.
Girvan, Norman. Copper in Chile: A Study in Conflict Between Corporate and National Economy. Surrey, England: Unwin Brothers and Gresham Press, 1972.
_____. "MNC's and Dependent Underdevelopment in Mineral Export Economics." Social and Economic Studies 19 (December 1970): 490-526.
Goeller, H. E. and Alvin M. Weinberg. "The Age of Substitutability." American Economic Review 68 (December
_____. "Alternatives to Oil and Natural Gas." Proceedings of the Academy of Political Science 31 (December 1973): 74-86.
Goldsmith, Maurice, Han Waalwijk and Niels Wiedenhof (eds.). A Strategy For Resources: A Science Policy Foundation Symposium held in Eindhoven, The Netherlands, September 18 and 19, 1975. Amsterdam, New York and Oxford: North Holland Publishing Company, 1977.
Goldstein, Walter. "Canada's Constitutional Crisis: The Uncertain Development of Alberta's Energy Resources." Energy Policy 9 (March 1981): 4-13.

Gordon, Richard L. "A Reinterpretation of the Pure Theory of Exhaustion." Journal of Political Economy. 75 (June 1967): 274-286.
____. "Conservation and The Theory of Exhaustible Resources." Canadian Journal of Economics 32 (August 1966): 319-326.
____. "Mythology and Reality in Energy Policy." Energy Policy 2 (September 1974): 189-203.
____. The Evolution of Energy Policy in Western Europe: The Reluctant Retreat from Coal. New York: Praeger, 1971.
Gordon, Scott. "Natural Resources as a Constraint on Economic Growth: Today's Apocalypses and Yesterday's." American Economic Review 63 (May 1973): 106-110.
Gould, Ed. Oil: A History of Canada's Oil and Gas Industry. Victoria, British Columbia: Harrnock House Publishers, 1976.
Gray, Earle. The Great Canadian Oil Patch. Toronto: Maclean-Hunter, 1970.
Gray, John E. Energy Policy: Industry Perspectives. Cambridge, Mass.: Ballinger, 1975.
Gray, J. Lorne. "Nuclear Power: An Energy Source for Canada." In Ian E. Efford (ed.) Energy and the Environment, pp. 45-68. Vancouver: Institute of Resource Ecology, 1972.
Gray, L. C. "Rent under the Assumption of Exhaustibility." Quarterly Journal of Economics 28 (May 1914): 466-89.
Grayson, Leslie G. Economics of Energy. Princeton, N.J.: Darwin Press, 1975.
Greenwood, Ted. "Canadian-American Trade in Energy Resources." International Organization 28 (Autumn 1974): 689-710.
Grenon, Michel. "Global Energy Resources." Annual Review of Energy 2 (1977): 67-94.
Griffiths, J. C. "Exploration for Natural Resources." Operations Research (March-April 1966): 189-209.
Gross, Andrew C. and Warren W. Ware. "Energy Prospects to 1990." Business Horizons 18 (June 1975): 5-18.
Gulf Oil Canada Limited. Submission to the National Energy Board in the Matter of the Exportation of Oil. Mimeo, December, 1973.
Hafele, Wolf. "A Systems Approach to Energy." American Scientist 62 (July-August 1974): 438-447.
Hall, Robert E. L. "Domestic Coal vs. Foreign Residual Oil." Natural Resources Lawyer 3 (May 1970): 266-270.
____, and Robert S. Pindyck. "The Conflicting Goals of National Energy Policy." Public Interest 47 (Spring 1977): 3-15.

Hammond, Allen L. "Energy and The Future: Research Priorities and National Policy." Science 179 (January 12, 1973): 164-166.
Hamilton, Richard E. "Canada's 'Exportable Surplus' Natural Gas Policy: A Theoretical Analysis." Land Economics 49 (August 1973a): 251-259.
_____. "A Marketing Board to Regulate Exports of Natural Gas?" Canadian Public Administration 16 (Spring 1973b): 83-95.
Hardin, Garrett. "Living on a Lifeboat." Bioscience 24 (October 1974): 561-568.
Harris, W. R. Intergovernmental Relations in Energy Policy, Or How to Get Along with the In-Laws. Santa Monica, California: Rand Corporation, 1974.
Hass, Jerome E., Edward J. Mitchell and Bernell K. Stone. Financing the Energy Industry. Cambridge, Mass: Ballinger, 1974.
Helleiner, G. K. "Canada and the New International Economic Order." Canadian Public Policy 2 (Summer 1976): 451-465.
Hellman, Hal. Energy in the World of the Future. New York: M. Evans and Company, 1973.
Helliwell, John. "Mineral Resources in the New International Order." Current History 69 (July-August 1975): 28-31.
_____. Public Policies and Private Investment. Oxford: Clarendon Press, 1968.
Helms, Robert B. Natural Gas Regulation: An Evaluation of FPC Price Controls. Washington: American Enterprise Institute for Public Policy Research, 1974.
Herfindahl, O. C. "Depletion and Economic Theory." In Goffney Mason (ed.). Extractive Resources and Taxation, pp. 63-90. Milwaukee: University of Wisconsin Press, 1967.
_____. "Some Fundamentals of Mineral Economics." Land Economics 31 (May 1955): 131-138.
Himle, Erik. "The Development in Norwegian Petroleum Activities." Financial Review of the Norwegian Banker's Association 3 (September 1978): 1-4.
Hirshleifer, J. and John G. Riley, "The Analytics of Uncertainty and Information--An Expository Survey." Journal of Economic Literature 17 (December 1979): 1375-1421.
Hirst, Eric, William Fulkerson, Roger Carlsmith and Thomas Wilbanks. "Improving Energy Efficiency: The Effectiveness of Government Action." Energy Policy 10 (June 1982): 131-142.
Hoel, M. "Resource Extraction When a Future Substitution Has An Uncertain Cost." Review of Economic Studies 45 (October 1978): 637-644.
Holcomb, Robert W. "Power and Fuel Resources." Current History 58 (June 1970): 330-336.

Holdren, John P. "Energy and Prosperity." Bulletin of the Atomic Scientists 31 (January 1975): 26-28.

Hooley, Richard W. Financing the Natural Gas Industry: The Role of Life Insurance Investment Policies. New York: Columbia University Press, 1961.

Hotelling, Harold. "The Economics of Exhaustible Resources." The Journal of Political Economy 39 (April 1931): 137-175.

Hottel, Hoyt C. and Jack B. Howard. "An Agenda for Energy." Technology Review 74 (January 1972): 38-48.

Hubbert, M. King. "Energy Resources of the Earth." Scientific American 225 (September 1971): 60-70.

_____. "Survey of World Energy Resources." The Canadian Institute of Mining and Metallurgy (CIM) Bulletin 66 (July 1973): 37-53.

Hunter, Alex. "The Indonesian Oil Industry." In Bruce Glassburner (ed.) The Economy of Indonesia. Ithaca: Cornell University Press, 1971.

Hürni, B.S. "The International Energy Programme." Journal of World Trade Law 9 (Nov.-Dec. 1975): 701-710.

Ikard, Frank N. "Competition in the Petroleum Industry: Separating Fact from Myth." Oregon Law Review 54 (1975): 583-605.

Industrial Gas Users Association of Canada. "Energy Policy for Canada with Particular Reference to Natural Gas." Unpublished mimeograph. Ottawa: Industrial Gas Users Association, 1973.

Innis, H. A. Essays in Canadian Economic History. Toronto: University of Toronto Press, 1956a.

_____. The Cod Fisheries. rev. ed. Toronto: University of Toronto Press, 1954.

_____. The Fur Trade in Canada. rev. ed. Toronto: University of Toronto Press, 1956b.

International Bank for Reconstruction and Development. "Opportunities for OPEC-type Action in Agricultural Commodities," Commodity Paper No. 1 (March 1973).

International Coffee Organization. International Coffee Agreement 1976. London: International Coffee Organization, 1976.

_____. International Coffee Agreement 1980. London: International Coffee Organization, 1980.

Jacoby, Neil H. Multinational Oil: A Study in Industrial Dynamics. New York: Macmillan, 1974.

Jarrett, James and Dick Howard. State Energy Management: The California Energy Resources Conservation and Development Commission. Lexington, Kentucky: Council of State Governments, 1976.

Jensen, Walter G. W. Energy and the Economy of Nations. Henley-on-Thames, United Kingdom: G. T. Foulis, 1970.

Jevons, W. S. The Coal Question: An Inquiry Concerning the Progress of the Nation, and the Probable Exhaustion of our Coal Mines, 3rd Edition, Revised. A. W. Flux (ed.). London: Macmillan, 1906.

Johnson, Harry G. "Commodities: Less Developed Countries' Demands and Developing Countries' Responses." in Jagdish N. Bhagwati (ed.) The New International Economic Order: The North-South Debate, pp. 240-251. Cambridge, Mass. and London, U.K.: MIT Press, 1977.

Johony, Ali D. The Myth of the OPEC Cartel: The Role of Saudi Arabia. New York: Wiley, 1982.

Kahail, Mohammed Abu al (Saudi Minister for Finance and National Economy). "The Oil Price in Perspective." International Affairs (October, 1979): 517-530.

Kahn, Alfred E. "The Combined Effects of Prorationing, The Depletion Allowance and Import Quotas on the Cost of Producing Crude Oil in the United States." Natural Resources Journal 10 (January 1970): 53-61.

Kash, Don E. "Energy in the 1970's--The Problem of Abundance to Scarcity." In Walter F. Scheffer (ed.) Energy Impacts on Public Policy and Administration, pp. 23-32. Norman, Oklahoma: University of Oklahoma Press, 1976.

____, et al. Energy Alternatives: A Comparative Analysis. Washington, D.C.: Government Printing Office, 1975.

Kaufman, Alvin. "Are We Running Out Of Natural Gas?" Albany: State of New York, Office of Economic Research. OER Report No. IV. August 9, 1971.

Kaufman, G. M. Statistical Decision and Related Techniques in Oil and Gas Exploration. Englewood Cliffs, N.J.: Prentice Hall, 1963.

Katzenstein, Peter ed. Between Poverty and Plenty: Foreign Economic Policies of Advanced Industrial States. International Organization 31 (Autumn 1977).

Khazzoom, J. Daniel. An Econometric Model of U.S. Natural Gas Supply. Federal Power Commission, Docket No. AR69-1, September, 1970.

____. "Gas Production Directionality." Public Utilities Fortnightly 84 (December 18, 1969): 20-25.

____. "The FPC staff's econometric model of natural gas supply in the United States." Bell Journal of Economics and Management Science 2 (Spring 1971): 51-93.

Kilbourn, William. Pipeline: Trans Canada and the Great Debate. Toronto: Clarke Irwin, 1970.

Kindleberger, Charles P. Power and Money. New York: Basic Books, 1970.

———. "U.S. Foreign Economic Policy, 1776-1976." Foreign Affairs 55 (January 1977): 395-417.

Kindred, Hugh M. and Warren F. Schwartz. "American Regulation of Oil Imports: Law, Policy and Institutional Responsibility." Journal of World Trade Law 5 (May-June 1971): 267-302.

Kissinger, Henry. "Energy: The Necessity of Decision." Atlantic Community Quarterly 13 (Spring 1975): 7-22.

Knorr, Klaus. "The Oil Crisis in Perspective: The Limits of Economic and Military Power." Daedalus 104 (Fall 1975): 229-243.

Kravis, I. B. "International Commodity Agreements to Promote Aid and Efficiency: The Case of Coffee." Canadian Journal of Economics 1 (May 1968): 295-317.

Krutilla, John V. and R. Talbot Page. "Towards a Responsible Energy Policy." Policy Analysis 1 (Winter 1975): 77-100.

Kubinski, Z. M. The Small Firm in the Albertan Oil and Gas Industry. Ottawa: Department of Industry, Trade and Commerce, 1979. Laird, Melvin R. et al. Energy Policy: A New War Between the States? Washington, D.C.: American Enterprise Institute for Public Policy Research Round Table, October 2, 1975.

Lall, S. "Transfer-pricing by Multinational Manufacturing Firms." Oxford Bulletin of Economics and Statistics (August 1973).

Lamm, Richard D. "States Rights vs. National Energy Needs." Natural Resources Lawyer 9 (1976): 41-48.

Langdon, Jim C. "The Energy Crisis and the Producer States." Natural Resources Lawyer 6 (Fall 1973): 485-494.

Lawrence, Robert M. "Energy Policy." Policy Studies Journal 2 (Winter 1973): 141-146.

Laxer, James. "The Norhern Pipeline and Canadian Economic Strategy." Canadian Forum (August 1977): 19-22.

———, and Anne Martin (eds.). The Big Tough Expensive Job: Imperial Oil and the Canadian Economy. Toronto: Press Porcépic, 1976.

Lee, J. E. "Longer Range Viewpoints on Energy." Futurist 8 (October 1974): 243-244.

Leeman, W. A. "The Functions of Market and Government in Coping With the Energy Crisis." Nebraska Journal of Economics and Business 13 (Autumn 1974): 117-121.

Leiss, William. The Limits to Satisfaction: An Essay on the Problem of Needs and Commodities. Toronto and Buffalo: University of Toronto Press, 1976.

Lewis, Tracy and Philip Neher. Consistent and Revised Plans for Natural Resource Use. Vancouver: University of British Columbia, Programme in Natural Resource Economics, Resources Paper No. 50 April, 1980.

Levitt, Kari. Silent Surrender: The Multinational Corporation in Canada. Toronto: Macmillan, 1970.

Lichtenberg, Allan J. and Richard B. Norgaard. "Energy Policy and the Taxation of Oil and Gas Income." Natural Resources Journal 14 (October 1974): 501-518.

Lieber, Robert J. "Europe and America in the World Energy Crisis." International Affairs (October, 1979): 531-545.

____. Oil and the Middle East War: Europe in the Energy Crisis. Boston: Harvard University Center for International Affairs, 1976.

Lieberman, Marvin S. "The Energy Quandary: State Attitudes, Activities, and Concerns." Public Utilities Fortnightly 94 (August 15, 1974): 25-29.

Light, Alfred R. "Federalism and the Energy Crisis: A View from the States." Publius 6 (Winter 1976): 81-96.

Lindeman, John and Donald Armstrong. Policies and Practices of United States Subsidiaries in Canada. Montreal: Canadian-American Committee, 1961.

Lindqvist, Sven. Land and Power in South America. Middlesex, England: Penguin Books, 1979.

Lippitt, Henry F., II. "State and Federal Regulatory Agencies--Conflict or Co-operation?" Public Utilities Fortnightly 85 (March 26, 1970): 33-38.

Long, Norman. An Introduction to the Sociology of Rural Development. London: Tavistock, 1977.

Loomis, Carol J. "How to Think About Oil Company Profits." Fortune 89 (April 1974): 98-103.

Lovejoy, Wallace F. The Regulation of Natural Gas and Its Economic Background. Unpublished Ph.D Thesis. University of Wisconsin, 1953.

Lovins, Amory B. "The Case for Long-Term Planning." Bulletin of the Atomic Scientists 30 (June 1974): 38-50.

____, and John H. Price. Non-Nuclear Futures: The Case for an Ethical Energy Strategy. New York: Friends of the Earth, 1975.

Lucas, Harry, Jr. "Energy: The Case for Self-Sufficiency." World Today 31 (July 1975): 283-290.

Lucas, Nigel and Dimitros Papaconstantinou. "Electricity Planning under Uncertainty: Risks, Margins and the Uncertain Planner." Energy Policy 10 (June 1982) 143-152.

Lumsden, Ian (ed.). Close to the 49th Parallel: The Americanization of Canada. Toronto and Buffalo: University of Toronto Press, 1970.

Luttrell, Clifton B. "A Bushel of Wheat for a Barrel of Oil: Can We Offset OPEC'S Gains With a Grain Cartel?" Review of the Federal Reserve Bank of St. Louis 63 (April 1981): 13-21.

MacAvoy, Paul, W. and Robert S. Pindyck. "Alternative Regulatory Policies for Dealing With the Natural Gas Shortage." Bell Journal of Economics 4 (Autumn 1973): 454-498.

_____, and Robert S. Pindyck. Price Controls and The Natural Gas Shortage. Washington: American Enterprise Institute for Public Policy Research, 1975.

_____, Paul A. Samuelson and Lester C. Thurow. "The Economics of the Energy Crisis." Technology Review 76 (March-April 1974): 49-59.

_____. "The Effectiveness of the Federal Power Commision." Bell Journal of Economics 1 (Autumn 1970): 271-303.

McCleskey, Clifton. The Government and Politics of Texas. 3rd edition. Boston: Little Brown and Company, 1969.

McDougall, I. "The Canadian National Energy Board: 'Economic Jurisprudence' in the National Interest or Symbolic Reassurance?" Alberta Law Review 11 (1973): 327-338.

_____. "The National Energy Board: Solving American Problems, Creating Canadian Dilemmas." Canadian Forum (August 1977): 16-18.

McDougall, John N. Fuels and the National Policy. Toronto: Butterworths, 1982.

McFarland, Carl. "The Unique Role of Discretion in Public Land Law." Rocky Mountain Mineral Law Institute 16 (1970): 35-58.

McKelvey, Vincent E. "Approaches to the Mineral Supply Problem." Technology Review 76 (March-April 1974): 13-23.

McKean, Roland N. "Growth Versus No Growth: An Evaluation." Daedalus 102 (Fall 1973): 207-228.

McKetta, John J. "The Energy Crisis: On and On and On." Chemical Engineering Progress 69 (August 1973): 51-56.

McKie, James W. "Energy Policy and the Long Run." Texas Business Review 47 (January 1975): 4-10.

_____. "Market Structure and Uncertainty in Oil and Gas Exploration." *Quarterly Journal of Economics* 74 (November 1960): 543-571.

_____. "The Oil Crisis in Perspective: The United States." *Daedalus* 104 (Fall 1975): 73-90.

_____. "The Political Economy of World Petroleum." *American Economic Review* 64 (May 1974): 51-57.

McLane, James. "Energy Goals and Institutional Reform." *Futurist* 8 (October 1974): 239-242.

McLean, John G. "The United States Energy Outlook and Its Implications for National Policy." *Annals of the American Academy of Political and Social Science* 410 (November 1973): 97-105.

Maddison, Angus. *Economic Progress and Policy in Developing Countries.* New York: W. W. Norton, 1970.

Maddox, John P. *Beyond the Energy Crisis.* New York: McGraw-Hill, 1975.

Makin, John H. "Facing the Tough Facts About Global Debt". *Business Week* (November 18, 1985): 22.

Malin, H. Martin, Jr. "Toward a National Energy Policy." *Environmental Science and Technology* 7 (May 1973): 392-397.

Mancke, Richard B. "Petroleum Conspiracy: A Costly Myth." *Public Policy* 12 (Winter 1974a): 1-13.

_____. *The Failure of U.S. Energy Policy.* New York: Columbia University Press, 1974b.

Manecon Associates Ltd. (A Monenco Company). *Report in Response to the National Energy Board Order GHR-1-78.* (For Alberta and Southern Gas Co. Ltd. and Canadian Montana Pipe Line Company). Calgary: Manecon, 1978.

Mankabady, S. "The Affreightment of Liquefied Natural Gas." *Journal of World Trade Law* 9 (Nov-Dec. 1975): 654-664.

Mansfield, Edwin. *The Economics of Technological Change.* New York: W. W. Norton and Company, 1968.

Marion, Jerry B. *Energy in Perspective.* New York: Academic Press, 1974.

Marr, William L. and Donald G. Paterson. *Canada: An Economic History.* Toronto: Macmillan, 1980.

Mathews, R. O. "The Third World: Powerful or Powerless" in Alkis Kontos (ed.). *Domination.* Toronto and Buffalo: University of Toronto Press, 1975.

Matuszewski, T. "Presidential Address to the General Assembly of the Canadian Economics Association, Montreal, 1980: Misére de l'économique'." *Canadian Journal of Economics* 13 (November 1980): 539-555.

Mead, Walter J. "The System of Government Subsidies to the Oil Industry." *Natural Resources Journal* 10 (January 1970): 113-125.

Meadows, Donnela H., Dennis L. Meadows, Jorgen Randers and William W. Behrens III. The Limits to Growth: A Report for the Club of Rome's Project on the Predicament of Mankind. New York: Universe Books, 1972.

Meier, R. C., W. T. Newell, and H. C. Pazer. Simulation in Business and Economics. Englewood Cliffs, N.J.: Prentice Hall, 1969.

Melkus, Rolf A. "Toward a Rational Future Energy Policy." Natural Resources Journal 14 (April 1974): 239-256.

Mersarovic, Mihajlo and Eduard Pestel. Mankind at the Turning Point: The Second Report to the Club of Rome. New York: Dutton, 1974.

Mikdashi, Zuhayr. The Community of Oil Exporting Countries: A Study in Governmental Cooperation. Ithaca, N.Y.: Cornell University Press, 1972.

_____. The International Politics of National Resources. Ithaca, N.Y.: Cornell University Press, 1976.

Mikesell, Raymond F. Foreign Investment in the Petroleum and Mineral Industries. Baltimore: John Hopkins Press, 1971.

_____. International Collusive Action in World Markets for Nonfuel Metals. Department of State, Bureau of Public Affairs, Office of Media Services, Special Report No. 4 (September 1974).

Millard, Reed et al. How Will We Meet the Energy Crisis? New York: Julian Messner, 1971.

Miller, Edward J. "Some Implications of Land Ownership Patterns for Petroleum Policy." Land Economics 49 (November 1973): 414-423.

Miller, John T. Jr. Foreign Trade in Gas and Electricity in North America, A Legal and Historical Study. New York: Praeger, 1970.

Miller, Roger L. "Economics of Energy: How Price Controls Did Us In." Business and Society Review (Spring 1974): 73-81.

_____. The Economics of Energy. New York: W. Morrow, 1974.

Mitchell, Edward J. U.S. Energy Policy: A Primer. Washington, D.C.: American Enterprise Institute for Public Policy Research, 1974.

_____. (ed.). Vertical Integration in the Oil Industry. Washington, D. C.: American Enterprise Institute for Public Research, 1976.

Molot, Maureen. "The Domestic Determinants of Canadian Foreign Economic Policy. Beavers Build Dams." Paper presented at the Annual Meeting of the American Political Association. Washington (September, 1977).

Moran, Theodore. *Multinational Corporations and the Politics of Dependence: Copper in Chile.* Princeton, New Jersey: Princeton University Press, 1974.

———. *Oil Prices and the Future of OPEC.* Baltimore: John Hopkins, 1978.

———. "The Theory of International Exploitation in Large Natural Resource Investments." In Seven Rosen and James Kurth (eds.) *Testing Theories of Economic Imperialism.* Lexington: Heath Publishing, 1974.

Morgenthau, Hans J. "World Politics and the Politics of Oil." In Gary D. Eppen (ed.) *Energy: The Policy Issues*, pp. 43-51. Chicago: University of Chicago Press, 1975.

Morrison, Denton E. et. al. *Energy: A Bibliography of Social Science and Related Literature.* New York: Garland Publishers, 1975.

Moyer, Reed. "Energy: Some Unresolved Problems." *California Management Review* 17 (Winter 1974): 64-73.

Muir, J. D. "Mineral Scarcities: A Political Problem With an Economic Solution or an Economic Problem With Political Solutions?" *American University Law Review* 24 (Summer 1975): 1209-1215.

Murphy, Earl F. "The Effect of Law, Economics and Politics on Energy Resources Development." *Case Western Reserve Journal of International Law* 5 (Winter 1972): 81-86.

Murphy, John J. (ed.). *Energy and Public Policy—1972.* New York: Conference Board, 1972.

Myint, H. *Economic Theory and the Underdeveloped Countries.* New York, London, Toronto: Oxford University Press, 1971.

Mytelka, Lynn K. *Regional Development in a Global Economy.* New Haven: Yale University Press, 1979.

———. "Technological dependence in the Andean Group." *International Organization* 32 (Winter 1978): 101-139.

N.V. Nederlandse Gasunie. *Annual Report 1977.* Groningen: N.V. Nederlandse Gasunie, 1977.

———. *1978 Gas Marketing Plan.* Groningen: N.V. Nederlandse Gasunie, 1978a.

———. *Facts.* Groningen: N.V. Nederlandse Gasunie, 1978b.

Naill, Roger F., Dennis L. Meadows and John Stanley-Miller. "The Transition to Coal." *Technology Review* 78 (October-November 1975): 19-29.

National Academy of Engineering. *U.S. Energy Prospects.* Washington, D. C.: National Academy of Engineering, 1974.

National Academy of Sciences. Energy: Future Alternatives and Risks. Cambridge, Mass,: Ballinger, 1975.

National Conference of State Legislatures (USA). Energy: The States' Response. 3 volumes. Washington, D. C.: National Conference of State Legislatures, 1975.

National Petroleum Council (USA). US Energy Outlook: Gas Demand. Washington, D. C.: National Petroleum Council 1973.

Naylor, R. T. "Dominion of Capital: Canada and International Investment." in Alkis Kontos (ed.). Domination. Toronto and Buffalo: University of Toronto Press, 1975.

Nelson, L. D. and Julie A. Honnold. "Planning for Resource Scarcity: A Critique of Prevalent Proposals." Social Science Quarterly 57 (September 1976): 339-347.

Newfarmer, Richard and Willard Mueller. Multinational Corporations in Brazil and Mexico: Structural Sources of Economic and Noneconomic Power. Report to the Subcommittee on Multinational Corporations, Committee on Foreign Relations, United States Senate (August 1975). Washington: United States Government Printing Office, 1975.

Nordhaus, William D. "Resources as a Constraint on Growth." American Economic Review 64 (May 1974): 22-

———. "The Allocation of Energy Resources." In Brookings Paper on Economic Activity No.3, pp. 529-576. Washington, D. C.: Brookings Institution, 1973.

Nordhauser, Norman. "Origins of Federal Oil Regulations in the 1920's." Business History Review 47 (Spring 1973): 53-71.

Norway. Royal Norwegian Ministry of Foreign Affairs. Norway and the North Sea Oil. (UDO 004/77). Oslo: March, 1977.

———. Norway During and After the Oil Era: Petroleum and Social Policy. Extract from Prime Minister Odvar Nordli's address at the Norrona Conference on Friday 14 April 1978. (DOC 007/78). Oslo: April, 1978a.

———. Norway's Energy Supplies. (UDA 204/82 ENG). Oslo: June, 1982.

———. Norway's Petroleum Policy: Speech by Tygve Tamburstven, Under-secretary of State in the Ministry of Petroleum and Energy, at the annual meeting of the Foreign Diplomats in Oslo, 9 May 1979. DOC 043/79. Oslo: May, 1979.

_____. Norwegian Oil and Gas Policy. Speech by Bjartmar Gjerde, Norwegian Petroleum and Energy Minister, at the Petroleum Policy and Decision Making Seminar at Sanderstolen, 8 February 1978. DOC (003/78). Oslo: February, 1978b.

_____. Norwegian Petroleum Activities: 30 Questions and Answers. (UDP 014/79). 2nd edition. Oslo: May, 1979.

_____. Norwegian Petroleum Activities: 30 Questions and Answers. (UDA 202/82 ENG). Oslo: April, 1982.

_____. Petroleum Industry in Norwegian Society (Exerpt from Parliamentary Report No. 25). Oslo: 1974.

_____. The Activity on The Norwegian Continental Shelf: Report to the Storting No. 53 (1979-80). (STM 053/80). Oslo: February, 1980.

Norway. Royal Ministry of Petroleum and Energy. Fact Sheet: The Norwegian Continental Shelf. (Unofficial translation). Oslo: January, 1979.

_____. Fact Sheet: The Norwegian Continental Shelf 1982: 1. (Unofficial translation) Oslo: 1982.

Norway. Statoil. Petroleum Activity in Northern Norway. Oslo: August, 1982a.

_____. Statpipe Gas Gathering System. Oslo: August, 1982b.

Novick, Sheldon. "Federal Energy Policy." Environment 18 (October 1976): 17-20.

O'Brien, Phillip J. "A critique of Latin American theories of dependency", in Ivan Oxaal, Tony Barnett and David Booth (eds.), Beyond the Sociology of Development: Economy and Society in Latin America and Africa. London and Boston: Routledge and Kegan Paul, 1975.

Odell, Peter R. Oil and World Power. 4th edition. London: Penguin, 1975.

_____. "The Future of Oil: A Rejoinder." Geographical Journal 139 (October 1973): 436-454.

_____, and Kenneth E. Rosing. The Future of Oil: A Simulation Study of the Inter-relationships of Resources, Reserves and Use, 1980-2080. London: Kogan Page Limited, 1980.

Ogden, William J. "Natural Gas Legislation." Public Utilities Fortnightly 93 (March 14, 1974): 20-24.

Ohlin, Bertil, Per-Ove Hesselborn, Per Magnus Wijkman (eds.). The International Allocation of Economic Activity. New York: Holmes and Meier, 1977.

Onyemelukwe, C. C. Economic Development: An Inside View. Longman: London, 1974.

OPEC. "Natural Gas in the OPEC area." A Statement Presented by G. Al-Ukaili, OPEC Delegate to the Second Symposium on the Development of Petroleum Resources of Asia and the Far East, Organized by the Economic Commission for Asia and the Far East. Tehran, September 1962.

Organization for Economic Co-operation and Development. International Energy Agency. Standing Group on Long Term Co-operation. Country Report on the Netherlands. (IEA/SLT (78) 129.5) Paris: January 29, 1979.

Oxaal, Ivan, Tony Barnett and David Booth (eds.). Beyond the Sociology of Development: Economy and Society in Latin America and Africa. London and Boston: Routledge and Kegan Paul, 1975.

Page, William. "Mining and Development: Are they compatible in South America?" Resources Policy 2 (December 1976): 235-246.

Patton, Janet W. "Administering State Energy Programs." Public Affairs Analyst 2 (1975): 2-4.

Payer, Cheryl. The Debt Trap: The I. M. F. and the Third World. New York: Monthly Review Press, 1975.

Pearce, D. W. (ed.). The Economics of Natural Resource Depletion. New York: Macmillan, 1975.

_____, and Richard Grace. "Stabilizing secondary materials markets." Resources Policy 2 (June 1976): 118-127.

Penrose, Edith. The Growth of Firms, Middle East Oil and Other Essays. London: Frank Cass and Co., 1971.

_____. The Large International Firm in Developing Countries. London: George Allen and Unwin Ltd., 1968.

_____. "The Oil Crisis in Perspective: The Development of a Crisis." Daedalus 104 (Fall 1975): 39-57.

Perry, Harry. A Review of Energy Issues and the 91st Congress. Washington, D. C.: Government Printing Office, 1971.

Peters, Charles and Glen Allerhand. "The Case Against Energy Independence." Washington Monthly 7 (September 1975): 19-26.

Petro-Canada. Annual Report 1981. Calgary, March 31, 1982.

Phillips, Charles Franklin. The Economics of Regulation: Theory and Practice in the Transportation and Public Utility Industries. Revised Edition. Homewood, Ill.: R. D. Irwin, 1969.

Pikl, I. J. (ed.). Public Policy and the Future of the Petroleum Industry. Laramie, Wyoming: University of Wyoming Press, 1970.

Pincus, John. *Trade and Development: The Rich and Poor Nations.* New York, Toronto and London: McGraw-Hill, 1967.

Pindyck, R. "Gains to Producers from the Cartelization of Exhaustible Resources." *Review of Economics and Statistics* (1977).

Powelson, John P. "The LDC's and the Terms of Trade." *Economic Impact* 22 (1978): 33-37.

Powrie, T. L. "Static Redistributive and Welfare Effects of an Export Tax." In A. Scott (ed.) *Natural Resource Revenues: A Test of Federalism.* pp. 137-152. Vancouver: British Columbia Institute for Economic and Policy Analysis, 1976.

____, and W. D. Gainer. *Canadian Policy Toward Trade in Crude Oil and Natural Gas: A Review of the Alternatives.* Ottawa: Economic Council of Canada, 1976.

Pratt, Larry. "Petro-Canada." In A. Tupper and G. B. Doern (eds.) *Public Corporations and Public Policy in Canada.* Montreal: The Institute for Research on Public Policy, 1981.

Prebisch, Raul. *Change and Development - - Latin America's Great Task: Report Submitted to the Inter-American Development Bank.* New York, Washington, London: Praeger, 1971.

Prior, M. J. and M. Teper. "The Future Supply of Gas". *Energy Policy* 8 (December 1980): 308-317.

Pushkarev, Boris S. "Energy in the New York Region." *Proceedings of the Academy of Political Science* 31 (December 1973): 13-23.

Radetzki, Marian. "Mineral Commodity Stabilization: The Producer's View." *Resources Policy* 3 (June 1977): 118-126.

Rangarajan, L. N. *Commodity Conflict: The Political Economy of International Commodity Negotiations.* Ithaca, New York: Cornell University Press, 1978.

Reuber, G. L. *Private Foreign Investment in Development.* Oxford: Clarendon Press, 1973.

Reynolds, Alan. "The Federal Energy Agencies: The Solution or the Problem?" *Imprimis* 5 (September 1976): 1-6.

Richardson, Harry W. *Economic Aspects of the Energy Crisis.* Lexington, Mass.: D.C. Heath, 1975.

Riddick, Winston W. "The Nature of the Petroleum Industry." *Proceedings of the Academy of Political Science* 31 (December 1973): 148-158.

Ridgeway, James. *The Last Play: The Struggle to Monopolize the World's Energy Resources.* New York: E. P. Dutton, 1973.

Rinfret Associates, P. and F. M. Peterson. "The Exploitation of Extractive Resources. A Survey." *Economic Journal* (December 1977): 681-721.

Ritchie, Ronald S. "Canada's Energy Situation in a World Context." <u>International Perspectives</u> (March-April 1974): 13-17.

Roberts, Marc J. "Is There An Energy Crisis?" <u>The Public Interest</u> 31 (Spring 1973): 17-37.

Roberts, W. G. <u>The Quest for Oil</u>. London: Metheun, 1970.

Rockefeller, M. W. and R. L. Schantz. <u>An Analysis of the Regulatory Aspects of Natural Gas Supply</u>. Washington, D.C: U.S. Environmental Protection Agency, Report No. APTD 1459 March 1973.

Rogers, Christopher. "Agreement about Commodity Agreements?" <u>Resources Policy</u> 2 (June 1976): 97-105.

Rosenberg, Nathan. "Innovative Responses to Materials Shortages." <u>American Economic Review</u> 63 (May 1973): 111-118.

Ross, Marc H. and Robert H. Williams. <u>Our Energy-Regaining Control: A Stratagy for Economic Revival through Redesign in Energy Use</u>. New York: McGraw-Hill, 1982.

Rouhani, Faud. <u>A History of O.P.E.C.</u> New York: Praeger, 1971.

Russell, Milton and Lawrence Toenjes. <u>Natural Gas Producer Regulation and Taxation: Interaction Between Federal Producer Regulation and State Severance Taxation</u>. East Lansing, Michigan: University of Michigan, 1971.

Rustow, Dankwart A. "U.S.-Saudi Relations and the Oil Crises of the 1980's." <u>Foreign Affairs</u> 55 (April 1977): 494-516.

Rycroft, Robert W., Timothy A. Hall, Don E. Kash and Irvin L. White. <u>Energy Policy-Making: A Selected Bibliography</u>. Norman, Oklahoma: University of Oklahoma Press, 1977.

Safarian, A. E. <u>Foreign Ownership of Canadian Industry</u>. Second Edition. Toronto and Buffalo: University of Toronto Press, 1973.

Sampson, Anthony. <u>The Seven Sisters: The Great Oil Companies and the World They Shaped</u>. New York: Viking, 1975.

Samuelson, P. A. <u>Foundation of Economic Analysis</u>. Cambridge, Mass.: Harvard University Press, 1974.

Schmidt, Herman J. "The Government's Role in Energy." <u>Conference Board Record</u> 11 (May 1974): 20-22.

Schumacher, E. F. <u>Small is Beautiful: Economics As If People Mattered</u>. New York: Harper and Row, 1973.

Scott, Anthony. <u>Natural Resources: The Economics of Conservation</u>. Toronto: McClelland and Stewart, 1973.

_____. "Who Should Get Natural Resource Revenues?" In A. Scott (ed.) *Natural Resource Revenues: A Test of Federalism.* pp. 1-51. Vancouver: Institute for Economic Policy Analysis, 1976.

Seidel, Marquis R. "Fuel Taxes and the Environment: A Primer." *Energy Systems and Policy* 1 (1976): 351-365.

Shapiro, Michael E. "Energy Development on the Public Domain: Federal/State Cooperation and Conflict Regarding Environmental Land Use Control." *Natural Resources Lawyer* 9 (1976): 397-440.

Shaw, Edward, S. *Financial Deepening in Economic Development.* New York, London, Toronto: Oxford University Press, 1973.

Singh, Shamsher. "The International Dialogue on Commodities." *Resources Policy* 2 (June 1976): 87-96.

Society for International Development. "Major New Agreement Signed Between EEC and 46 Developing Countries." *Survey of International Development* 12 (March-April 1975): 1-3.

Solow, Robert M. "The Economics of Resources or the Resources of Economics." *American Economic Review* 64 (May 1974): 1-14.

Sparrow, Roy L. "The Failure of Natural Resources Policy Making in the United States." Unpublished Ph.D. Thesis. Los Angeles: University of California, 1976.

Spraos, John. "The Terms of Trade of Primary Commodities of Developing Countries." In *Thames Essays.* London: Trade Policy Research Centre, 1978.

Stauffer, Thomas R. "Economic Cost of U.S. Crude Oil Production." *Journal of Petroleum Technology* 25 (June 1973): 643-658.

Stern, Jonathan P. *Soviet Natural Gas Development to Nineteen Ninety: The Implications for the CMEA and the West.* Lexington, Mass.: Lexington Books, 1980.

Steward, R. F. "Energy Consumption in Canada Since Confederation." *Energy Policy* 6 (September 1978): 239-244.

_____. "A Survey of Energy Consumption Within Canada Since Confederation: Some Comparisons with the United States." Unpublished mimeograph. Fredericton, N. B.: Department of Chemical Engineering, University of New Brunswick, 1977.

Stiglitz, Joseph E. "Monopoly and the Rate of Extraction of Exhaustible Resources." *American Economic Review* 66 (September 1976): 655-661.

Stobaugh, Robert and Daniel Yergin (eds.). *Energy Future: Report of the Energy Project at the Harvard Business School.* New York: Random House, 1979.

Strange, Susan. "The Study of Transnational Relations." *International Affairs* 52 (July 1976): 333-345.

____, and Roger Tooze (eds.). *The International Politics of Surplus Capacity: Competition for Market Shares in the World Recession.* London: Allen Unwin, 1981.

Street, James and Dilmus D. James. "Institutionalism, Structuralism, and Dependency in Latin America." *Journal of Economic Issues* 16 (September 1982): 673-689.

Streeten Paul. "The Dynamics of the New Poor Power." *Resources Policy* 2 (June 1976): 73-86.

____. "World Trade in Agricultural Commodities and the Terms of Trade in Industrial Goods." In Nural Islam (ed.) *Agricultural Policy in Developing Countries,* pp. 207-223. London: Macmillan, 1974.

Stuart, Alexander. "The Blazing Battle to Free Natural Gas." *Fortune* (October 19, 1981): 152-179.

Sunkel, O. "Big Business and Dependencia." *Foreign Affairs* 50 (1972a): 517-531.

____. "National Development Policy and External Dependency in Latin America." In Y. H. Ferguson (ed.), *Contemporary Inter-American Relations.* Englewood Cliffs, N. J.: Prentice-Hall, 1972b.

____. "The Pattern of Latin American Dependence." In V. L. Urquidi and R. Thorp (eds.), *Latin America in the International Economy.* New York and Toronto: John Wiley & Sons, 1973a.

____. "Transnational Capitalism and National Disintegration in Latin America." *Social and Economic Studies* 22 (1973b): 132-176.

Swidler, Joseph C. "The Challenge of State Regulation Agencies: The Experience of New York State." *Annals of the American Academy of Political and Social Science* 410 (November 1973): 106-119.

Talley, William. "The Role of the State in Energy." In Walter F. Scheffer (ed.) *Energy Impacts on Public Policy and Administration,* pp. 185-199. Norman, Oklahoma: University of Oklahoma Press, 1976.

Tanzer, Michael. *The Political Economy of International Oil and the Underdeveloped Countries.* Boston: Beacon Press, 1969. Texas. Railroad Commission of Texas, Oil and Natural Gas Division. *Annual Reports.* Austin: 1980, 1982.

Tilton, E. J. "The Choice of Trading Partners: An Analysis of International Trade in Aluminum, Copper, Lead, Manganese, Tin and Zinc." *Yale Economic Essays* (Fall 1966): 419-474.

Tinbergen, Jan. *Shaping the World Economy: Suggestions for an International Economic Policy.* New York: The Twentieth Century Fund, 1962.

Train, Russell R. "The Long-Term Value of the Energy Crisis." *Futurist* 8 (February 1974): 14-18.

TransCanada Pipelines. *Annual Report 1981.* Toronto: TransCanada Pipelines, 1982.

Tribus, Myron. "The Case for an Energy Commission." *Public Administration Review* 35 (July-August 1975): 317-327.

Toner, Glen and François Bregha. "The Political Economy of Energy." In Michael S. Whittington and Glen Williams (eds.) *Canadian Politics in the 1980s,* pp. 1-26. Toronto: Meuthen, 1981.

Toronto Dominion Bank. *The Canadian Petroleum Industry.* Toronto: Toronto Dominion Bank, 1968.

Tullock, G. "Monopoly and the Rate of Extraction of Exhaustible Resources: Note." *American Economic Review* 69 (March 1979): 231-233.

Turner, Louis. *Multinational Companies and the Third World.* New York: Hill and Wang, 1973.

_____. *Oil Companies in the International System.* London: Allen and Unwin, 1978.

Tussing, Arlon R. "Toward a Rational Policy for Oil and Gas Imports." In Harold Wolozin (ed.) *Energy and the Environment,* pp. 59-88. Morristown, N. J.: General Learning Press, 1974.

_____, and Connie C. Barlow. *The Natural Gas Industry: Evolution, Structure, and Economics.* Cambridge, Massachusetts: Ballinger Publishing Company, 1984.

Uhler, Russell S. "Costs and Supply in Petroleum Exploration: The Case of Alberta." *Canadian Journal of Economics* 9 (February 1976): 72-90.

_____. *Petroleum Finding Costs.* Mineograph. Vancouver: University of British Columbia, Department of Economics, January 1979.

United Nations. Center for Economic and Social Information. "Thorough Examination of U.N. Role in International Economic Co-operation Expected." OPI/CES I Features ESA/146 (February 11, 1975a).

_____. Centre for Economic and Social Information, UNCTAD Information Unit. "An Integrated Programme for Commodities." TD/B/C.1/166/supp. 1-5, (December 9, 1974 - January 14, 1975b).

_____. *Economic Survey for Latin America, 1974.* E/CEPAL/982/Rev. 1, October 1975c. New York: United Nations, 1976a.

_____. Office of Public Information. *Charter of Economic Rights and Duties of States.* OPI/542-75-38308 (February 1975d), p. 2.

_____. UNCTAD Information Unit. TD/214; TD/215, 9 June 1976b.

Uri, Noel D. The Demand for Energy and Conservation in the United States. Greenwich, Connecticut and London, England: JAI Press, 1982.

U.S. Congress. Canadian Foreign Investment Screening Procedures and the Role of Foreign Investment in the Canadian Economy: Hearings Before the Subcommittee on Inter-American Economic Relationships of the Joint Economic Committee. 94th Congress, 1st and 2nd Sessions (1975-76).

_____. The National Energy Act. Publication No. 96-1. 96th Congress, 1st Session, 1979.

U.S. Congress, Congressional Budget Office. Energy Policy Alternatives. Washington, D.C.: Government Printing Office, 1977.

U.S. Federal Energy Administration. Natural Gas Facts and Figures for 1974. Washington, D.C.: National Technical Information Service, May, 1976. Report No. FEA/B-76/125.

_____. Windfall Profits in the Coal Industry. Washington, D.C.: Government Printing Office, 1975a.

_____. Report to Congress on the Economic Impact of Energy Actions. Washington, D.C.: Federal Energy Administration, 1975b.

_____. The Petroleum Industry: A Report on Corporate and Industry Structure and Ownership. 2 Volumes. Washington, D.C.: Government Printing Office, 1975c.

_____. The Relationship of Oil Companies and Foreign Governments. Washington, D.C.: Government Printing Office, 1975d.

U.S. Federal Power Commission. The Gas Supplies of Interstate Natural Gas Pipeline Companies 1969. Washington, D.C.: U.S. Government Printing office, 1969.

U.S. General Accounting Office. Natural Gas Price Increases: A Preliminary Analysis. Report No. GAO/RCED-83-76. Washington: General Accounting Office, December 9, 1982.

U.S. Geological Survey. "The Oil Supply of the United States." Bulletin of the American Association of Petroleum Geologists 6 (1922): 42-46.

U.S. House, Committee on Interior and Insular Affairs. America's Energy Potential: A Summary and Explanation. Washington, D.C.: Government Printing Office, 1973.

U.S. House Committee on Science and Astronautics. Energy - The Ultimate Resource. Washington, D.C.: Government Printing Office, 1971.

U.S. Senate, Committee on Interior and Insular Affairs. Goals and Objectives of Federal Agencies in Fuels and Energy. Washington, D.C.: Government Printing Office, 1971.
_____. Federal Leasing and Disposal Policies. Washington, D.C.: Government Printing Office, 1972a.
_____. History of Federal Energy Organization. Washington, D.C.: Government Printing Office, 1973a.
_____. Legislative Authority of Federal Agencies With Respect to Fuels and Energy. Washington, D.C.: Government Printing Office, 1973b.
_____. Natural Gas Policy Issues. Washington, D.C.: Government Printing Office, 1972b.
Vaitsos, Constantine. Intercountry Income Distribution and Transnational Enterprises. Oxford: Clarendon Press, 1974.
_____. Power, Knowledge and Development Policy: Relations Between Transnational Enterprises and Developing Countries. Mimeograph of paper presented at the 1974 Dag Hammarskjold Seminar on the Third World and International Economic Change. Uppsala, Sweden: 8 February, 1975.
Valenzuela, J. Samuel and Arturo Valenzuela. "Modernization and Dependency: Alternative Perspectives in the Study of Latin American Underdevelopment." Comparative Politics 19 (July 1978): 535-538.
Van Loon, Richard J. and Michael S. Whittington. The Canadian Political System: Environment, Structure and Process. Toronto: McGraw-Hill, 1971.
Van Meurs, A. P. H. Petroleum Economics and Offshore Mining Legislation. Amsterdam: Elsevier Publishing Company, 1971.
_____. Modern Petroleum Economics. Ottawa: Van Meurs and Associates Limited, 1981.
Vernon, Raymond. "Multinational Enterprise and National Sovereignty." Harvard Business Review 45 (March-April 1967): 156-172.
_____. Sovereignty at Bay. New York: Basic Books, 1971.
_____. Storm Over the Multinationals: The Real Issues. Cambridge, Mass.: Harvard University Press, 1977.
_____. "The Oil Crisis in Perspective: The Distribution of Power." Daedalus 104 (Fall 1975): 245-247.
Ward, Barbara. The Rich Nations and the Poor Nations. Toronto: Canadian Broadcasting Corporation (The Massey Lectures Inaugural Series), 1961.

Walker, R. A. "Economics of Energy Extravagance." Ecology Law Quarterly 4 (1975): 963-985.
Walsh, J. H. and R. P. Overend. "Energy Consumption Patterns in Canadian and World Economics." Energy Policy 9 (March 1981): 39-46.
Watkins, G. Campbell and Michael Walker, (eds.). Oil In The Seventies. Vancouver: Fraser Institute, 1977.
Watkins, M. "A Staple Theory of Economic Growth." Canadian Journal of Economics and Political Science. 29 (May, 1963): 141-158.
Waverman, Leonard. "Estimating the Demand for Energy: Heat Without Light." Energy Policy 5 (March 1977): 2-11.
_____. Natural Gas and National Policy: A Linear Programming Model of North American Gas Flows. Toronto: University of Toronto Press, 1973.
_____. "The Distribution of Resource Rents: For Whom the Firm Tolls." in Peter Nemetz (ed.). Energy Crisis: Policy Response, pp. 225-279. Montreal: Institute for Research on Public Policy, 1981.
_____, and Edward W. Erickson (eds.). The Energy Question: An International Failure of Policy. 2 Volumes. Toronto: University of Toronto Press, 1974.
Webb, Michael and David Pearce. "The Economics of Energy Analysis." Energy Policy 3 (December 1975): 318-331.
Weinberg, Alvin M. and R. Philip Hammond. "Limits to the Use of Energy." American Scientist 58 (July-August 1970): 412-418.
Weinrich, John E. Economic Impact of the Canadian Gas Industry: Local, Provincial and Regional. Calgary: Gas Committee of the Calgary Chamber of Commerce, 1966.
Westcoast Transmission Company Limited. Annual Reports. Vancouver: 1958 to 1980.
Wheatley, Charles F., Jr. "Natural Gas: Crisis in Regulation." Public Power 29 (March-April 1971): 20-23.
White, Irvin L. "Policy and Technology: Options for Our Energy Future." Norman, Oklahoma: Science and Public Policy Program, University of Oklahoma, 1974.
White, M. D. and H. J. Barry III. "Energy Development in the West: Conflict and Cooperation of Governmental Decision-Making." North Dakota Law Review 52 (Spring 1976): 451-528.
Whittington, Michael S. and Glen Williams. (eds.). Canadian Politics in the 1980s. Toronto: Meuthen, 1981.

Willrich, Mason. Energy and World Politics. New York: Free Press, 1975.
_____. "International Energy Issues and Options." In Jack M. Hollander (ed.) Annual Review of Energy, pp. 743-772. Palo Alto, California: Annual Reviews, 1976.
Willson, Bruce F. "Natural Gas and the Public Interest." Canadian Forum (August 1977): 5-22.
Wilson, John W. "Adam Smith Abandoned: Big Oil Is Big Coal Is Big Natural Gas." Business and Society Review (Spring 1974): 65-72.
Winberg, Alan R. "International Coffee Market: Implications for Latin American Exporters." In L. Alschuler (ed.) Dependent Agricultural Development and Agrarian Reform in Latin America, pp. 89-99. Ottawa: University of Ottawa Press, 1981.
_____. "Law of the Sea: Who will manage the oceans' riches? How will developing countries be affected?" In Papers and Documents of the I.C.I. Ottawa: University of Ottawa, 1976a.
_____. "Power Diffusion Through Raw Material Producer Associations in the Third World." Journal of International and Comparative Public Policy 1 (Spring 1977): 149-160.
_____. "Raw Material Producer Associations and Canadian Policy." Behind the Headlines 34 (Fall 1976b).
_____. "Resource Politics: The Future of International Markets for Raw Materials." In Marvin S. Sorros and David Orr (eds.) The Global Predicament: Ecological Perspectives on World Order, pp. 178-194. Raleigh, North Carolina: University of North Carolina Press, 1979.
Workshop On Alternative Energy Strategies. Energy: Global Prospects, 1985-2000. (Carroll Wilson-Director). New York: McGraw Hill, 1977.
Wu, Yuan-li. Japan's Search for Oil: A Case Study in Economic Nationalism and International Security. Stanford, California: Hoover Institution Press of Stanford University, 1977.
Young, H. W. "Conservation of Natural Resources -- Ecology, Economics and Energy." West Virginia Law Review 78 (May 1976): 315-333.
Zarb, Frank G. "The Seven Truths of Energy." Wall Street Journal 186 (September 10, 1975): 24.

Index

Agip, 140
Alberta, 68-73, 75, 180, 196
Alberta and Southern Gas Company, 88, 209
Alberta-California Project, 88
Alberta Energy Corporation, 92
Alberta Natural Gas Company, 69, 88
Algeria, 136, 199
Amerada Minerals, 157
Amoco, 140
  See Amoco Canada
Amoco Canada, 157
  See Amoco
Anaconda Copper Mining Company, 70
Appalachian region
  early gas production from, 52
Arctic Pilot Project 43
Athabasca, 104
Atlantic Richfield Canada Ltd., 104
Atomic Energy Control Board, 171
Australia 31, 153

Belgium, 134
Board of Transport Commissioners, 68, 71
Borden Commission
  See Royal Commission on Energy
British American Oil Company Limited, 48

British Columbia Electric, 189
British Columbia Hydro and Power Authority, 18
British Columbia Petroleum Corporation, 92
British North America Act, 8, 66, 185

California, 162
  Canadian gas supply to, 97 (table)
Canadair, 105
Canada Wildlife Foundation, 118
Canadian Delhi Oil, 70, 75
Canadian-Montana Pipeline Company, 70-72, 209
Candian Occidental, 157
Canadian Pacific Railway, 67
Carter, President J., 60-61, 181
Chevron, 157
China, 105
Clark, Joe, 105
Club of Rome, 23, 24, 135
Coal, 115-118
Coffee
  See International Coffee Agreements
Colorado
  Canadian gas supply to, 97 (table)
Commodity agreements
  See International commodity agreements

Commodity-value, 99-100, 198-199
  See also Substitution value
Common Fund, 35, 152
  See International commodity agreements
Compensatory financing, 38-39
  See International commodity agreements
  See also, Stabex; Lomé Convention
Conoco, 140, 165
Cross-subsidization, 237

Dehaviland Aircraft, 105
Den norske stats oljeselskap a/s
  See Statoil
Diefenbaker, John, 80
Dining Commission, 69
Distrigas Corporation, 43
Dome Petroleum, 108, 165
Dominion Coal Board, 171
Drake's Well (Pennsylvania), 119
Dualism, 32
Duncan-Lalonde formula, 200

Eisenhower, U.S. President, 87
Ekofisk, 136, 139-140, 142
Eldorado Nuclear, 105
Electricity and Fluid Exportation Act, 3, 66, 68, 71, 169, 185-186, 203
Elf, 140
Elmworth, 241
El Paso, 197
Emmen, 140
Energy Resources Conservation Act (1971), 69
Essex County (Ontario), 65-66
Esso, 140
  See Exxon
  See Imperial Oil

Esso Holding Company Holland Inc., 134
Export controls, 36-37
  See International commodity agreements
Export licences, transferable, 219-220
Export marketing board, 222-225
Export tax, 225-226
Exxon, 155, 157
  See Esso
  See Imperial Oil

Farwell, storage area 90
F.E.R.C.
  See Federal Energy Regulatory Commission
Federal Energy Regulatory Commission (FERC), 61, 169, 181, 183
Federal Power Commission (FPC), 8, 52, 71-72, 169-170, 176, 181, 183, 195, 197
  price regulation by, 50-61
  See also Natural Gas Act of 1938
Fina, 140
Forecasts, 114-126
  sensitivity in, 122
  See also Uncertainty, Substitution
Foothills pipeline, 93
F.P.C.
  See Federal Power Commission
France, 134

Gas Resources Preservation Act (1949), 69
Gelsenberg AG., 43
Germany, 140
Great Britain, 153
Great Lakes Project, 90
Great Pipeline Debate, 80, 170
Greene, J.J., 197

Groningen gas field, 134-135, 137
Group of 77, 28
  See also Less developed countries
  See also Third world countries
Gulf Canada, 157
  See Gulf Oil

Heritage Fund, 180
Holland, 133-137
  See Netherlands
Howe, C.D., 75-78, 203
Hudson's Bay Oil and Gas, 165
Huntingdon (British Columbia), 197

Idaho
  Canadian gas supply to, 97 (table)
Illinois, 162
  Canadian gas supply to, 97 (table)
Imperial Oil, 155, 157
  See Esso
  See Exxon
Indexing, 37-38
  See International commodity agreements
Indonesia, 105, 217
Inter-City Gas, 209
International coffee agreements, 36-37
International commodity agreements (ICA's), 33-39
Interprovincial Pipeline Company, 69
Italy, 134

Jamaica, 38
Japan, 7, 43, 108, 162
Jevons, William Stanley, 117-119

Kansas
  discoveries in, 44
  imports from, 220
King Christian Island, 43
Korean War, 70

Leduc oil fields, 68, 153
Less developed countries (LDC,s), 27-31
  See also Third World countries
Liquid natural gas (LNG), 43, 142-143, 239
Liquified natural gas (LNG)
  See Liquid natural gas
LNG
  See Liquid natural gas
Lomé Convention, 39, 133
Louisiana
  discoveries in, 44

Mackenzie Delta, 20, 93
Malthus, Thomas, 23
Manning, E., 75
Market cycle, 241-243
McMahon, F., 189
Mexico, 104, 153, 199
  U.S. imports from, 2, 7, 63
  exemption from U.S. quotas, 87
Michigan, 66, 90
  Canadian gas supply to, 97 (table)
Middle East War (1973), 92
Midwestern Gas Transmission, 79
Minnesota
  Canadian gas supply to, 97 (table)
Mobil Canada, 157
Montana, 70-72
  Canadian gas supply to, 97 (table)
Montana Power, 70-72
Mulroney, Brian, 105

National Energy Board (N.E.B.), 81, 83-84, 169-177, 186, 195, 240
  exportable surplus determination, 204-214
  export price recommendations, 97-102

forecasts, 125
See also Royal
 Commission on Energy
National Energy Program of
 1980, 164, 233
National Oil Policy (NOP),
 86-87
Natural Gas Act of 1938,
 52-54
Natural Gas Policy Act of
 1978, 21, 59-61
Natural gas reserves
 growth in the U.S.,
 47-48 (table)
N.E.B.
 See National Energy
 Board
Netherlands, xi, 129
 See Holland
Nevada
 Canadian gas supply
 to, 97 (table)
New Mexico, 56, 73
 discoveries in, 44
New York State, 66
 See also St. Lawrence
 County
Nigeria, 136
Norsk Hydro a/s, 140
North Dakota
 Canadian gas supply
 to, 97 (table)
Northern Ontario Pipeline
 Crown Corporation,
 80-81
Northern Tier states, 162
North Sea, 43, 105, 138
 141 (map)
North South dialogue, 31
 See also United
 Nations Conference on
 Trade and Development
Norway, xi, 129, 133,
 136-144, 153
N.V. Netherlands Gasunie,
 134

Ohio, 162
 early gas production
 from, 52
Oil and Gas Conservaion
 Board (of Alberta), 75

Oklahoma
 discoveries in, 44
 imports from, 220
Oklahoma Corporation
 Commission, 59
Olympia and York Ltd.,
 157
Ontario, 17, 66
Ontario Energy
 Corporation, 92, 165
Oregon, 68
 Canadian gas supply
 to, 97 (table)
Organization of Petroleum
 Exporting Countries
 (OPEC), 18, 24, 25,
 126, 153
Ostry, S., 125
Ottawa River Valley, 86

Pacific Gas and Electric
 Company, 88
Pacific Northwest
 Pipeline, 72, 74, 167,
 189, 191, 193, 195
Pacific Petroleum, 196
Pan American, 196
Peace River district,
 187-190, 192-193, 199
 exports from 19, 72-74
Pennsylvania
 early gas production
 from, 52
Petro-Canada, 43, 92,
 103-106, 108, 165
Petrofina, 165
Petroleum and Natural Gas
 Conservation Board, 67
Phillips Case of 1954,
 54
Phillips Petroleum Co.,
 138, 140, 142
Pipelines Act (1949),
 68, 71, 169, 186
Portland, 189
Prairie Transmission Lines
 Limited, 70
Price stabilization,
 232-234
Producer associations, 25,
 243

Quotas, import of crude oil, 87

Railroad Commission of Texas, 150-152
Ratemaking, 147-152
Rate regulation
 See Ratemaking
Regulation 11A, 98-99, 197
Renewables, 4
Reserves
 proven, 14
 recoverable, 14
Royal Commission on Canada's Economic Prospects, 74, 80-81
Royal Commission on Energy, 48, 74, 169, 186, 188-190, 194
Royal Decree of 9 April, 1965, 139
Royal Dutch Shell, 157
Ruhrgas AG., 43

Saga Petroleum a/s and Co., 140
Saudi Arabia, 25, 26
Seattle, 189, 191, 193
Shell Canada, 157
 See Shell Oil Co.
Shell Oil Co., 140
 See Shell Canada
Shell Netherlands B.V., 134
Société québecoise d'initiatives pétrolières (SOQUIP), 72
Solar energy, 121
Soviet Union (USSR), 31, 43, 236
South Africa, 31
Spot market
 natural gas, 2, 21, 218
Stabex, 39
Statoil, 140
St. Laurent, Louis, 80
St. Lawrence County (New York)
 Canadian gas supply to, 97 (table)
Strategic commodities, 12-15, 133
 natural gas considered 12-21
Substitute energy sources, 119-121, 129-132
Substitution value, 100-101, 198-200
 See also Commodity-value
Sunoco, 165
Sun Oil, 165
Swaps, 111
Sweden, 31

Teesside, 140
Teleglobe, 105
Tennessee Gas Transmission, 79
Texas, xi, 56, 129, 133, 144-152
 discoveries in, 44
 regulation of pipelines by, 51
Third World countries, 27
 See also Less developed countries
Tidal power, 121
Tin, 33-34
Trans-Canada Pipelines, 43, 75, 170, 197, 203, 207, 209
Trans-Canada Railroad, 77
Transferable export licences, 219-220
Trends
 perceptions of, 232-234
Trudeau, Pierre, 105

Uncertainty, 113-128
Union Gas, 220
United Nations Conference on Trade and Development (UNCTAD), 28, 31
 See also International commodity agreements
United Kingdom, 140, 144

Vancouver, 189, 193
Venezuela, 87, 104
Vermont,
  Canadian gas supply to, 97 (table)

Washington, 68
  Canadian gas supply to, 97 (table)
Water power, 121
Welland County (Ontario), 65
Westcoast Gas Transmission, 72, 185-197

Western Pipelines, 75
West Germany, 134
West Virginia
  early gas production from, 52
Wind power, 121
Wisconsin, 90
  Canadian gas supply to, 97 (table)
Wood, as a source of energy, 114-116
Wyoming
  Canadian gas supply to, 97 (table)